Paul Beauchamp

Psalms Night and Day

Translated by

Peter Rogers, SJ

MARQUETTE
UNIVERSITY
PRESS

MARQUETTE STUDIES IN THEOLOGY
NO. 84
ANDREW TALLON, SERIES EDITOR

LIBRARY OF CONGRESS CATALOGING-IN-PUBLICATION DATA

Beauchamp, Paul.
  [Psaumes nuit et jour. English]
  Psalms, night and day / by Paul Beauchamp ; translated by Peter Rogers, SJ. — first [edition].
       pages cm. — (Marquette studies in theology ; No. 84)
  Includes bibliographical references and index.
  ISBN 978-1-62600-706-2 (pbk. : alk. paper) — ISBN 1-62600-706-3 (pbk. : alk. paper)
  1. Bible. Psalms—Criticism, interpretation, etc. I. Title.
  BS1430.52.B42513 2015
  223'.206—dc23
                                                              2015010188

Copyright Acknowledgment:
All English biblical citations are from *The Holy Bible containing the Old and New Testaments with the Apocryphal/Deuterocanonical Books, New Revised Standard Version.* New York: Collins, 1989.

Cover art by Dailey Thibeaux
http://www.daileythibeaux.com

♾ The paper used in this publication meets the minimum requirements of the American National Standard for Information Sciences—
Permanence of Paper for Printed Library Materials, ANSI Z39.48-1992.

Association of American University Presses

Marquette University Press
MILWAUKEE

The Association of Jesuit University Presses

Psalms Night and Day

Table of Contents

Preface 7

Numbering the Psalms 11

Bibliography 13

Part One: The Psalms and Us 15
1. Opening the Book 15
2. Prayer of All in One 21
3. The Dense Land of the Psalms 27
4. The Psalms of Christ and Our Own 33
5. The Model and the Unique 39

Part Two: Supplication 45
6. In the Midst of Enemies 45
7. Prayer of the Body 53
8. Prosecution of the Ill 59
9. The Resemblance of Sin 65
10. The System of Evil 71
11. Images of Salvation 77

Part Three: Praise 85
12. Praise and Freedom 85
13. Begin with Praise 91
14. Ending with Praise.—But Now What 99
15. Time of the Psalms 107
16. Praise Night and Day 113

Part Four: Promise 119
17. Response 119
18. Memorial 125
19. Desire 131
20. Promise of Life 137
21. True Bread 143
22. Path 149

Part Five: The Psalms and the World 155
A. Near Creation 157
23. Psalm 8 157
24. Psalm 19 163
25. Psalm 104 171
26. Psalm 139 179
B. Distant Creation 189
27. Psalm 136 193
28. Psalms 74 and 89 203
C. Creation to Come 213
29. Psalms of the Kingdom of God 213

Recapitulation: Psalm 22 223
30. A. Commentary 225
30. B. Interpretation 239

Index 259

Acknowledgments 272

Preface

What did most Christians know about the Psalms except that they were the substance of the breviary for priests, the divine office of men and women religious. They were hardly used by lay people outside the time of vespers and a few verses during Mass. Even those who have heard the *De Profundis* often do not know that it was a Psalm.

Today, at the invitation of the Second Vatican Council, the use of the Psalms in modern languages has awakened, in men and women who make it their ordinary prayer, an urgent desire to perceive their meaning. But that is not all. Christians who may never have sung *Dixit Dominus Domino meo ... Beatus vir qui timet Dominum ... In exitu Israel de Aegypto, domus Jacob de populo barbaro, ...* happy to join the choir of religious communities, feel spontaneously attracted to biblical prayer. The Psalms have experienced a new growth, with new demands.

Today more than yesterday, we recognize the need for outside guidance. Neither a tradition of reading nor one of prayer can be invented. By virtue of the attraction that hidden things have on us, an initiation is desirable.

The simple definition of "psalm" by our *Petit Larousse* dictionary immediately signals an enigma. "Psalm, masculine gender. Canticle or sacred song of the Hebrews and of the Christians." By reciting for centuries the prayer of Israel, Christians recognize that this people knew how to speak as a witness for all humanity. Chosen for that, they found a cry far from themselves and from us. By the cry of the Psalms, we come closer to our ancestors and they to us. If it is true that this cry is stronger before God than death, it is profound! Therefore, it is normal that it comes to us from so far away.

Who will hear, who will understand this language but what is human in every reader? Yet the Psalms do not have us ignore other cries, and reading them, as I propose, is for anyone.

The Psalms are not there in order to keep the faithful from singing other compositions to God. Believers have always renewed their songs.

Irreplaceable because of their unique identity of Christ, the Psalms do not prevent one from using other forms of prayer.

Whether it be a question of universal outlook or the richness of biblical prayer for the future, praying the Psalms is to be experienced rather than demonstrated.

But what is especially to be experienced—with the help of God and neighbor—is that Christian faith that delves deeply into its early roots finds unheard of newness every time. Let us call Gospel what is given to us and what we believe. This Gospel acquires all its luminosity when it shines on the mountain of the Old Testament and the Psalms that summarize it as prayer. This Gospel is not deduced from the older text; if it had been, it would surprise us less. This Gospel respects the former text, because it has the same origin, and both shine in recognition of each other.

I present two intentions, two hopes that have inspired this work: to help one pray with the Psalms and to clarify what we believe.

I have yet to mention the circumstances that encouraged me to write this book.

First, there was the renewal of the liturgical text of the Psalms in French. *Le Psautier, version oecuménique, texte liturgique* was published in 1977 as the approved version of the Episcopal Conferences of France and of the countries where French is spoken. In 1980, this version was introduced in a new edition of the French breviary or *Liturgie des heures*. This is the version that I quote. It was composed from the original Hebrew text, reviewed and corrected several times during the collaboration and for several years between exegetes and specialists of modern and ancient languages.

Then I had occasion to write an introductory essay regarding the biblical language of the Psalms. This was in 1974-1975, in the course of six French television programs of the "Jour du Seigneur" ("Day of the Lord") with Michel Farin. I then wrote twenty of the thirty chapters of this book, first as articles for two journals. Sister Annick Leroux and Sister Jeanne-Marie Grassignoux had invited me to collaborate with the journal *Religieuses dans les professions de santé* and Fr. J. Mesny with *Recherches. Conscience chrétienne et Handicap*. Thus took shape my desire to articulate different aspects of biblical prayer that affect every man. I knew well that it was not necessary to be complete, but I wanted to add, before the publication of the book, a dozen small chapters, notably those dealing with "Creation" in the Psalms. This allowed me to better show how biblical prayer is articulated with expressions of faith. Encountering these chapters at the end of the book, the reader will have been well prepared by what preceded, or such is my hope, to approach certain theoretical aspects of the subject. We understand the Psalms when we apply ourselves to them. As an example, I suggest a patient reading, perhaps closer to a commentary, of Psalm 22: "My God, my God, why have you forsaken me?" I would be pleased if these last words could incite the reader, in turn, to comment on other texts, first of all for him or herself, and then for others.

Something could have kept me from writing about the Psalms. It is that I had announced, two years ago, a sequel to my *Essai de lecture* (Essay in Reading) entitled *L'Un et l'Autre Testament* (The One and the Other Testament), and which was especially concerned with the Old Testament. But as a reader will note, the Psalms did not keep me from exploring the relationship of the two Testaments

Paul Beauchamp
Paris, 4 May 1979

Numbering the Psalms

The numbering of the Psalms is not a problem for everyone who is interested in exegesis and not at all in the liturgy. They follow the numbering of the Hebrew that is used for all modern editions of the Bible. For those who are interested in the liturgy and not in exegesis, the situation is also simple: the Psalms follow the numbering of the liturgical books, which is that of the Greek and Latin, even when the translation was redone from Hebrew.

Unfortunately, for the majority of people who are interested in exegesis and liturgy, the situation is complicated because it is necessary to change the number according to the book that one is reading. I have used the Hebrew numbering, but I provide a table with the corresponding numbers.

Modern editions of the Bible and all books which quote the Psalms: numbering according to the Hebrew edition	Liturgical Psalters which follow the numbering of the Greek & Latin editions
Psalm 1-8	Psalm 1-8
9	9, 1-21
10	9, 22-39
11 to 13	10-112
114	113, 1-8
115	113, 9-26
116, 1-9	114
116, 10-19	115
117 to 146	116-145
147, 1-11	146
147, 12-20	147
148-150	148-150
In this book, each Psalm is indicated according to the number of the column above.	In *Le Psautier, version oecuménique, texte liturgique*, the first number, in large print, reflects the numbering of the column above; the second, smaller, number corresponds to the numbering to the left.

Bibliography

TEXTS

Before comparing one translation with another, it would be good to use a commentary or, this lacking, an edition where the main difficulties of the original text are signaled, as in these accessible volumes:

1. *Les Psaumes, fasciule de la Bible de Jerusalem*, R. Tournay; Paris: Le Cerf, 1964; also found in *La Bible de Jerusalem*, 1973. This is an excellent introduction, with a fine note of Raymond Schwab.
2. *Traduction oecuménique de la Bible, Ancien Testament*, 1975.

INTRODUCTIONS AND COMMENTARIES

3. Marina Mannati, *Les Psaumes* (Collection Cahiers de la Pierre qui Vire), 4 volumes; Paris: Desclée De Brouwer, 1966-1968. The author presents a detailed and in-depth scientific study to a wide group of readers.
4. Marina Mannati, *Pour prier avec les Psaumes* (Cahiers Evangile numéro 13). Paris: Le Cerf, 1975. Short pedagogical synthesis, introduction to modern exegesis.
5. Évode Beaucamp, *Le Psautier*, 2 vol. (Collection Sources bibliques); Paris: Gabalda 1976-1979). After many years given to the study of the Psalms, a Franciscan exegete offers an informed and personal perspective.

FUNDAMENTAL RESEARCH

6. *Supplément au Dictionnaire de la Bible*, fascicule 48. Paris: Letouzey & Ané, 1973. The article "Psaumes" which consists of 245 dense pages of the 255 of this volume, is the work of E. Lipinski, E. Beaucamp, I. Saint-Arnaud: researchers list an almost exhaustive repertory of the actual scholarship.

PATRISTIC READING

7. Saint Augustin, *Prier Dieu. Les Psaumes, Présentation et choix de texts augustiniens*. A.-M. Besnard, O.P.; Paris: Le Cerf, 1964. These passages replace those of Humeau, more numerous, but out-of-print.

THEMES AND FORMS

8. Claus Westermann, *Lob und Klage in den Psalmen* (5e édition augmentée de Das Loben Gottes in den Psalmen). Göttingen: Vandenhoeck & Ruprecht, 1977). Unfortunately not yet in French, this fine work excels at showing how different forms are articulated in the Psalter, notably praise and supplication.

9. Olivier Odelain and Raymond Seguineau, *Concordance des Psaumes*, Desclée De Brouwer, 1980. An inventory of the main words, with an exhaustive list of their uses and a classification by themes. A way of rereading the Psalter, subject by subject, on the basis of known French translations with some references in Hebrew.

PART ONE
THE PSALMS AND US

I

Opening the Book

When we open the Book of Psalms, it may be that fear seizes us: should we not know many things before reading the Bible? It is true that we should learn a certain number of things, but it is better to learn while we read, as our reading becomes the occasion for asking questions. Without that, the prerequisites, the conditions frequently serve as an excuse for putting off a serious encounter with the Word of God. Today let us take Psalm 77, according to the numbering of our Bibles, which is Psalm 76 in the numbering used for the Liturgy of the Hours (which in that follows the old translations, both Greek and Latin).

Since this Psalm is taken from the middle of the Psalter, I am also keeping a verse (v. 10) that is itself from the middle of the Psalm:

And I say, "It is my grief
 that the right hand of the Most High has changed."

This means that the arm of God "is no longer what it was ... ." When we talk about his wondrous deeds, astounding interventions in the midst of history, we always speak about them in the past. We no longer see that today. Perhaps we even see the opposite: we no longer see victories of God but, rather, the victories of those who refuse him, a distancing of those who believe in him. And, as the Psalmist says, "... . it is my grief ..." Yes, this hurts. We cannot accuse this Psalmist of speaking an incomprehensible language!

Who is the Psalmist?

Is he a voice without a body, even more anonymous than those that we hear when we turn on a transistor at any station? There is no single answer to this (good) question: "Who is speaking? Who is saying that the right hand of the Most High has changed?" In earlier times one would have answered: "It is David," because the people of Israel, including those of the New Testament, attributed the Psalms to David. History has taught us that this attribution can only have a symbolic value: this proper name is the sign in which Israel has recognized itself; it rallies all the anonymous cantors who have written the Psalms. Except for rare cases, one cannot identify the Psalmist according to what he says. This people has had many occasions to say that it has no longer seen the hand of God acting in the world, and the Bible relates these times because it not only talks about marvelous things but also about their opposite. Today when we pronounce the words quoted above, in placing "Me" in "I say," we accept a long historical experience of misfortune, and we form one body with a people. One of the effects of praying the Psalms is that even the cry of solitude is no longer solitary, because it melts many cries into one that is repeated. To shout out this cry with our own breath, in our isolation, or to say it aloud with our companion the Psalmist is not the same thing!

Why with him rather than with someone else? Why should I borrow these words translated from Hebrew? There is a reason for that. The first time that God spoke to Abraham, he promised him that "all the families of the earth" would place the benediction of God in relation to his name (Genesis 12: 1-3). This promise is being realized by the simple fact that our benediction and our ordeal are also expressed through the words of an anonymous son of Abraham. Because Abraham and all his sons have only been chosen by God for all of us. We are going towards "David," son of Abraham, because he was going towards us. We believe that he was going towards us because he was going towards Jesus Christ. Praying with the words of the Psalmist is a manner of praying "through Jesus Christ our Lord," as the Church does.

This Psalm is a psalm of supplication:

> I cry aloud to God,
>   aloud to God, that he may hear me. (Ps. 77: 1)

1 *Opening the Book*

Verses 2 to 5 continue on the same note. Because he speaks in the first person, exegetes classify this Psalm in the series "individual supplications." But we should go beyond the surface. What does not at first appear in these stanzas is that the supplicant is inhabited by a misfortune that goes beyond his individual case. The horizon is broader, and we understand this by comparing this text with others. When one evokes, in such a context, "the right hand of the Most High," it is in order to recall the grand events of Sacred History, recited and repeated by all the children of this time in what was the equivalent of their "catechism." This Psalm (v. 10-21) is clearly alluding to the exodus from Egypt. In short, it is saying this: "In our time we no longer see any exodus from Egypt but rather slavery, oppression and defeat." The Psalmist is pleading on account of a "change" of this kind, rather than for his own case.

> I consider the days of old,
>   and remember the years of long ago.
> I commune with my heart in the night;
>   I meditate and search my spirit:
> "Will the Lord spurn forever,
>   and never again be favorable?
> Has his steadfast love ceased forever?
>   Are his promises at an end for all time? ..." (Ps. 77: 5-9)

At times one wonders whether this or that text is contemporary. Faced with this one, we would like to say that it only contains what is current. The present is its one theme. The true reality, in effect, is the crisis, what comes about because a difference has broken up any continuity. About what is this Psalm talking? The subject is change.

If that is the case, should we not also change our ideas about the Bible? Questioned, we would probably answer that the Bible is Sacred History, all the while thinking about a well-known series of resounding actions made by God. Faced with this series, we think invincibly that what it relates is distant from us. The call of Abraham, the revelation to Moses, and the Passover of Exodus are far from us. Thus, in our imagination, we reduce the Bible to a book that relates distant and wondrous deeds; it even gives us the impression, at times, that these are present. Children, at least during a brief period of their early years, are subject to the illusion that what one tells them is quite real. When we do not know the Bible well, it is reduced to this screen of our childhood where images are projected. The Bible does have these stories and it has something else. It includes, with what is wondrous, the experience of the next day and of the following day with its wonder; and the experience that the wonder is far away. It is truly an experience that bites the flesh and wears it out:

> You keep my eyelids from closing:
> I am so troubled that I cannot speak.
> I consider the days of old,
> and remember the years of long ago. (Ps. 77: 4-5)

Those who have lived this wonder are far from us. But the ones who lived its absence, its disappearance—the shadow rather than the spark—they are near us. Their today is the same as our own. This today speaks in the Bible, at length and frequently, particularly in the Psalms that we refer to as "supplications." It is more than just some kind of nearness: we touch them. For these, the wondrous deeds of God are a tradition, a learned narrative.

> I will open my mouth in a parable;
> I will utter dark sayings from of old,
> things that we have heard and known,
> that our ancestors have told us.
> We will not hide them from their children;
> we will tell to the coming generation
> the glorious deeds of the Lord, and his might,
> and the wonders that he has done. (Ps. 78: 2-4)

Thus speaks the Psalm that follows our own: Psalm 78 in our Bibles. To "have heard" from the mouth of relatives and to teach by repeating to others, that is a rather clear description of tradition and of catechism. The voice of the Bible has us hear quite often the voice of those who held only the words to describe "the glorious deeds of the Lord." Similarly, we, though lacking direct experience of these events, can use the same words.

Is this a paradox, an exaggeration? Rather it is a reality, because in effect reality is often paradoxical and often exaggerated. For one generation that lived the Exodus, more than a hundred followed who

1 Opening the Book

only possessed the narrative, only the words. But it was not enough for the words to be repeated by father to son without any change. It was probably necessary. And like many necessary things, it was also at times soporific and even dangerous. One could believe that one experienced the deeds of which words were said, and even contemplate in the words the reflection of oneself, as in a mirror. This could no longer be done in a time of radical misfortune; all illusions were taken away. One day, the Philistines capture the Ark of the Covenant. Another day, the sons of David revolt against him and he flees. One prolonged day beginning around the eighth century before our era, the world is led by peoples whose Lord is not the Lord of Israel, and it is they who accomplish "wonders." And then Israel becomes divided, because the people of God are no longer faithful in witnessing, in close order, to their Lord: they reflect more often in themselves the state of the world that surrounded them. The grand day, "the day of anger," was sensed at the time of exile, which imprinted upon all these changes of the right hand of the Most High the evident mark of the irreversible, from the very beginning of the sixth century:

Are his promises at an end for all time? (Ps. 77: 8)

It was not enough for the word of the Fathers, the ancestors—the Law—to be stated once again. The prophets and the Psalms needed to add their own cry to it as they do here, the cry of the sons. Life passes through the supplication of those who follow, after the time of the wondrous deeds.

In the Psalms, supplication is different every time and, every time, so is the response. Here we could say that the Psalmist who remembers his song finds an answer in it: "I commune with my heart in the night; I meditate and search my spirit" (Ps. 77: 6). His song accompanied him all the days of his life. He modulated the narrative of past deeds. Now, in supplication, he finds a new modulation for it:

The crash of your thunder was in the whirlwind,
   your lightning lit up the world;
   the earth trembled and shook.
Your way was through the sea,
   your path through the mighty waters;
   yet your footprints were unseen. (Ps. 77: 18-19)

These verses offer an original reading of Exodus. It is, indeed, a question of this great day when God opened up a path in the sea for his people. But an attentive look discovers in the sea the place of the unknowable, at the same time as the place of the present. God does wondrous things, but he erases their traces.

Who will again find the path of Israel, the path of God, once the waters have flowed back? It is with this question that the Psalmist finishes his meditation and finds his light that is night, his night that is light. No archeology of the Exodus is possible, nor of any past wondrous act of God. The Exodus is of yesterday. The sea is of yesterday and today, it is the same. And this dangerous sea of today is the path of always for the God of Israel:

> ... yet your footsteps were unseen.
> You led your people like a flock
>   by the hand of Moses and Aaron. (Ps. 77: 19-20)

We cannot "know" the Exodus but only that today the people of God are near the same death, and that God is leading them. Is it necessary to explain that we say the same thing about the path that God had his Son follow and which he indicates to his Church: Does no one know his path?

2

Prayer of All in One

When we read Psalm 77, we said that the Psalms very often give the word to the ordinary person, particularly to the one who saw, like us, these wondrous deeds the following day or even the one after that, that is to say, at a time when they are very distant in history, in the past.

But if these wonderful deeds of salvation are far from us, or if they are present in the form of beautiful narratives, the danger itself is near. Let us take as our point of departure Psalm 3:

> O Lord, how many are my foes!
>   many are rising against me;
> many are saying to me,
>   "There is no help for you in God." (Ps. 3: 1-2)

We cannot get over how frequently we see those who speak in the Psalms exposed to the worst troubles. This is already an important theme of reflection for us.

"There is no help for you ..." That is the same as saying, in our everyday language: "You are lost," and God can do nothing about it or is not interested. Death then appears on the horizon, not only in this Psalm but also in many others. When we are young, we wonder by what unfortunate accident did so many Psalmists "put themselves," as we say, in such terrible situations. They seem to belong to a very particular category of human beings. But this is a rather short view that time, encounters, and some experiences will correct.

If the Psalmists speak, if they have something to say, it is because something has happened to them. Even if it is a question of happiness, this rarely exists without some hardships and danger, before, during, and after. Many times, what has happened and what makes a man speak is to have been visited by, shaken by or thrown down by a danger stronger than himself, a danger that threatens life and the reasons for living. We would not have any Psalms if their authors had not gone through these things, quite near death.

The mystery is that passing through all this should have one come to the point of talking to all men. I open the collection of the 150 Psalms and I find on each page a man who "sinks" (Ps. 69), prey to those who seek his life (see Psalms 38, 56, 70, etc.). He hears them talk:

They think that a deadly thing has fastened on me,
   that I will not rise again from where I lie. (Ps. 41: 8)

They are already digging his grave (Ps. 57:6); they share his belongings (Ps. 22: 18):

... the terrors of death have fallen upon me. (Ps. 55: 4)

... and there is no soundness in my flesh. (Ps. 38: 7)

It is easy for each of us to multiply these examples by going through the book at random. It is a good way to take into account how much this tone differs from that of so many prayers where we tell God our difficulties or even our boredom. Here everything is radical and that is why we might feel ourselves separated, by some kind of threshold, from the Psalms. We resist saying what it is on days and in those circumstances where we feel less threatened: our misfortunes do not reach these proportions.

However, this prayer is a good daily bread.

Let us take every man, every woman in particular. Let us suppose that misfortune strikes them only once in their lives. From that moment on, "once" becomes "every day." By that I do not mean that the misfortune is necessarily repeated, but this day of misfortune is always present, it always marks one. It is worthwhile to note that, in each of our days, we live in reality many days at once:

"...often have they attacked me from my youth ...
The plowers plowed on my back;
   they made their furrows long." (Ps. 129: 2-3)

2 Psalms of All in One

It is not that we remain sad, but that we have become another person. Let us go further. We do not have to suppose it; it is a fact: every man is marked in advance by death. It is already active in us and works in every manner in the depths of our being, in an inexplicable way. That moment, like the test in the past that may be in the future, is also present every day, and it is radical. It marks, as the Psalms say, the "sons of Adam":

> Remember how short my time is—
> for what vanity you have created all mortals? (Ps. 89: 47)

From this we must conclude that the radicalness of the Psalms is at a level that truly corresponds to our daily existence. It reveals the true level of this existence, the precarious reality that is threatened each day, even if appearances hide this.

That is not all. I have taken the perspective of some individuals. But there are others who literally experience the words of the Psalms:

> ... or like a lion they will tear me apart;
> they will drag me away, with no one to rescue. (Ps. 7: 2)

> ... my bones cling to my skin. (Ps. 102: 5)

Although they may feel alone, many people are tracked by injustice, or they are starving, sick, or frightened. When it concerns them, the Psalms neither dramatize nor exaggerate. Dramatization becomes the reality when it concerns the history of humanity, including that of today. It is precisely for this reason that thousands of men and women go to the theatre and to the movies to see horrible things more terrible than those that they experience. They are right to tell themselves "interested" and attracted by images of a reality which the more calm surface of their life and the isolation of their preserved existence make invisible. That is the reality of the world, and how can we not receive a text that places our prayer at its level? Is not this what we seek? Prayer for those who are tested on the five continents has today become a reflex, at times a bit mechanical one, of the prayer of Christian assemblies. The Psalms stamp upon this habit an apparently light change: instead of praying for "those who ...," let us say "I" in their place. Every time that I open this book, I am the man who is tracked by injustice; I am the one who is starving, sick, and frightened. I was going to say:

it is as though God, in our prayer, is not only looking at our particular case, but at the drama of all humanity today.

But here there is no fiction, no "as if." In the time of an individual, a moment of misfortune is more than a moment; it marks an entire life. In the space covered by all living men, those who are offered to injustice and to death occupy more than their place in a prison or in a hospital. If we accept the manner of praying the Psalms, the cry of men who are threatened and oppressed invades our own space, occupies our prayer and, perhaps, melts our problems into their misfortune. This is more than giving a gift of prayer to the unfortunate, because they are the ones who transform us by their cry. The prayer of the Psalms is at times a bit cramped in our hearts, but it is there in order to broaden them.

It could be a fiction to believe that all these cries form just one, to want to pray with the cry of someone else. Who tells me that I am able to cross so much space and place myself before God, as though I am carrying the cry of all, or even that I am carried by the cry of those who suffer most? With this question, prayer very much questions us:

> But I am lowly and in pain;
> let your salvation, O God, protect me. (Ps. 69: 29)

It goes without saying that this cry questions us, if we walk with our head held too high and if we have done everything in life so as not to be disturbed. On the one hand, as we have seen, most often words pass us by and perhaps that is always the case. On the other hand, they question us, as does the drama that is played out in humanity and about which we are now talking. The prayer of the Psalms is a strong wine, and it would be a pity, through some distraction, not to notice this surprise. To pray and to say "I" in the place of those who are most tested is also to be called towards them, and this call has concrete consequences in our lives.

We shall answer this call if we understand its origin. If a man or a woman, who finds it difficult to hope, discovers in the Psalms an individual prayer, that is a sufficient reason to justify the writing of the Psalms. But it is still surprising that such distant words can touch any of us. What has brought these cries together? By what cement have so many men, scattered and touched by death, been able to express their desire with the same words?

2 Psalms of All in One

For the people of Israel, it was the solidarity of one and the same promise that, already, was no stranger to the concerns of humanity at large. In the human race in general, solidarity in one cry is perceived as a possibility, a desire, and a hope. Christians did not invent it. Christians only hold, facing this hope when it exists, or confronted with its opposite, a divine attestation given them as a deposit confided to a passerby who is no more worthy of it than any other. A message that is received: God sees all of humanity as one body, takes its cry as one cry that he hears through the cry of Jesus offered to injustice and to death. Before answering the cry of evil, God has made it his own. Jesus has thus sealed the unity of all sufferings in his own. He has signed the prayer of the Psalms as a virtual prayer for all men and women and he has given us the right, without pretending, to say "I" in the place of the humiliated, to learn from them what he bore.

The "I" of the humiliated man, tracked and dying, is that of Jesus Christ. It is no surprise that this prayer should at once pass through us and go beyond us. Who tells me that I can recite the prayer of the Psalms in the name of all? Faith tells me by having me believe that the death of Christ, who assumes the death of all, is imprinted in me by baptism. The "I" of the Psalms is that of Christ, but he does not exclude anyone from them because effacement is his sign. He attracts in them. He gives passage. Thus understood, the prayers of the Psalms become alive. Their words are like the breads of the miracle: they are held in a basket and they are good for a multitude of people. To believe is to believe that they are truly worthwhile. In this sharing of the words at such a grand distance in time and in space, the faith expressed in tradition, recognizes in it the work of the Spirit. It animates, it has one breathe, it unifies.

But by what can all these sufferings of death be already cemented, if not by the opposite of death, by life? Some men who have experienced them have declared that the words of Scripture were inspired. This does not mean only that they have some authority but that a breath carries them.

To say everything, the cross of Christ is a sign that marks all humanity and, through this sign, the Spirit of life and hope passes which rallies all, as Ezekiel says, from the four winds. If that is the case, we shall again meet this sign as we go through the Psalms. Just now we have encountered what authorizes us to take from the Psalms words for the prayer of all humanity.

In the prayer that gathers those who are distant, living or dead, we have recognized the motion that tradition calls the movement of the Spirit.

As this Spirit is already present when the words, which connect one suffering to another, quite behind and beyond them, are written and read, it is not surprising that it manifests itself so suddenly, arising from the heart of supplication in each of the Psalms. Sleep and night-time hold a great place in our texts. Night: time of choice for prayer, but especially for an answer from God; like a turn that man would not be able to take all alone; where he falls each day under what he cannot bear, night arranges some transition towards hope:

> I lie down and sleep;
>   I wake again, for the Lord sustains me. (Ps. 3: 5)

3

THE DENSE LAND OF THE PSALMS

The reading of the Psalter encounters some obstacles. After reading a few pages, we might have a different perspective about the text and even some questions. Perhaps some old questions, a bit sluggish because frequently asked. But there are better remedies than habit when a biblical text astonishes us. The difficulties, when confronted, often become luminous points.

I shall choose two points that might perplex us:

Why does our companion, the Psalmist, so often say that he is just? Why does he have such harsh words for his enemies?

He thus places himself on the opposite side of behaviors that offer confession and pardon.

Certain verses have us hesitate and we hurry, while singing them, to come to those that follow. Nevertheless, there are not just a few of these:

… judge me, O Lord, according to my righteousness (Ps. 7: 8)

… my feet have not slipped. (Ps. 17: 5)

or these lines:

Therefore the Lord has recompensed me
   according to my righteousness,
   according to the cleanness of my
   hands in his sight. (Ps. 18: 24)

On the one hand, these verses have not displeased the Church: before the offertory at Mass, the priest used to recite them when he washed his hands "as a sign of innocence" ("I wash my hands in innocence, and go around your altar, O Lord ..." Ps. 26: 6). On the other, cannot such an attitude have one pray in a different manner, one that Saint Luke mentions? "'God, I thank you that I am not like other people: thieves, rogues, adulterers, or even like this tax collector ...'" (Luke 18: 11). If the person who speaks in this way does not go home justified, it is not because he is a Pharisee but because of his manner of praying. Saint Luke shows what made everything wrong in the Pharisee's prayer: the man singles out as a sinner, to God, a tax collector who has done him no wrong; whereas this tax collector does not even notice him and only thinks of his own sins. The parable stands as a kind of warning; it is not a judgment about the prayer of the Psalms.

In order to judge objectively, we need to find what exegetes call the "form" or the "literary genre," or the place where these prayers originated. Unlike a geographical place, distant from us, it is an institutional place, similar to the one where we can also find ourselves. For example, a tribunal is a place where someone can state that he is innocent without passing for a proud person. In comparison, the words of Luke take on all their importance: "... not like this tax collector." No one has come to accuse the Pharisee in order to oblige him to declare himself innocent; on the contrary, he wants to make himself the accuser and he does not do this in order to answer an attack or to defend himself. The Psalmist, on the contrary, is practically always the accused. That does not mean that he always prays as though he were on trial, but he refers to this situation, where the unique question is not knowing whether one is modest but whether one says the truth before men and even before God. Luke's Pharisee gives a monologue; the Psalmist a dialogue. He pleads his defense.

Given a particular circumstance, the tribunal might become symbolic or universal. The Book of Job presents us with a perpetual accuser of the just, who pursues Job before the heavenly tribunal: his name is Satan. "Accuser" and "Satan" have become synonyms. Behind the friends of Job who accuse him (although it no longer be before a tribunal) stands the invisible Accuser. The similarities between the Book of Job and the Psalms are so great that it is reasonable to relate them on this point. In fact, the more the Psalms were read at a distance from the events experienced by the Psalmist, all the more were the traits of the Accuser revealed. The Book of Revelation will call Satan "the accuser of our comrades ... , who accuses them day and night before our God" (Revelation 12: 10).

3 The Dense Land of the Psalms

This transformation of particular circumstances of the life of the Psalmist into a durable reality, visible or invisible, but shared by the Psalmist and the reader, has always accompanied the reading of the Psalter since biblical times, and it is indispensable for it. What is this reality? It is quite substantial and runs throughout our life.

First of all, it is curious that any declarations of innocence are rather rare in our spontaneous prayers. And so we are not truly tempted on that side. Expressions of this feeling of personal justice do not attract us; rather we tend to avoid them. This is a significant indication, but of what? Is it that we are humble? … In this case, the continuous confession of our faults should give us some relief, make us less difficult and less harsh towards every kind of publican; in a word, joyous. But there is an alternative; the Accuser Satan can easily enter by the door of our readiness to accuse us, and he knows, I imagine, this weak characteristic of Christians. And if only to refuse him entry, let the Psalms propose that we say, "I am without reproach."

The Old Testament is full of these indirect teachings and instructs us while setting up some traps. We are scandalized when a man declares that he is just when we feel that we are not more humble than he is. The accusation then turns against us. We are ready to acknowledge that we are sinners, but the willingness to declare oneself a sinner is often a roundabout way to believe in one's own justice. The accusation that we pronounce against ourselves, is it not the "absolute just self" that we secretly nurture in our hearts that has it come forth? An *imaginary* "just" self that is quite lively persecutes a "sinful self" in us. This system lets our true sins remain hidden from us: our "just" self is the true sinner who hides in us under humility. This kind of pride, less candid than that of the Pharisee, also loses its mask: when we can just no longer put up with tax collectors, we betray ourselves.

It is necessary to pray before the tribunal of truth. The Psalmists say that they are sinners and they call themselves just. In order to be able to say truthfully: "Here I have done badly," one must be able to say truthfully: "Here I have done well." This is a lesson of the Psalms and its effects are far-reaching, if it teaches us to be reflective.

There is more. As we already know, the Psalms lose all meaning if they close us in on ourselves. In order to make us pray with others, they have us say words written by others. Why not say that this Assembly which sings with us is "without reproach," since it is a part of the Church, holy and without stain? It is true that, in one's thought if not in the prayer of many, the Church is seen from afar and has replaced the accused tax collector. Let us learn to see the Church with the compassion that God has for it. He sees his son in it and, made in the name of Christ, the prayer of the Psalms confesses our justice as coming entirely from him, as being his own. To believe that God sees us as just in Jesus Christ would perhaps be most in conformity with the Gospel in that we would—finally—have shame for our sins and more pity for those of others.

The second point that leaves us perplexed are the imprecations, the cries expressed before God against men who destroy others and what is good. Here again, what we must first do is establish the facts in order to have an objective appreciation. For example, some serious exegetes think that a great part of the curses in the long Psalm 109 (verses 6 to 15) is not uttered by the Psalmist, but by his enemy, defined at verse 6 as the "accuser." The Psalmist, here again, counterattacks:

He loved to curse; let curses come on him. (Ps. 109: 17)

This supposes that the Psalmist himself does not like to curse. But, indisputably, he wishes that the curse would turn on those who take pleasure in it. In other cases, we hear, more than the curses of the persecutors (who are supposed or evoked), the curses of the Psalmist himself:

Let them be blotted out of the book of the living,
  let them not be enrolled among the righteous. (Ps. 69: 28)

We could choose not to read or sing these verses, but those that we do sing are from the same source. It is normal, if we are interested in the source itself, and not only in a few verses, to seek the unity of its manifestations. It was a source for the Gospels also. Matthew takes up another passage of Psalm 69 that I have just quoted, in the narrative of the Passion (Mt. 27: 34, 48, see Ps. 69: 21). It is true that the Psalter comprises diverse texts from several periods. Certain war songs, or of a more national inspiration (cf. Ps. 68: 22-23), may reflect more primitive times. However, Psalm 69 is quite near the experience of a prophet such as Jeremiah, who would not have erased a line from it (see Jeremiah 11: 20 and 12: 1-3): Jeremiah could teach us much about the love of God and of neighbor. We should not speak too quickly about

3 The Dense Land of the Psalms

some progressive mellowing of men during sacred history. Psalm 149 is not that old.

Here are some facts: the curses in the Psalms already quoted (Pss. 109: 8 and 69: 25) are applied by Saint Peter to Judas (Acts 1: 20) and those in Psalm 69, by Saint Paul, to those of his people who have remained hard-hearted (Romans 11: 7-10). And what should we say about the curses of the Book of Revelation against Great Babylon! All that does not make these words sweeter on our lips. Yet such a difficulty has us be attentive to one point: besides uttering at times the words "Woe to you" for the benefit of several cities and groups of people (Matthew 23: 13-29; see Luke 6: 24-26, parallel to the Beatitudes), Jesus also states a definitive judgment when he says, "You that are accursed, depart from me ..." (Matthew 25: 41).

The use of the New Testament shows us that the words of the Psalmist go further than the particular circumstances that occasioned them. Otherwise, since the persecutor and the persecuted are not with us, why would we have kept these words for such a long time? Two dimensions should remain present to our minds. First of all, the words of the Old Testament, going beyond the truth of their passing moment, inscribe in an enigmatic way the trace of the mystery of faith, and this comprises the mystery of evil and the judgment of God. Secondly, if this mystery goes beyond experiences, it has effectively encountered them. It has been present in the ordeals of real men before Christ. The Gospels reveal this mystery in Jesus Christ. They teach us that sin is the effective will to destroy life, goodness, and hope. Sin is death seeking both partisans and complicity for itself; it is not necessarily what awakens feelings of guilt in us. And why always think about ourselves? The death wish is at work everywhere in the world. The Psalms are greatly effective in teaching us to read it where it is and to hate it. They have us understand the violence of Jesus Christ; the least that one can say is that the Gospels do not hide it.

"Father, forgive them; for they do not know what they are doing" (Luke 23: 34). With his hatred of evil, a liberating hatred, Jesus has no hatred for bad men. He forgives his executioners, but his words have not always been gentle. Love your enemies and pray for those who persecute you (Matthew 5: 44). This prayer is not in the Psalter. That is evident. Let us wish that it be in our hearts and on our lips. But let us fear any forgiveness that, in our hearts, would not be sincere.

It is more perfect to say, "Forgive us," than to say, "I am without reproach." It is more perfect to say, "We forgive those who have offended us," than to appeal to the justice of God. More perfect, and more beautiful. But our prayer also needs to start from the level where our humility and our forgiveness are not perfect, already composed: they have to traverse in us this thick layer of experience of which the Psalms record a trace. We shall then see our pardon traverse curses and, joyfully, undo them. The roots of the avowal of our faults and of our forgiveness of another person absolutely need this more obscure terrain. Confession and forgiveness are not performances, but gifts of the Spirit. The Spirit has to rise through all our roots, through the thickness of our being. Is it because we have forgotten[1] the roots of the tree that we have tasted so rarely the savor of its fruits?

---

1   When certain words against enemies are between brackets in a Psalter, this means that assemblies are not *obliged* to sing them, and it is good that they have this choice. There is less liberty when the same words do not appear and, in this case, it is even necessary, in order to notice it, to pay attention to the numbering of the verses.

In all these cases, these measures should not have it that the Bible becomes a censored book. We do not sing *other* Psalms than those of the Bible. It would be troubling to remark that we are using a Bible that has been reviewed, corrected, and in some way muffled. The past teaches us that the manipulations of masterpieces only entail spiritual anemias ...

... Teresa of Avila was not afraid of the "difficult" passages of the Psalter. When she is persecuted, not by invisible spirits, but by well placed people in religion, she quotes Psalm 141, 10 to apply it to them: "... the wicked fall into their own nets, / while I alone escape (Letter of 31 January 1579). We shall not find these words in certain official Psalters, which have omitted them, and we shall not even realize it, since we shall not see that verse 10 is the last one ... However, the verse clarifies the traditional meaning of the Resurrection of Jesus.

# 4

The Psalms of Christ and Our Own

How do we refer to Christians, when they hold the Psalter in their hands? "Readers" of the Psalms? That does not quite satisfy us because, when we address the text of a prayer to God, we do something else and more than just read it. It happens that we sometimes sing this prayer. Were we only to recite it, that is, already, more than reading it. I agree that this word "recite" is not very attractive as it makes us think of our school exercises. However, if we hide this shadow for a moment, as we do when we place our hand on a part of a painting in order to see the other parts better, we shall perhaps discover that the word "recite" has some advantages. It signifies an absence and a presence.

An absence: when I recite a poem, I express that it is not my own and I honor it. (If I had written it, I would recite it in order to say that it is no longer mine, I would thus honor it and detach myself from it: this would be the same.) But to recite is also to make an "act of presence," because it is to make interiorly one's own the text by adhering to it with sincerity. I conclude from these two aspects that the "recitation" of the Psalms is an act of tradition, in the true (living) meaning of the term: to be oneself the actualization of a message that does not have its origin in us. The recitation, the tradition, is an act, taken up by "actors," people who play the role of another. Saint Paul says that it is necessary "to put on Christ" like a piece of clothing that is not ourselves. This clothing is, par excellence, the gift that God gives us. And when we have received a beautiful garment, we wear it: it was not ours; it is a part of us. It is the same for the words of Scripture: we enter into them and they enter into us; we are "actors."

Naturally, "to put on Christ" does not mean having to put on the garment of the Psalms. But tradition teaches and shows that it is a good way to put on Christ. I am going to try to connect to this tradition.

Let us begin with a clarification. The good phrasing is that of Luke (24: 44) "... . that everything written about me in the law of Moses, the prophets, and the Psalms must be fulfilled." Jesus puts on the totality of Scripture, what was, in his time, the Bible. When we talk about the relationship that Jesus lived with the Psalms, it is a question of the Psalms as an essential part of a unit, not of the Psalms as if they went beyond the rest of the Book. The place of the Psalms is rather precise: whereas the Law and the Prophets say "You" to man, the Psalms say "I" to God. "Happy are those who ... delight ... in the law of the Lord, and on his law they meditate day and night" (Ps. 1). And so the Psalms designated the place of the "narrator," of the reader, which was the place of Jesus. When we look again at the sentence of Luke, we see that naming the Psalms as the third term in the list of the great biblical writings, after the Law and the Prophets, was not an absolute given. This has us remark that the Psalms are indispensable for understanding the destiny of Jesus Christ.

Jesus himself recited the Psalms. "... . he went to the synagogue on the sabbath day, as was his custom" (Luke 4: 16). This type of indication, rather frequent in the Gospels, informs us quite well: if Jesus thus situated himself among the religious practices of his people, the prayer of the Psalms was his own. Another indication, very significant, comes to us from the writings of the New Testament itself; all its authors show themselves to be so close to the writings of the Old Testament that they use them as though they were a mother tongue. They reproduce sentences of Scripture and, notably, at the right place, those of the Psalms, often without any indication that they are quoting them, aptly and with ease, as though giving no thought to it. Taking into account the differences between these authors, and their writing at different times, it would not be reasonable to imagine that they were filled with the texts of Scripture and the Psalms and that Jesus would have been less so than they.

These indications are indirect, for they are deduced from the general behavior of Christ and of that of the generation of the New Testament in regard to the texts of the Old Testament. There are also some direct affirmations. According to the Gospel writers, Jesus quotes the Psalms. Before his Passion, the Passover supper includes the singing of the Psalms (Matthew 26: 30). On the cross, Jesus's cry, "Elî Elî lemâh sabachtanî," is the beginning of Psalm 22. After his resurrection, Jesus appears to the Eleven, according to the text that we have quoted above, and tells them that he has accomplished the Law, the Prophets and the Psalms. According to Matthew, the first words of the resurrected Jesus to the two Marys is a return to a Psalm: "… . go and tell my brothers …" (Matthew 28: 10). It is a question of Psalm 22, the Psalm of the "lemâh sabachtanî" which then becomes praise with verse 22: "I will tell of your name to my brothers and sisters …" This last case provides us with an example of the way by which the Psalms flourish in the Gospels and on the lips of Christ, without their always being recognized as sources.

So there was a rich and narrow relation between the Psalms and the person of Jesus. But the question is to know what there is within this relation, what it offers us that is essential.

It proposes to us, in fact, knowledge of Christ at a fundamental level. If we know Jesus Christ through the Psalms, I will admit that this is surprising and paradoxical, because it consists in knowing a man by what is not of him. Is this like delving into the past environment of the deceased? Let us suppose that we are allowed to visit his apartment: then his preferred books and his records tell us much about him, but little about his originality, his secret, his newness. Here, the question is of a quite different order. To find through the Scriptures of the Old Testament the ambiance of the days of Christ and the impressions that came to him is not insignificant, but it remains uncertain and unstable. It is not a solid foundation for knowledge of Jesus Christ. What one does find is more radical.

Jesus Christ defines himself as the one who has done the will of another, in other words, as the one who obeys. We can look for, guess, and reconstitute the ways by which Jesus has known what he calls the will of his Father. One thing is certain: the witnesses who proclaim Jesus Christ in the New Testament all say that the will of the Father for Jesus is inscribed in the Scriptures:

> … . Christ died for our sins in accordance with the scriptures, and that he was buried, and that he was raised on the third day in accordance with the scriptures … (1 Corinthians 15: 3-4).

The consequence for us is very precise. We might think (and this would be unreasonable) that Jesus knew the will of his Father and the path to follow only at the times, reported by the Gospels, when he was alone in prayer, but we can only know the will of the Father for Jesus through what was, for him, Scripture, through the Law, the Prophets, and the Psalms. The Gospels have made for us this reading of the plan of God in the Old Testament, designating Jesus Christ, and they complement in part this work. But the Law, the Prophets, and the Psalms again present themselves to us in order to accompany, clarify, and orchestrate the Gospel—in biblical terms—in order to "glorify" him. And so it is meaningful to say that we know Christ by knowing what is not from him: we know the path traced for him. He recognized the will of the Father in it, the will of the Father from whom he proceeds entirely. The way which is not "of him" is "he."

The Gospels are written entirely in order to show us that Jesus accomplishes a plan, one by which we recognize that he is the Christ. A plan posits a sense of fullness, especially since it is a question of God's plan. So we should not think that Jesus only accomplishes some isolated verses to be selected from Scripture. That would be a paralyzing way of considering things. We can be a victim of this, because the Evangelists often quote a particular text of the Old Testament in order to found the narrative of an isolated action of Jesus. But they proceed in this manner because, for them, just one verse evokes an entire world, whereas that is not the case for us. They thus proceed differently than we. We see this in Luke: it is probably in his Gospel that we find the simplest declaration of the relation of Jesus to the Scriptures.

I am referring to the episode of Emmaus. It is the resurrected Jesus who reads the Gospel to the two disciples: "Then beginning with Moses and all the prophets, he interpreted to them the things about himself in all the scriptures" (Luke 24: 27). In this verse we have the word "all" mentioned twice. This "all" contains a message: "Was it not necessary that the Messiah should suffer these things and then enter into his glory?" (Luke 24: 26). Thus understanding the Scriptures, the disciples believe that Jesus has risen from the dead. By experiences less representative than that of Emmaus, many disciples had to believe through this way of reading which runs throughout the book. We are missing one thing, knowing what Jesus explained. Luke does not tell us.

Unless ... it is not missing at all! Let us read the Gospel. It indicates, one by one, the passages of Scripture in order to show us fulfillment in Jesus Christ. Emmaus is almost a signature of the entire Lukan Gospel, the birth certificate of the narrative of the Gospel based on the Scriptures that precede the Gospel. Through the path of the Scriptures, the Gospels give a beginning to the life of Jesus, that

4 The Psalms of Christ and Our Own

of "the only Son, who is close to the Father's heart" (John 1: 18), and show that he returns to the Father by his offering, such as the Psalms describe it:

> Sacrifice and offering you do not desire,
>   but you have given me an open ear.
> Burnt offering and sin offering
>   you have not required.
> Then I said, "Here I am;
>   in the scroll of the book it is written of me.
> I delight to do your will, O my God;
>   your law is within my heart." (Ps. 40: 6-10)

There is something else in the Emmaus narrative: "Were not our hearts burning within us while he was talking to us on the road, while he was opening the scriptures to us?" (Luke 24: 32). The experience of the disciples, the experience of the conformity of Jesus to the Scriptures, is not just a reflection. It moves through the depths of one's being and revives its roots. The question is precisely that of knowing why we are concerned, touched, by the fact that Jesus Christ fulfills the former Scriptures. The example of obedience to his Father would not be enough. We would remain outside it.

Rather are we concerned because the obedience of Jesus to his Father is dictated to him through men. Where is "the plan of the Father" written if not on men, on an entire people before him? Of course, it is written on a book. But, if the paper speaks, it is because it sends us back to other lives, similar to our own, which God has taken in order to write on them the plan that he formed for his Christ. Here the Book of Psalms can claim its rightful place, because some men, who say "I," here face life and death and tell of their own passion.

We know how the Psalms were the cry of an anonymous people in difficulty, devoid of grand deeds, stretched to the breaking point in moments of crisis, in the trial that the enemy within gave to the unhappy and poor people of Yahweh. The inscription of this trajectory in an entire people is, I recall, the work of the Spirit, sent by the Father to a people in order to gather them around the only Son. Between the Son and the Father, there is the work of the Spirit in a people. And, as this people are like us, our heart can be "burning" when we recognize in us the passage, not only of Jesus, for he is "not alone" (John 8: 16 and 29; 16: 32) but of Jesus with the Father and the Spirit.

By "reciting" the Psalms, we "put on" Christ. But this is possible only because he has "put on" us. That is the only way. It consists in knowing Christ while knowing ourselves. There is no other way. But this also has us know ourselves where we do not want to know ourselves, in our carnal weakness. At times the Psalms seem to us to be less beautiful than our ideal and almost not elevated enough for us. By placing them in the mouth of Christ, we understand what Saint Paul wants to say, that he bore "the likeness of sinful flesh" (Romans 8: 3).

Let us conclude with two words: we should not read the Psalms "quite simply" as though the Jewish people spoke in them, nor "quite simply" as though Christ spoke in them, nor "quite simply" as though they related my own life or the life of the Church. There is no "quite simply." The text is all of its rings, taken one in the other, passing from one to the other. The narrator can change rings from one day to another and thus work at accomplishing this passage.

5

The Model and the Unique

We have said that the Gospels often quote the Old Testament and particularly the Psalms. "Often" is not a precise enough term; we count, in fact, 16 strict quotations (more than recalls or allusions) in Matthew, 11 in Mark, 17 in Luke and 10 in John, referring us to a text of the Psalms. As for the allusions that, for an attentive reader, certainly evoke the Psalms, these are more difficult to list, but they are numerous. Behind these literary rapprochements, which assume in the Evangelist a learned knowledge, and which thus call for a learned exam, there hides a more simple experience, one which was universally shared by the first witnesses of the Gospel and its first intended audience. Simple as it is, this experience is also foundational for our faith. I shall try to find its source while admitting that we shall have to face several obstacles.

In order to begin, let us describe the experience that we are discussing: the life and death of Jesus Christ seemed to the witness to fulfill a program and bear the mark of a resemblance.

The consciousness of an accomplished program is expressed in the formula dear to St. John: "... to fulfill the scripture." He uses it frequently: John 13: 18; 15: 25; 19: 24, 28, 36. The Psalms thus introduced in these five passages are all considered as prophecies of the Passion. Other quotations express the astonishment caused by a resemblance that we suddenly notice. Let us suppose that after the visit of some unknown person, we recognize him in a portrait that we have possessed for some time without knowing whom it portrays. The surprise is inscribed in this question:

"Have you never read in the scriptures: 'The stone that the builders rejected has become the cornerstone; this was the Lord's doing, and it is amazing in our eyes'?"

Here Matthew (21:42) quotes Psalm 118: 22-23. Luke and Mark do much the same and almost in the same terms. It always concerns the Passion, because it always regards the rejection of Jesus by the authorities of Jerusalem. The text is addressed during the last days of his life to the immediate interlocutors of Jesus. It is also addressed, in a permanent manner, to the readers of the Gospel who—it is understood—have also read the Psalter. The text expresses two surprises: first, the Messiah has come and so the living model of the portrait traced by the Psalm truly exists; he is not invented, he is not imaginary. Secondly, he came and I let him leave without recognizing him, although I had his portrait.

Surprise is a capital element of the coming of the expected Christ. One could object, in effect, that fulfilling a program (in biblical terms: a "design") or even resembling a model does not take with it any shock of newness and approaches more repetition, fixity, and finally boredom. But whether it is a question of conformity to the program or to the portrait, its discovery by witnesses of the Gospel makes it appear rather astounding. We have to talk about an unexpected resemblance. This is a paradox that is stronger than an "ordinary paradox," if one can thus talk; a paradox that is more paradoxical.

The Gospel gave and still gives joyful news: he has come, the unknown person whom I awaited. He came, the one about whom I already possessed some kind of signal. That is the certainty, and the Gospel of John gives us an example of its function when Phillip goes to look for Nathanael and tells him, "We have found him about whom Moses in the law and also the prophets wrote, Jesus son of Joseph from Nazareth" (John 1: 45).

But Nathanael, neither touched nor convinced by his words, answers: "Can anything good come out of Nazareth?" (John 1: 46). At first, all that one learns from this kind of exchange is that the witness is certain about what he says. This is a necessary condition but it is not enough to convince us. One always talks about dialogue, but dialogue is not sufficient. Sometimes, it does not advance anything. In effect, the experience of the witness is always stronger and more radical than any proof that he might offer. That is why Phillip tells Nathanael, "Come and see" (John 1: 46). Testimony is only effective if it incites

5 The Model and the Unique

the listener, not to acquiesce when faced with proof but to have his own experience.

Can we experience what the Gospels tell us when they quote texts of the Old Testament and, notably, those of the Psalter? When the Gospel establishes relationships between the Passion of Jesus (since that is the main point) and proclamations of the Psalter that are taken to be prophetic, do we feel ourselves concerned? Nathanael's experience prepares us to encounter some obstacles.

Let us try to go through this itinerary of recognition by again reading some Johannine quotes of the Psalter that we already mentioned.

> Even my bosom friend in whom I trusted,
> who ate of my bread, has lifted the heel against me. (Ps. 41: 9)

This quote from the Psalms shows that the betrayal of Judas fulfills the Scriptures (John 13: 18). It is the same for Psalm 35: 19 (or 69: 4):

> ... or those who hate me without cause ...

Here John sees prophesized the hostility of the world towards Jesus and his Father (John 15: 25). As for dividing his garments and casting lots for his tunic, the Evangelists refer to Psalm 22: 18. John, like the three synoptic writers, underlines this aspect of dividing the clothes, but he offers more detail while insisting on the seamless tunic.

> ... they divide my clothes among themselves;
> and for my clothing they cast lots. (Ps. 22: 18)

As in Psalm 69: 21, Jesus is thirsty and is given vinegar to drink (John 19: 28). Finally the bones of Jesus are spared; the soldiers do not break them in order to fulfill Psalm 34: 20:

> He keeps all their bones; not one of them will be broken.

There are other quotations from the Psalms in the Gospel of John and in the synoptics. Some of the similarities that are noted have a very general air: betrayal of the friend, unmotivated hatred of the just one, thirst experienced by the tortured victim and even the sharing of his clothing by the guards. Thousands of men and women have experienced such misfortunes. They experienced them before Jesus, since the Psalms sing of real suffering. Other men, and how many, have experienced them after him. What is astounding is that, possessing the portrait of the Just One suffering in the Psalms and elsewhere, witnesses were able to say, while seeing Jesus suffer, that they referred to him, that these texts were fulfilled by him and by no other person. The portrait could have been applied to many other people!

Next to these general aspects, the Gospel of John probably presents some that are rather special and accidental. Judas shares the bread of the Supper at the very moment that Satan enters into him (John 13: 27), which perhaps gives more relief to the quotation of Psalm 41 made a bit earlier. Jesus's seamless garment (John 19: 23) seems to be made expressly in order for it to be placed separately from the other clothing, so that the model of Psalm 22: 18 is more carefully followed. But it is especially because his legs are not broken that Jesus is not executed as others are. In the entire composition of the suffering Just One as John presents it, this detail constitutes a particular sign. This is very little with which to identify Jesus; it is almost nothing.

We should admit two facts. First, it is a fact that Jesus was recognized by these details or, at least, that these details were retained; so there is a lesson for us in this. Secondly, it is a fact that these details do not constitute a proof. Let us even be frank and say that they are very subjective. But that is precisely why they have an important role when it comes to witnessing. Is it not normal to question witnesses: "When did you see him?"—"... when he broke the bread" (cf. Luke 24: 31). "And you?"—"... when we caught so many fish" (John 21: 7). Likewise, it is not because Jesus was given vinegar to drink that he accomplishes the Psalms; but it is when the narrative or the spectacle of this suffering was connected to a Psalm that the first believers understood: "It is the Lord!"

These indications are valuable even if they are not proofs. They teach us how witnesses have believed. But these witnesses tell us as Phillip told Nathanael: "Come and see." They do not say, "Agree with me" but, rather, "Having learned how I believe, come ... !"

We must distinguish between an indication and a proof. An indication, while it is weak, accidental and vulnerable in itself, is nevertheless quite valuable in having us approach truth, when this truth belongs to the order of life. Regarding what is essential to life, proofs play an important role, but they play it down. They do not fight at the front

5 The Model and the Unique

because, the more a proof is solid, the more the mind resists it. That is why so much evidence escapes us and we do not see what is obvious. That is also why, when we tell our neighbor that a truth that he refuses to accept is obvious, we are wasting our time. On the front line of fighting for the truth, indications are much more effective in coming to a decision, which proofs only confirm later.

The Gospel witnesses provide indications of their faith from the writings of the Old Testament. They do not give proofs. But they send the listener to what he will himself find. This is because no one can show another what is essential regarding truth; he can only send him forth by showing him that he himself has gone down a certain path. Let us remember what the Samaritans said to the woman who had first spoken to them about Christ: "It is no longer because of what you said that we believe, for we have heard for ourselves, and we know that this is truly the Savior of the world" (John 4: 42).

But witnesses do lead us somewhere. If they lead us towards the testimony of the Old Testament, it is because, for us, there is something of life in these texts. The Psalms give witness to Jesus Christ. He says that Moses "wrote" about him (John 5: 46; cf. 1: 45), and this testimony extends to all of Scripture. But the truth that we will find in this way must become our own.

The prophecy of Jesus Christ that is in the Psalms can only reach us if it is also a prophecy about ourselves. And there is a different prophecy for each person and for each epoch from the same texts. Each person must find his path.

If we think about it, the Gospel witnesses recognized in the model given by the Scriptures the one who was the Unique. That is quite a paradox! Several knowledgeable commentators proclaim, "There is no model of the Unique!" They refuse all these connections. But it is not easy to admit that the Gospel writers were intent on communicating an idea that was so fragile and inconsistent. Let us try to understand them. They did not give, as proof, subject to calm reason, a paradox of experience: there is a model for the Unique. The Psalms describe the just man as betrayed, stripped of everything, hated and rejected. It was necessary that Jesus Christ have a model, since he came to bear our image. The model for Jesus Christ is our weakness. With this little book in hand where the model is traced, who will be able to say, standing before Jesus Christ, whether the model is well realized? One should have some experience of the model in order to say whether

Jesus Christ is its truth. In reality, the Gospels answer in different ways. They say that it is necessary to be poor or tested in order to understand whether Jesus Christ is the perfect poor person. They also say that it is necessary for God to cry out in order for one to recognize Jesus Christ in his model; only the perfect one reveals the perfect.

We could conclude that the path of our life is a part of our faith. Or even this: that recognizing the work of the Spirit in the Scriptures is to recognize the work of the Spirit that leads us towards the Unique. The Spirit attests in the Scriptures that the Unique is not alone and that we also are not alone.

The Unique has followed the model of all, but he is also the model who has attracted every man since the beginning.

PART TWO

SUPPLICATION

6

IN THE MIDST OF ENEMIES

Let us recall with a few broad strokes different stages of our reading:

1. The Psalms assign a large place to ordeals and they especially stress the times when the grand acts of God, his "wondrous deeds," distance themselves in the past. In this the Psalmists make themselves closer to us.

2. Because of its extreme character, the suffering of the Psalmist finds the crucial moments of each life in their root and it gathers the traits that are applicable to the immense number of those who are most downtrodden. Everything in this collection of prayers is a "question of life or death."

3. The Psalmists declare themselves to be just, not always, but often enough for this position to surprise us. In addition, they proclaim before God words against their enemies that are sometimes terrible. So where is the admission of their own faults, where is the pardon of those of another? But if the Psalmists resemble more what we are than what we dream to be, is it in order that we reject this mirror?

4. Jesus Christ himself put on the text of the Psalms, as we do when we "recite" them. Obedience to the will of the Father showed him a path in the fulfillment of the Scriptures and particularly of the Psalms. The Psalms have shown the path where Christ has joined all men of yesterday and today.

5. Jesus fulfills the Scriptures. The editors of the Gospels have given us this certainty as the echo of an experience that has overwhelmed

them. This is the experience of an unexpected resemblance, where the Unique sent by God takes as a model the image of men who were tested before he was.

All that precedes has prepared us to discover that the point where the Psalter most enlightens us is the Passion of Jesus Christ. This clarity, this light, is of a prophetic nature, one that the witnesses of the New Testament recognized. The revelation that it brings to us is not unilateral. On the contrary, it is necessary that the weight of the prophecy of the Old Testament be distributed equitably between the announcement of the sufferings to be undergone and that of glory, between the Passion and the Resurrection:

> ... Christ died for our sins in accordance with the scriptures, and that he was buried, and that he was raised on the third day, in accordance with the scriptures ... (I Corinthians 15: 3-4)

We find the same equilibrium in The First Letter of Peter:

> Concerning this salvation, the prophets who prophesied of the grace that was to be yours made careful search and inquiry, inquiring about the person or time that the Spirit of Christ within them indicated when it testified in advance to the sufferings destined for Christ and the subsequent glory. (1 Peter 1: 10-11)

In effect, the Prophets as well as the prophetic prayer of the Psalms present, as front and back, tears and joy, the bitter end and the new beginning. So it is not a question of granting some privilege to only one side. Here, any preference of one over the other would be a mistake. But we cannot say everything at the same time.

Since we must begin by one of the two sides, I would like to show in what follows that the Psalms are a commentary on the Passion.

We had thought that we knew the Passion of Christ and that this was somehow revealed to us through a reading of the Psalms. We had not paid attention to what is, however, clear in the Gospels: the Psalms do underline it.

We had some difficulty in noticing the passivity that the word "passion" expresses. However, we should know that Christ is taken to his cross by numerous human wills. But the stature of Christ is so great for us that we would see him alone determining to walk towards his death. For us he becomes like the saints whose qualities hagiographers signal to us without being able to describe what their situation was, so like the portraits that a frame separates from the wall. The "Passion" of Christ is, indeed, the "action" of others, at the center of a whirlwind. The Passion of Jesus and the action of others come together in a relationship, in which everything becomes clear, on the condition that one look at it. Did Christ not come in order to make visible what is hidden, to humble himself in order to place the mystery within our reach? So whoever wants to be enlightened by Jesus Christ must look at, first of all, what is most visible and most simple.

What is most simple is that, in his death, Jesus Christ is the victim of an injustice. When the Psalms place us in the mob, the antagonisms, the violence, the strident noise of the "enemies," they have us enter into that place where Jesus wanted to put himself, and this from the very first moment of his public appearance.

I have often been asked if there is not, in the Christian tradition or also in other religions, some books that are more elevated or more serene than the Psalter, developing more easily the paths of prayer such as it is sometimes understood. There may be some books. Indeed, they do exist. Libraries are full of them. Even today some people have the talent to write them. But perhaps we realize that this is not the question. Certainly, the Psalter lacks neither the sublime nor the serene. Let us not underestimate it. But we shall not find Jesus Christ in some competitive exam for excellence; that is not a sure path.

The divinity, in effect, is not only better than we, but also quite other than we, and that is revealed if it takes our most common paths.

When it is a question of prayer, the Psalms cannot escape dust. Yet, this is not just the "dust and ashes" towards which the ascetic freely directs his gaze. It is also the dust of the street, of the crowd, of the riots that engulf anyone who would not like to be a part of them:

And I say, "O that I had wings like a dove!
   I would fly away and be at rest;
truly I would flee far away;
   I would lodge in the wilderness ..." (Ps. 55: 6-7)

Such a wish is very understandable, but reality is quite different:

... for I see violence and strife in the city.
Day and night they go around it on its walls.
... oppression and fraud

do not depart from its marketplace. (Ps. 55: 9-10, 11)

For the Bible, the good confronts evil, and this confrontation takes place everywhere, because the just person does not exist without the wicked one, as Ben Sira states: "... so the sinner is the opposite of the godly" (Sirach 34: 14).

How much dust flies about in these encounters! Saint Paul evokes the time of Genesis: "Just as at that time the child who was born according to the flesh persecuted the child who was born according to the spirit, so it is now also" (Galatians 4: 29). The biblical narratives bend all their characters to this law. The Psalter connects to these stories; among the Psalms attributed to David by an explicit title, many are related by these same titles to the struggles of Saul, of the Philistines, of Absalom against David (Pss. 7; 18, 34; 52; 54; 56; 57; 59; 63; 142).

The term that has become banal, oppression, is true in its full physical meaning when it is applied to the Psalmist confronted by the force of many:

Consider how many are my foes,
 and with what violent hatred they hate me. (Ps. 25: 19)

Those who are my foes without cause are mighty,
 and many are those who hate me wrongfully.
Those who render me evil for good
 are my adversaries because I follow after good. (Ps. 38: 19-20)

How long will you assail a person,
 will you batter your victim, all of you,
 as you would a leaning wall, a tottering fence? (Ps. 62: 3)

That is the situation of a man who is totally helpless. Before being assaulted, the victim is touched by the will to do evil, and first of all by noise and cries, the conspiring of the nations (Ps. 2: 1) and their "uproar" (Ps. 46: 6). Closer to the victim are the "empty words" and whispers that are spread about (Ps. 41: 6-7), the "howling" and "growl" of a dog (Ps. 59: 14-15), cries of triumphs (Ps. 70: 3):

They scoff and speak with malice;
 loftily they threaten oppression.

6 In the Midst of Enemies

they set their mouths against heaven,
   and their tongues range over the earth. (Ps. 73, 8-9).

There is no doubt; the wicked are stronger than the just man:

He delivered me from my strong enemy;
   and from those who hated me ... (Ps. 18: 17)

Save me from my persecutors,
   for they are too strong for me. (Ps. 142: 6)

This is a physical force. It is also psychological and it excels at making one afraid. This force also has a reason and a plan. Some wicked blows are secretly prepared (Ps. 36: 4; see Ps. 52: 3); plans and projects are made (Ps. 33: 10).

The success of these machinations horrifies the spirit of the just person (Ps. 73) before it takes his life. It is not only in our time that the believer witnesses the irresistible movement that seems to reduce faith to nothingness (Ps. 53: 4). What is most strange, if we believe the Psalms, is that the powerful organism of evil seems to find it important for the just person to die. This death fulfills a desire of the enemy; the just man fascinates him:

I have been like a portent to many ... (Ps. 71: 7)

They stare and gloat over me ... (Ps. 22: 17)

But at my stumbling they gathered in glee,
   they gathered together against me;
ruffians whom I did not know
   tore at me without ceasing ... (Ps. 35: 15)

I am the subject of gossip for those who
   sit in the gate ... (Ps. 69: 12)

For my enemies speak concerning me,
   and those who watch for my life consult together.
They say, "Pursue and seize that person
   whom God has forsaken,

for there is no one to deliver." (Ps. 71: 10-11)

Starting with these references, it would be good to read not only them but also their contexts. We cannot reproduce everything here, but I wanted the reader to have a sense of the abundant cases that do exist, so as not to appear to base myself on some isolated examples, which I would have chosen to prove my point.

The Psalter traces a schema of the drama lived by the just person, of his ordeal and suffering, and of his salvation. At times this vision was considered excessive, a kind of sudden foreshadowing, granted to an isolated Psalmist, of what Jesus Christ was supposed to experience. Today, we are struck by a detail that is probably more substantial; this drama was not only a revelation made to one person about the future of another. It was lived in the present by many, and it is precisely into this lived reality that Jesus entered in order to take it to the end and to reveal its entire meaning. His Passion placed him in the decisive struggle between good and evil.

The Psalms call evil "lying and violence:"

... the bloodthirsty and treacherous
   shall not live out half their days. (Ps. 55: 23)

Their mouths are filled with cursing and
   deceit and oppression ... (Ps. 10: 7)

Saint John will be marvelously faithful to this schema by describing Satan as a "'murderer from the beginning'" and one "who does not stand in the truth'" (John 8: 44). In a more general manner, the Evangelists take from the Psalms words that they need to describe the project of evil that is directed towards the death of the just person.

The traps and the plots that beset the Psalmist make him the figure of Jesus tracked by the machinations of hypocrites:

All day long they seek to injure my cause;
   all their thoughts are against me for evil.
They stir up strife, they lurk,
   they watch my steps.
As they hoped to have my life ... (Ps. 56: 5-6)

This passage of the Psalter, which summarizes many others, is one that Saint Luke makes his own in order to describe what threatens Jesus: "... so they watched him and sent spies who pretended to be honest, in order to trap him by what he said ..." (Luke 20: 20; see 11: 54). Matthew (22: 15) and John (11: 56-57) use the same framework. The justice of Jesus obliges evil to betray itself: "They hated me without a cause" (John 15: 25 quoting Psalm 35: 19; 69: 4).

This hatred that has no cause reveals sin and obliges it to leave its shelter, the definite hiding place from which it destroyed man (Ps. 10). The sinful man, placed in the presence of the Just One par excellence, will be moved by hatred to accomplish the actions that he himself, in words, declares to be wrong. Thus will the trial unfold in broad daylight around the body of Jesus Christ condemned to death. The Psalms prepare us to understand this drama by the place that they give to suffering bodies.

7

Prayer of the Body

In the Psalms, the one who implores often speaks of himself as though he were sick, and he does it so well that we should consider sickness as an essential given of biblical prayer.

But it concerns what illness? We may well ask because, throughout three thousand years of history, the phenomenon of sickness is not without some change. First of all, the attitude of society towards the sick person is quite capable of evolving, during such a long period, for better or for worse. Then, the physical ills themselves assume different forms throughout the ages, either because one treats them differently or because of other reasons having to do with their nature. There are ancient illnesses that no longer exist, at least in some societies, and there are new ones, permanent ones. Is there something that we should recognize in the concerns left by biblical prayer? Only a doctor would be competent to say so. I shall propose at least a very partial inventory of some data.

We easily recognize what many societies call "the fire of the body" and which, for us, is fever, with thirst and dehydration:

… my mouth is dried up like a potsherd,
 and my tongue sticks to my jaws … (Ps. 22: 15)

For my loins are filled with burning,
 and there is no soundness in my flesh. (Ps. 38: 7)

… and my bones burn like a furnace. (Ps. 102: 3)

This last quotation presents the difficulty that our questioning faces. "Bones" play a significant role in the range of described symptoms. But the term is often a synonym for force or, quite simply, for the capacity to stand up. In this language, the weakness of the "bones" means that one should go to bed! Also, when the text indicates, literally: "... my bones waste away," has not the translator preferred to render it thus: "... my strength is fading"? The equivalence is at times very clear:

> ... my strength fails because of my misery,
> and my bones waste away. (Ps. 31: 10)

The repercussion of sickness on one's sight offers a most instructive and striking characteristic:

> ... my eye wastes away from grief,
> my soul and body also. (Ps. 31: 9)

> My heart throbs, my strength fails me;
> as for the light of my eyes—it also has
> gone from me. (Ps. 38: 10)

> ... my eye grows dim through sorrow. (Ps. 88: 9)

We can take an important indication from this detail. Losing the enjoyment of the light of day, which is so beautiful in the Orient, the light that God created from the first day, losing that is the equivalent of death. Acuity of vision is equal to integrity of life. It is the same for the mobility of the body, the rhythm of breathing. All this means that we are alive. The Psalms do not describe one sickness rather than another. They describe death by varying the disposition of its signs according to the experience of the moment or according to the inspiration of the poet. We are not sure which one is at play. These are, until some better information comes our way, the modest conclusions of our study.

As life disappears, all that remains of it finds refuge in the cry of prayer.

> My eyes waste away because of grief ... (Ps. 6: 7)

> For my life is spent with sorrow,
> and my years with sighing. (Ps. 31: 10)

> While I kept silence, my body wasted away,

7 Prayer of the Body

through my groaning all day long ... (Ps. 32: 3)

I am weary with my crying;
  my throat is parched.
My eyes grow dim
  with waiting for my God. (Ps. 69: 3)

Because of my loud groaning,
  my bones cling to my skin. (Ps. 102: 5)

The last expenditure of energy is spent in these cries, the last risk is taken; to lose one's life while asking for life; to lose one's life while hoping for life.

The substance, the last essence of life is the desire for life. But neither life nor death are confused with the good or the bad state of this or that part of the body. And this is the moment to notice a very curious aspect of the Bible. Its religion appears, at first sight—and, in certain ways, it is—not to be very "spiritualist." In effect, the Bible generally has very little to do with the invisible and seems to know nothing about it, unless it is that God the All-Powerful continuously acts in this world! However, when the Psalms talk about the body and its struggle in corporal terms, it is really about a struggle where two unequal and absolute principles confront each other at another level. In man, life and death combat each other and both are directly submissive to God. If we desire life before God, in his presence, we live. Not very "spiritualist," the Bible never forgets the body and at times seems to think only about it. But when it thinks about the body, the Bible sees in it the place of a struggle that goes beyond it.

Travelers and ethnologists have revealed the same phenomenon in many archaic societies. Every attack upon the body is already experienced as an approach of death, a bite of its absolute on the absolute of life. In this there is the tendency not to distinguish between the degrees of seriousness of a sickness. Why would one do this, since any illness, serious or not, shows the face of death itself? Foreigners are surprised that, in these societies, the sick express themselves, almost ritually, with grand cries as soon as they take to bed. But foreigners do not see that these very cries have a therapeutic value and conjure death, by the fact that they recognize it. As for us, after we have censored and gagged death, we then have no way of getting rid of it. The cry of the Psalms keeps for us something of this open and frank complaint. A doctor might speak of a mild sickness, but the supplicant cries out:

> ... and my life draws near to Sheol.
> I am counted among those who go down
>   to the Pit;
> I am like those who have no help,
> like those forsaken among the dead ... (Ps. 88: 3-5)

Inversely, perhaps very sick people (medically speaking) have not cried out in this way. To interpret the language of the Psalms, I shall suggest an image that will seem to be new, but it is not quite that. Everything happens as if each man had two bodies. The first body, immediately visible, may be healthy or sick, and it always remains at a certain distance from the struggle between life and death, not without receiving some repercussions. The second body, which is not visible to the naked eye, is, on the contrary, taken up with, in direct contact with the struggle between life and death and immediately implicated in the two unequal absolutes. This second body has neither members nor separate parts, and that is why it can see when the first body is blind and why it can walk when the first is still. The state of the second body has great influence on the state of the first, but it is far from commanding it in an absolute manner.

One might ask: why not call this second body the "soul," as everyone does? For many reasons. First of all, because, in our present use of language, we would not understand it as much. We would not see it as so concrete, as so concerned about death and about what changes. If I read the quotations that I just mentioned while telling myself that the Psalmist talks about his soul, I think that I would be betraying him. However, he does not always talk to me about his body as a doctor would see it. We could also say that he speaks about his "symbolic body." This could be another possible name for the "second body." Then, there is still another reason for me to use this language: it is that the language which opposes "the soul and the body" in the theology of the West had a much more nuanced form in the biblical tradition. The Scriptures not only distinguish between soul and body (Matthew 10: 28) but between spirit, soul and body (1 Thessalonians 5: 23), or between psychological body and spiritual body (1 Corinthians 15:

7 Prayer of the Body

44). Finally, by speaking of the "second body," not only do I make the biblical tradition more readable but I get closer to the traditions of the Far East which, less ready than we are to establish a distance between body and soul, suggest a way by which we can avoid "spiritualism" and "materialism."

The "second body," the "symbolic body," is like an image of the first, but an image that is more profound and more real than it. One traditionally gives it the name of "form," a substantial form, a moving one, a form that is hard, living, and secret. Since it is spiritual, the second body cannot live without being involved in a relationship. It is sustained by the loving gaze and vivifying word of another. This second body is the seat of true life, which is nurtured by love and communion. We should thus hear its cry in the moaning of the sick:

> I have passed out of mind like one who is dead;
> I have become like a broken vessel. (Ps. 31: 12)
>
> My friends and companions stand aloof from my affliction,
> and my neighbors stand far off. (Ps. 38: 11)
>
> You have caused friend and neighbor to shun me;
> my companions are in darkness. (Ps. 88: 18)
>
> I lie awake;
> I am like a lonely bird on the housetop. (Ps. 102: 7)

This abandonment is capable of killing. But the content of the Psalms often goes further than solitude. It extends to rejection. Here we encounter something particular that has always surprised commentators. The position of the sick person, such as the Psalms present it, is not the one that our system of thought (our conscious system) attributes to it. In our consciousness (our clear consciousness), misfortunes are distinguished and placed separately from each other; but the case of the sick person is different, as is the case of the person who is rejected or that of a prisoner or the accused. On the contrary, in the Psalms, misfortunes always tend to come together; the accused who appears before a judgment seat is nearly always a sick person, and a sick person is nearly always also one who is accused.

We shall return to such a striking fact. But it is already clarified by what has preceded: the "second body" risks its life on the gift or the refusal of solidarity and mutual presence.

8

Prosecution of the Ill

Usually the sick person who complains in the prayer of the Psalms is also a victim of men. He suffers not only because his body is ill but because he has been abandoned by another. Not only abandoned, but rejected, and more than rejected; pursued, and even accused, condemned and hated.

In Psalm 6, verse 3, the person who says, "O Lord, heal me … ," speaks as a sick person would speak. The same man sees in his mind's eye the day when, the Lord having heard him, his enemies will draw back (v. 10). There is not just one ordeal.

A supplicant is affected in his eyes, his throat, his bowels, his life, his vigor, his bones. His friends flee him, and his enemies also work at plotting his death:

> For I hear the whispering of many—
>   terror all around!—
> as they scheme together against me,
>   as they plot to take my life. (Ps. 31: 13)

But why are such plots directed towards a man whom sickness already gravely threatens?

Elsewhere, in the context of a trial, a man, victim of false witnesses, complains. He remembers another time when his enemies of today were sick. Then he fasted and prayed for them (Ps. 35).

After a very complete description of the illness, we learn in another Psalm that the person who is suffering is kept at a distance by his friends (Ps. 38: 11). Yet others go much farther:

> Those who seek my life lay their snares … (Ps. 38: 12)

> Those who render me evil for good
>   are my adversaries because I follow after good. (Ps. 38: 20)

A bedridden person cries out, "... heal me ..." (Ps. 41: 4-5). Not only his enemies condemn him:

> Even my bosom friend in whom I trusted,
> who ate of my bread, has lifted the heel against me. (Ps. 41: 9)

The man who can no longer eat and whose skin sticks to his bones does not sleep at night, but that is not all:

> All day long my enemies taunt me;
> those who deride me use my name for a curse. (Ps. 102: 8)

These are accounts that the texts give us. They have surprised commentators who have found them to be unnatural. The wisdom of the nations, observation, common sense, and personal experience can find explanations for them by remaining at the level where these data are the same, always, on every part of the globe.

Besides, certain scholars prefer to seek what is proper to some bygone epochs and faraway climates, and it is true that this level (I call it ethnological) is important. Numerous commentaries have resulted from the research that has gone on in different directions. I will try to present what, from them, is essential.

Let us begin with a practical explanation: we find in all these prisons (and more particularly in certain ones, which are not always just those that are farthest from us) men who are both accused and sick.

In the extreme case, the man condemned to death is exposed at once to losing all human friendship and his life. This is the situation that we find in Psalm 22 ("... why have you forsaken me?"). In such a case, one will say that the supplicant is sick because he has some enemies.

An ethnological variant of the same explanation has been proposed: the enemies of the plaintiff have made him sick by putting a curse on him. There may be allusions to these evil spells in some of the texts (Ps. 38: 12; see Ps. 69: 22; 2 Samuel 3: 29).

The relation between hostility and sickness can carry many other nuances: the simple perception of hatred is enough to make one sick, with there being no need for the enemy to do anything; and at times we forget this terrible effectiveness of hatred, as we seek to understand those who are persecuted. There is no need to have magic formulas in order for hatred to act. The Psalms illustrate this all the more since,

8 Prosecution of the Ill

often, sickness is confused with the horror that one has when facing death, with the action that death already exercises from afar.

But other commentators have reversed the explanation: the plaintiff has enemies because he is sick. This can be verified at the ethnological level when a people believe that sickness has come to punish a hidden sin. Naturally, having recourse to the beliefs of a people is only a stage in every explanation. First of all, because it will be necessary to make these distant and particular beliefs comprehensible, if it can be done. Then, because we notice that they are often less special than one thought, and also less old.

It is true that the Jews spontaneously explained sickness by sin. But others did the same. And so, the inhabitants of Malta, pagans, see a serpent bite Saint Paul who has barely survived a shipwreck, and from this they conclude: "This man must be a murderer" whom the gods are pursuing (Acts 28: 4). As for Israel, the Book of Job shows how the friends of a sick person who have come to comfort him end up by becoming his enemies and accusing him. The perfect type of the man who is both sick and accused, Job talks like the Psalmists. Job the leper has no hesitation in saying: "God gives me up to the ungodly, and casts me into the hands of the wicked" (Job 16: 11; see the context). And it is true that the friends of Job, the leprous just man, accuse him harshly: "If iniquity is in your hand, put it far away ..." (Job 11: 14).

And Job will answer in a terrible struggle: "If you say, 'How we will persecute him!' ... be afraid of the sword ..." (Job 19: 28-29). This is the sword of the judgment of God that they risk receiving when they judge the leprous just man.

But here we are led to go beyond the ethnological level where explanation has recourse to particular habits. Job is not a victim of any particular thing. His drama unfolds at the level of all humanity, whichever it may be.

It is not always obligatory to choose between the explanations of several commentaries, such as some of the principal ones to which we have alluded. We should let them sink slowly into the depths of our mind, where they will form a kind of residue that, with time, will provide an explanation, nurtured by others, and perhaps a better one.

I shall begin again with the wisdom of the nations, which has observed for a long time that "Misfortune never comes alone." Misfortunes are accumulated and attract one another. They come together from all points of the horizon on the same base. Sickness, poverty, and solitude (or rejection) tend to meet; they often converge. That is not what (unfortunately) is surprising. What is astonishing is that the center for coming together, that the point of saturation of misfortunes is precisely the place where new central figures of the Bible are reformed. There we find the plaintiff of the Psalms. We find Job there, and we find, in particular, the One whom the late prophecies of the Book of Isaiah announce.

That One is touched, like Job, in his body. His appearance makes us think of a leper:

> He was despised and rejected by others;
>   a man of suffering and acquainted with infirmity;
> and as one from whom others hide their faces
>   he was despised ... (Isaiah 53: 3)

He is, at the same time, victim of an unjust trial:

> By a perversion of justice he was taken away ... (Isaiah 53: 8)

These prophecies designate the type of the suffering man, such as he has been lived by multitudes of men. The Bible sets up an encounter at this crossroads. We understand by prophecy the expectation, renewed from age to age, that a man would come to correspond perfectly to this place, would occupy it on the part of God.

If attention is attracted by this place of encounter between physical misfortune and injustice, it is because their relation holds a secret. The human soul is fascinated by this relation, and this fascination is not an "ancient" given. It is not only the men of antiquity who associate sin and misfortune. The human unconscious, beginning with that of the victim, does not distinguish between the one who experiences and the one who brings, who causes misfortune. The human unconscious sees a fault in every fall, every accident, and every disability.

Clear consciousness probably wants there to be no secret. It is mistaken as much as the unconscious. The more or less vehement and tense declarations of clear consciousness, in us and around us, will say that there is no relation between physical sickness and sin. But no one can change his unconscious being because of logical declarations. Physical sickness and moral sickness, in any case, have this in common: they are a sickness. There is a relation between the two since

8 Prosecution of the Ill

every physical sickness entails a process, a dialectic, a system of accusation and guilt, in the order of moral evil; accusation of self, accusation of others, accusation of God. One could even say condemnation, since this attitude neither expects nor seeks a response from the accused. As an indirect consequence, this trial entails one of justification, and it is not more productive.

This is precisely the lesson of the Book of Job; Job does not give in to this system. He refuses the logic of the unconscious as well as the logic of a consciousness that ignores the unconscious. He holds firmly onto one line; neither to declare himself guilty, nor to declare that God has already, once and for all, rendered justice. When Job accuses God, it is not in order to have the last word. On the contrary, it is, because of an impassioned faith, in order for God to speak. God does speak; he shows himself *in the act* of creating the world, now!

But, in the case of Job, there is a link between moral sickness and physical sickness. His physical sickness reveals the moral sickness of his bad friends, who have given in to the process of accusation. However, what good is this revelation, if it is only for these bad friends to be condemned? Things turn out differently; Job is the typical story of a sick person on trial. At the end of the trial, the bad friends, the accusers, are forgiven! And this by consideration for Job, the accused one. The confidence that the victim has actively placed in the justice of God suppresses all accusation. Job, because he has been sincere in these ordeals and was not afraid to speak before God, made his friends healthy, friends who did not seem to be ill! It is not because he has suffered for them, as it is said, but because he has revealed to them their true nature, which does not condemn them but rather heals them.

The man about whom the Book of Isaiah prophesizes reveals the same thing to those who said:

... yet we accounted him stricken,
   struck down by God, and afflicted. (Isaiah 53: 4)

A light that does not come from them shows them their own face in this accusation, and it is what saves them, if they want to see.

9

The Resemblance of Sin

It is easy to represent to oneself the good accusing evil, evil accusing the good. One can spontaneously think that the just person and the sinner accuse each other. And it is even more current to hold on to the image of a God who accuses man.

But the purpose of biblical reading, its recompense, its reward, is to heal us of easy representations and of their static and mechanical automatism by replacing them with other propositions, slower to come about but more concrete, more productive.

Rather than having good and evil accuse each other reciprocally, it is rather the fact of accusing that is evil. To have one's mouth dry because of the many accusations it has proffered is not really proper for the good. It is not becoming. It is probably inevitable that this happens, and the Scriptures certainly mention the indictments made by prophets, Psalmists and Jesus himself. But this is not the true place for the good, not its final place.

On the other hand, the place of the accuser, finally, would be made in order for it to be occupied by evil. I say "finally" since it is in the Book of Revelation, at the end of the Bible, that we read:

> ... for the accuser of our comrades has
>   been thrown down,
> who accuses them day and night
>   before our God. (Revelation 12: 10)

There is no doubt: "Accuser" is a name added to all the names given to Satan in the preceding verse:

> The great dragon was thrown down, that ancient serpent, which is called the Devil and Satan, the deceiver of the whole world—he was thrown down to the earth, and his angels were thrown down with him. Then I heard a loud voice in heaven, proclaiming, "Now have come the salvation and the power and the kingdom of our God

and the authority of his Messiah, for the accuser of our comrades has been thrown down, who accuses them day and night before our God. (Revelation 12: 9-10)

It is a question of the same evil, and this designation goes back to more ancient sources. In a vision granted to the prophet Zechariah, the high priest stood before the angel of the Lord, with "Satan standing at his right hand to accuse him" (Zechariah 3: 1).

In the prologue of the Book of Job, conceived somewhat like a "mystery play" of the Middle Ages, Satan opposes himself to God by taking on the role of an accuser. God believes in the goodness of Job: "Have you considered my servant Job …?", but Satan suspects Job (Job 1: 8). How many times have we pictured a suspecting God! But here, the suspicious one is not God but Satan. Satan cannot believe in the good because, in advance, he accuses Job before he has said anything:

" … he will curse you to your face." (Job 1: 11; 2: 6)

He repeats his accusation, even after the facts have proven him wrong. This proves that evil is in him, not in the one whom he accuses.

If we imagine a suspicious God, that is because we are suspicious.

The place of the accuser, finally, comes back to evil, because it is, finally, the place of the loser and that is why it is very dangerous to accuse. The accuser very quickly reveals his own fault. It is probably better to accuse at times than to be silent, especially when it happens that we find ourselves to be in a state of anger, which clears the atmosphere and which is soon forgotten. But choosing by a natural bent the place of the accuser is to choose to fall into the trap set for the bad person for his ruin. And this comes out clearly from a reading of the Psalms.

The Psalms are well acquainted with the Accuser about whom we have just spoken. They first know the visible accuser, since the Psalmists are victims of a perpetual trial:

For wicked and deceitful mouths
    are opened against me,
  speaking against me with lying tongues.
They beset me with words of hate,
    and attack me without cause. (Ps. 109: 2-3)

9 The Resemblance of Sin

But this visible accuser much resembles the Accuser who sets himself up against Job or against the high priest of Zachary. Wicked people, in effect, speak in these terms against the just one:

> They say, "Appoint a wicked man against him;
> let an accuser stand on his right.
> When he is tried, let him be found guilty ..." (Ps. 109: 6-7)

The Psalmist represents the defeat of his accuser in the effect of the words that the Accuser himself pronounces:

> He loved to curse; let curses come on him.
> He did not like blessing; may it be far from him.
> He clothed himself with cursing as his coat,
> may it soak into his body like water, like oil onto his bones.
> May it be like a garment that he wraps around himself,
> like a belt that he wears every day. (Ps. 109: 17-19)

This is related to a schema that is widespread in the Psalms and throughout the Bible. In a more general manner, evil is destroyed by itself. In this way we recognize that it is, precisely, evil:

> They make a pit, digging it out,
> and fall into the hole that they have made. (Ps. 7: 15; see Ps. 9: 15)

> The wicked draw the sword and bend their bows ...
> ... their sword shall enter their own heart ... (Ps. 37: 14-15)

The normal instrument for the destruction of evil by evil is, so to speak, the mouth. It is this hole that is going to close itself on the one who wanted to open it. The tongue is another instrument; it is the sword that will pierce the one who wanted to use it to kill:

> Because of their tongue he will bring them to ruin ... (Ps. 64: 8)

Insult is the stone that strikes those who throw it:

> Those who surround me lift up their heads;
> let the mischief of their lips overwhelm them! (Ps. 140: 9)

In order to receive the teaching of the Scriptures regarding its main points about evil and salvation, more than one reading is needed.

When one wants to talk about evil, one risks two evils.

The first is the vertigo of the chasms; the second is to stand so far from them that one remains deplorably superficial. The writings of the New Testament have never feared abysses and Saint Paul often has us approach them. But we risk vertigo less when we take the paths of the Old Testament in order to clarify the most difficult writings of the New.

For Saint Paul, Satan used the Law as an instrument of accusation in order to lose man before God:

> While we were living in the flesh, our sinful passions, aroused by the law, were at work in our members to bear fruit for death. (Romans 7: 5)

That is one of the main ideas of the Letter to the Romans:

> It was sin, working death in me through what is good, in order that sin might be shown to be sin, and through the commandment might become sinful beyond measure. (Romans 7: 13)

These words have always been judged to be difficult, and rightly so. But, in their own way, they join those of the Book of Revelation that we quoted earlier and which showed Satan occupying a place before the law tribunal and citing, in the name of the Law, the list of man's faults and demanding the death sentence for him. Saint Paul also keeps to this very old schema: Satan used the Law. He used something good; it was quite necessary to do so since, being sin, he is a liar. To do evil with something that is good is, all said, the definition of evil. So Satan used the Law in order that it be clear that he was sin, "that sin might be shown to be sin"!

Should we let fall to the side these difficult words of Scripture, since today the asphyxiation of a superficial religion in a superficial word threatens us? And yet this world continually touches upon the real questions. It "burns," since we sometimes sense it so near to us. Doubting that any good or evil exist, but multiplying to the point of saturation, by the press and speeches, thousands of "condemnations" of all the faults of another and of society. Is this not, in reality "to use a good thing" in order to explode its powerlessness to give birth to the

9 The Resemblance of Sin

good? Yes, Scripture is difficult, but perhaps the impasse lived around us is mortal. So let us listen to the difficult Saint Paul.

Lying is a sin that plays on appearances; it separates appearance from reality; it uses the Law for evil. Satan gives to his will for death the appearance of a justice of the Law. Thus do those who walk with Satan. Satan manifests an exterior appearance, the visibility of what is good, and so does the servant of Satan. Satan will fall into his own trap, and God will give to the holiness of the body of Jesus the appearance of injustice, since this holy body will be similar to that of a man shown to be dead for his injustice, like a sinner on the gallows, a place of "justice," which fascinates men because sin and corporal defeat come together on it. This is a place for meeting that the Psalms designate so clearly: appearance for appearance. The appearance of justice with Satan; appearance of the contrary with the condemned Jesus Christ. Because God has his son appear ...

> "... in the likeness of sinful flesh ..." (Romans 8: 3)
>
> For our sake he made him to be sin who knew no sin, so that in him we might become the righteousness of God. (2 Corinthians 5: 21)

Christ in effect has saved us ...

> ... by becoming a curse for us—for it is written, "Cursed is everyone who hangs on a tree— ..." (Galatians 3: 13).

We only understand this teaching of Saint Paul if we reread all the symmetry: Satan in the place of the accused; God in the place of the accused; Satan in the place of justice, since he perverts the Law that is good, just and holy; and God in the place of sin, since in sending his Son he has "made him to be sin ... " But—appearance against appearance—it is less a question of understanding than of seeing. To see in Jesus the one who resembles an accused sick person, a punished sinner. Why and how is it that sight saves? The Evangelist John remembers the days in the desert when serpents bit the people (John 3: 14). Then Moses raised a serpent on a pole: the one who looked at the cause of death made visible was healed. For us who are sick from appearances, from lies of justice, from false images of God, from an imaginary holiness or charity, for us to see all these visible things die and disappear on the cross of Christ is what heals us, and what makes our sight good.

If the appearances of evil, on the cross, save us, it is because appearances of the good were having us perish.

10

THE SYSTEM OF EVIL

A good diagnostic of evil is already a liberation. A big step is taken when the description of evil deals with the place that has been touched and obliges evil to come out of its hiding place. In the Psalms we find not only this simplicity of precision but an imaged form that places grand truths within our reach. And this happens while we search for the secret of the images.

Hope is thus born: when evil is discovered, the good is already proclaimed, because it is the contrary of evil.

Assured by all these reasons, we are going to take some steps down into the unknown in order to find what is underneath the "violence and lying" of the men who attack the Psalmist or, according to the Gospel, of the men who attack Jesus.

Evil is first of all a project that wants to go to the very end because enemies want to kill:

> ... they scheme together against me,
> as they plot to take my life. (Ps. 31: 13)

This is an obsessive theme: the Psalmist is always "sought" by the wicked who intend "to kill those who walk uprightly" (Ps. 37: 14); "Let them be put to shame and dishonor who seek after my life. / Let them be turned back and confounded who devise evil against me" (Ps. 35: 4; see Pss. 38: 12; 40: 14; 54: 3). The Psalmist tells himself that he is pursued and closely watched (Ps. 56: 6), subject to "violent hatred" (Ps. 25: 19). That may seem strange. And yet Cain did kill Abel, Esau wanted to kill his brother, the brothers of Joseph wanted his death, and an armed Saul pursued David. Is this an exaggeration of the Psalms? The question is asked again in the Gospel of John. Jesus said to the crowd: "Why are you looking for an opportunity to kill me? The crowd answered, 'You have a demon! Who is trying to kill you?'"

(John 7: 19-20). In effect, "All who hate a brother or sister are murderers ..." (1 John 3: 15).

The weapons of evil naturally comprise the classic offensive weapons: the sword, bow and arrows. But the most characteristic ones are instruments for capture: the net, the hole, and the trap. The enemy spies, imprisons, and ties one up. The images of biblical history approach these things: his own brothers put Joseph into the pit. Later, the King's men took Jeremiah "and threw him into the cistern of Malchiah, the king's son, which was in the court of the guard, letting Jeremiah down by ropes. Now there was no water in the cistern, but only mud, and Jeremiah sank in the mud" (Jeremiah 38: 6). The beginning of Psalm 69 seems to be made just for him:

Save me, O God,
   for the waters have come up to my neck,
I sink in deep mire,
   where there is no foothold ... (Ps. 69: 1-2)

There is also a precise reason for the choice of such weapons. There are those of calculated murder or in juridical terms, premeditated murder. This category is written in the Penal Code of Israel, as it is in our own: "Whoever strikes a person mortally shall be put to death. If it was not premeditated, ... then I will appoint for you a place to which the killer may flee. But if someone willfully attacks and kills another by treachery ..." (Exodus 21: 12-14). The term used in this law of Exodus to indicate "treachery" is a term for hunting, which corresponds to the behavior described in the Psalms:

They sit in ambush in the villages;
   in hiding places they murder the innocent.

Their eyes stealthily watch for the helpless;
   they lurk in secret like a lion in its covert;
they lurk that they may seize the poor;
   they seize the poor and drag them off. (Ps. 10: 8-9)

We can take out a sword against someone when we suddenly become violently angry, but it is only in cold blood that we await someone near a trap or a pit, or with a net. In such cases there is premeditation.

10 The System of Evil

The description of evil is at times more indirect: there is a sword that does not kill immediately. This is the tongue. And there is a hole that does not swallow up immediately; this is the wicked mouth. As Ben Sira says (Ecclesiasticus): "Many have fallen by the edge of the sword, / but not as many as have fallen because of the tongue" (Sirach 28: 18). The mouth is at once the sword that devours like teeth, the net that captures like the tongue, the pit that swallows one up. The mouth often destroys by false witness. We have only to think of a calumniated Joseph (Genesis 39), of Naboth, who was a victim to the parody of a trial set up by Jezebel (1 Kings 21), of Suzanne saved from defamation and death by Daniel (Daniel 13). Here again the law enlightens us in teaching that a false witness must undergo the punishment that he was going to have fall on his neighbor (Deuteronomy 19: 18). This places many of the curses of the Psalms in a juridical context. The case of the man led to death by false witnesses receives our attention, if one remembers that this is the case of Jesus. It reminds us at which level every lie is a part of the mechanism of death:

... their throats are open graves;
they flatter with their tongues. (Ps. 5: 9)

It is not for nothing that the mouth intervenes so often as a weapon of evil. Everything is there: the tongue, for lying, teeth of violence, the orifice that swallows one up. Often figured by the mouth of a devouring beast, the enemy wants "to eat"(Ps. 14: 4; 53: 4), "devour" (Ps. 27: 2), and "swallow" (see Ps. 35: 25; 124: 3) the people. The animal is sometimes like a dog "prowling about the city" (Ps. 29: 6). There is a word to translate this attraction and hunger. It is envy, and it is to be understood in all the meanings that one could give it, of appetite and jealousy. There is a wound in this contradiction to desire and to destroy. Throughout history the Bible follows this mysterious tendency and explains by it the hatred of Cain for Abel, the hatred that the brothers of Joseph had for him, and—what is important for the Psalms—the hatred of Saul for David. The Wisdom of Solomon even sees in it the origin of every human sin: "... but through the devil's envy death entered the world ..." (The Wisdom of Solomon 2: 24).

Envy is said to be the opposite of wisdom. Envy has us suffer on account of a good if it belongs to someone else, to savor a good if we deprive others of it. That is why envy leads us at once to desire the good and to destroy it, because the true good is always shared. Envy tends towards the good with the same violence as love.

The more that evil is radical, the more the Bible expresses it in images taken from nature, extended to all of creation. The mouth opened through envy that runs throughout history is the insatiable force of the sea that swallows up and kills. That is why the sea is often confused with death, with the sea monster that imprisons all that it can in its belly. This symbol of envy and avarice is universal: behind the bad enemies, the devouring beasts, the dragon in the depths, the sea pit bellows in order to swallow the earth up again (Ps. 104: 9). The symbol tells us that evil envelops the world. Behind all these images there is death, armed with all the weapons of the enemy:

The cords of death encompassed me;
  the torrents of perdition assailed me;
the cords of Sheol entangled me;
  the snares of death confronted me. (Ps. 18: 4-5)

With your faithful help rescue me
  from sinking in the mire;
let me be delivered from my enemies
  and from the deep waters.
Do not let the flood sweep over me,
  or the deep swallow me up,
  or the Pit close its mouth over me. (Ps. 69: 13-15)

We see that death is personified; its portrait is that of a destructive envy, of avarice. Envy, avarice is denounced: it is called death. To believe the Psalms, many realities of the world are explained by death. In the narrative of Exodus, Pharaoh wants to keep the people as slaves. His avarice is shown in the image of the Red Sea that wants to drown Israel. In the New Testament, a reading of the entire story is proposed through enigmas and symbols. This reading is the Revelation to John. A Woman gives birth; it is humanity, Eve, who bears a fruit of life. A dragon first threatens her: "… the dragon stood before the woman who was about to bear a child, so that he might devour her child as soon as it was born" (Revelation 12: 4). This Dragon is "the ancient serpent, who is called the devil and Satan …" (Revelation 12: 9). The origin of evil is thus described with total precision and continuity throughout the Bible. The Good is, since the beginning, desired, but not desired by the good: death is there.

It has always been said that reading the Bible required the work of mind and faith. If the stake of the prayers of the Psalms were the destiny of an innocent person who died a long time ago, the Psalter would only be a dead document. There was, in the origin of these prayers, particular cases, but the universal truth is hidden behind the words that describe these cases. Is this not the same in our own lives? The last truth of our lives is hidden safe from what seems to be very accidental. By deciphering the Psalter, we learn to decipher our lives.

Evil is death personified. I do not want to say that evil is in the fact of dying, nor essentially in what provokes death, but in what wants it. It is in the will that works for the victory of death. Because it is the strongest, evil works for it.

The teaching of Saint Paul has taught us that evil nourishes itself on the good. Therefore it is not enough to want the good. If one desires evil, one is able to kill the good. It is not enough to want some good for someone: if one wants it poorly or if one wants it badly, one is able to give death.

If there is a mystery of evil, it is in the fact that death can seduce. I am not talking about monstrous actions, but about all sin that merits this name, for sin is, in its root, a choice for death.

We should know that death, not only can, but wants to pass itself off as life. One of the ways by which Christ buys us back is by obliging evil to unveil itself. And what does one see? Men considered to be just and religious making an alliance with Herod and with the tribunal of the Romans: "they plot to take my life (Ps. 31: 13; see Acts 4: 25-27). The Law, the "holy," "spiritual," and "good" law, says Saint Paul, (Romans 7: 12, 14, 16) is what one opposes to the holiness of Christ: "'We have a law, and according to that law he ought to die …'" (John 19: 7).

The Psalms help us to decipher, behind the plan to kill Christ, the weapons of evil, such as they function before Christ and as they function after him. Hypocrisy, misappropriation of property, and lying are the grand weapons of sin and death; this lesson, inscribed in the Gospel, is, on the contrary, erased each time that we say: "Now that is how the Pharisees act …" No, that is the manner of evil that always wants to swallow up the good, today as yesterday.

Many things follow from this. First of all, the necessity to recognize our sin, as the first step to take in leaving our hypocrisy: we have committed sin in darkness and we confess it in the light. Then with the help of Wisdom granted by God according to our hopes and our needs, we should learn the signs of sin. It is true that there is an insolent sin that does not hide itself. Nevertheless, it is still a lie. There is still another that we must unmask. By what signs do we recognize it?

When something good resembles a hammer which dulls, or it resembles a mouth which swallows, or a net which paralyzes, then it is not something good. It is evil. When the means that the good adopts resemble a trap, it is evil that is acting. When the good imprisons, it is not the good. Whether it is a question of visible things, of virtues or of spirituality, the good that sticks to the fingers is not the good.

The Psalms should wake us up by making us see how evil attacks us. The worst evil is not to see it.

11

Images of Salvation

Evil imprisons, the good liberates. This liberation we call salvation.

There are several ways of expressing deliverance and salvation. One of the more current ones in the Psalms is the verb "to liberate" or, much more literally, "to uproot," to snatch, to seize, to take by force. The word, in Hebrew "hâtsil," appears more than forty times in the Psalter. It generally refers to God. This frequent recurrence is quite logical: since evil, death, and prison are equivalent to one another, one expects that the good be freedom. The symbol of evil is a mouth that swallows. According to the prophet Micah, God snatches; he forcefully removes his sheep from the mouth of the wild beast or, according to the prophet Amos, only, alas, what remains of the animal (Amos 3; see Micah, 5: 7). God also saves one from those who devour or tear up (Ps. 7: 3); he grabs one from the waters (Ps. 69: 15, 144: 7), from nets (Ps. 91: 3), from death (Pss. 33: 19; 56: 14; 86: 13) and generally from the hands of others, be they oppressors or enemies:

> He reached down from on high, he took me;
>   he drew me out of mighty waters.
> He delivered me from my strong enemy,
>   and from those who hated me;
>   for they were too mighty for me. (Ps. 18: 16-17)

Salvation understood in this way supposes that evil is, without any possible comparison, stronger than we are. The enemies of the Psalmist are always represented as being at once much more numerous and powerful than he is. If not, the one who cries out to God would be wasting his time, which he would better use by striking a few blows. But the first biblical formula of salvation may be thus written: evil is stronger than man; God is stronger than evil. This is why:

> I lift up my eyes to the hills—
> from where will my help come? (Ps. 121: 1)

In these conditions the hope of the supplicant is more often the desire to be snatched from evil than to become the conqueror and dominator.

> ... so I shall be saved from my enemies. (Ps. 18: 3)

At times we may be disconcerted that salvation can be thus received passively; the images of liberation granted from without have caused, among Christians, many misunderstandings, and even violent and muddled debates, or even dramatic ones. This calls for several remarks.

It is significant that the same men whom the Bible has speak in this manner would have used their weapons, and I do not believe that the two attitudes belie each other. The same texts, for example Psalm 18, describe the active struggle and salvation that is received. Keeping both aspects is a kind of guarantee of truth; we would not willingly receive lessons of confidence in God from those people who would have abandoned the common context of human life and avoided the struggles that we experience.

And then this experience is very human as well: to hope to encounter some bearer of a remedy that we do not have, of a key without which we remain imprisoned. Even those who struggle the most accept situations when there is nothing else to do but to call out, to hope, to await help:

> My help comes from the Lord,
> who made heaven and earth. (Ps. 121: 3)

Those who do not want any salvation, if it comes from elsewhere, forget that this experience is not only human but that it is beautiful. It is not at all human to believe that "to be saved" diminishes a man. On the contrary, humanity has known much in learning that a man could not do much all alone against certain evils. Even at this level we probably receive more greetings than we give, and man educates himself in learning how to be thankful.

By remaining very near to the description and to the biblical images, we see that they are coherent. Evil absorbs much like a swamp: we are swallowed up; we sink. Can we fight against a swamp? We need to be snatched up, grabbed out of it; the biblical word is quite precise. But we sometimes confuse the struggle against bad habits with the salvation that snatches us from sin. The first can perhaps be corrected through our own efforts or those of another. But the zone of sin properly called—what makes us sinners—is something quite different. We do not have to go far into the struggles of the spiritual life in order to believe that our own efforts are sufficient. What is tragic in all this is that we struggle against sin by means of sin. Our weapons against evil are all tainted with evil. The victim sinks and allies himself precisely to those movements that he makes in order to escape them. This experience is rather radical: if it is the sinner that struggles in us against the sinner, how will he become just? But if it is not the sinner, who else can it possibly be? However, it is at this level of the question that it becomes possible to understand that the help of God is neither imaginary nor some kind of compensation; it is the gift, freely made, of freedom. We call faith the waiting, assured by the promise, that God will freely make to us this gift of freedom. The supplicant addresses himself to the freedom of God through his plea.

Those are questions that the Doctors of the Church have long debated. They talked about them so much that they have left Christians an idea of salvation that might have seemed simple but was false. It excused one from desiring a promise, from turning towards the gift of God with faith, hope and charity. However, salvation, in its truth, is not announced first of all in the discourse of scholars. It is first inscribed in biblical images that reach a deep level of the conscience of every man, whoever he is.

Evil is a glue, a trap, a hole in the ground, a swamp. You do not fight against it. Rather do you flee and place yourself beyond its reach. This rule is proclaimed, written in large letters in the middle of the history of salvation, that is to say in the narrative of the Exodus that is so rich in images. Evil is the "envy" of Pharaoh, the prison which wants to keep people enslaved, the waters of the river into which Pharaoh wants to throw the first-born, the waters of the sea of reeds which threaten to engulf Israel. There is no aspect of this for which the prayer of the Psalms would not be appropriate, either in the description of evil and its weapons, or in the description of salvation. The people of God do not make war against Egypt; they flee its prisons, and they can do nothing against the Red Sea. If the people enter the water, it is not by their own choice. Regarding man, it is a question of flight. Regarding God, it is a question of his gesture that snatches one from evil because he has heard the cry of the people (Exodus 3: 7; 6: 5; Deuteronomy 27: 7; Joshua 24: 7).

If evil is the prison of Jonah, this sea stomach which envelops one and another insatiably, the good and freedom consist in recognizing the good and freedom outside of oneself and, for all humanity, in God. The good can be defined as what cannot be enclosed in a *self*. To call out, to cry out through the bars of our prison is already to be free. To call out seems to be what Jonah did when he "prayed to the Lord his God from the belly of the fish" (Jonah 2: 1).

> ... out of the belly of Sheol I cried ...
> The waters closed in over me;
>   the deep surrounded me;
> weeds were wrapped around my head ... (Jonah 2: 1 and 5)

Strangling seaweeds present an image of the abyss as a net. All comes together in the symbols.

Just as there are symbols of evil, there are also symbols of salvation. They are to be seen facing one another. Evil is the abyss, a hole, slippery and muddy ground. Salvation is the mountain, the rock, solid ground, the path. Evil is imprisonment; the good is agility, the freedom to move about. Agility par excellence is that of the body that leaps about the mountain instead of sinking "like lead in the mighty waters" (Exodus 15: 10).

> By you I can crush a troop,
>   and by my God I can leap over a wall.
>
> He made my feet like the feet of a deer,
>   and set me secure on the heights.
>
> You gave me a wide place for my steps under me,
>   and my feet did not slip. (Ps. 18: 29, 33 and 36)

We quote Psalm 18 again. It illustrates quite well salvation that is received and it also perfectly presents active salvation. This is not a contradiction. True spiritual freedom is certainly not in us. But we are made free through grace. The second formula of biblical salvation is that, if action does not give salvation, salvation gives action. Freedom cannot be immobile. The word "freedom" is a synonym for the ability to act. This lets us end our list of symbols. While the sea beast is the symbol of evil, the bird is the symbol of freedom, the animal that only our gaze can follow, captivated to see it go, more than we, where it wants to.

When God snatches his people from Pharaoh and from the sea, he does so by carrying them away on wings: "You have seen what I did to the Egyptians, and how I bore you on eagles' wings and brought you to myself" (Exodus 19 4; see Deuteronomy 32: 11). Starting from a typical grand moment of salvation, this figure is applied to all salvation:

... if it had not been the Lord who was on our side,
    when our enemies attacked us,
then they would have swallowed us up alive ...
... then over us would have gone the raging waters.

Blessed be the Lord, who has not given us
    as prey to their teeth.
We have escaped like a bird from the snare of the fowlers;
    the snare is broken, and we have escaped. (Ps. 124: 2, 5, 6 and 7)

The dragon, symbol of the abyss that terrifies us, is not only what causes fear; it is the symbol of fear itself. The bird is the symbol of the mountain to which it is attracted, "brought to me," says God (Exodus 19: 4). This symbol ends up by filling up everything when the Book of Revelation tells of salvation: "But the woman was given the two wings of the great eagle, so that she could fly from the serpent into the wilderness, to her place where she is nourished ..." (Revelation 12: 14). This evokes the people pursued by Pharaoh, carried by wings to the desert and to Mount Sinai. But we should also read in it the destiny of Jesus ("male Child") and the destiny of his saints, of the Church that the enemy wants to silence and whom God overwhelms with the gift of his freedom in face of fear. We meet again in these images of all humanity the struggle of the bird against the serpent. The Dragon, according to the Book of Revelation, is also "that ancient serpent" (Revelation 12: 9).

In nearly all the Psalms we shall find images that we can contrast in two columns:

abyss	mountain
sea, waters	rock
pit	ground
slippery mud	sound path
tied up, net	to run about, freedom
dragon	eagle, or bird
serpent	bird ...

The function of these images is to help us go from one situation to another, from visible things to what is invisible, from figures of biblical history to the mystery of Christ.

Christ has formulated this law for us, not to resist the evildoer (Matthew 5: 39). It should be interpreted with intelligence, courage and, because it is the law of Christ, complete freedom. But it is based on the schema of the Psalms and of all the Old Testament: "Evil brings death to the wicked" (Ps. 34: 21). So it is not the just man who must do something evil to the wicked; the wicked are victims of their own sin:

> ... in the net that they hid has their own
>   foot been caught. (Ps. 9: 15).

This schema repeats itself with the same regularity that we have noticed for the other elements. It completes, in order to form a more vast schema, the figure of salvation (Pss. 7: 16; 37: 15; 57: 6; 64: 8; 94: 23; 109: 17; 140:10).

> Let the wicked fall into their own nets,
>   while I alone escape. (Ps. 141: 10).

Thus does Jesus, pursued by those who seek his life, pass through them, while waiting to pass through death. He accomplishes the Exodus. Pharaoh, who wants to keep the Israelites, is kept by the sea. Pharaoh, who wants to throw the people into the sea, is himself thrown. Israel, on the contrary, passes through the sea. From the central place of the Exodus, the same truth is read in the Passion and Resurrection of Christ. Death, which usually engulfs, has been swallowed up (1 Corinthians 15: 54). Christ has let it have its way, in a freedom that anticipates his resurrection.

When he calls on us "not to resist the evildoer," it is not so that we might show that we possess the virtue of patience but rather to have us participate in the action of salvation, inscribed everywhere in the Bible, the Paschal act.

PART THREE
PRAISE

12

Praise and Freedom

"Praise" is not a word that we often find everyday on our lips. "Congratulations" is more frequently used. Likewise, "thanksgiving" translates, in the language of the Church, what one normally expresses when we say "thanks."

"Praise" and "thanksgiving" do not mean quite the same thing. The difference consists in this: we praise for something good even if this good does not belong to us ("Congratulations!"); we give thanks for something good which belongs to us because we have received it ("Thanks"). I give praise for a good granted to others (whether I benefit from it or not in some way); I am thankful for a good that comes to me from another. Parents give thanks to God for the birth of a child; their friends congratulate them, compliment them, and praise them.

For both of these, praise and giving thanks, it is a question of leaving self.

Praise and giving thanks are necessarily at the heart of prayer, because it is necessary to leave self in order to pray.

We share salvation with others and we receive it from another. The saved man will therefore praise for the salvation that he shares and gives thanks for the salvation that he receives. We recognize the saved man because of his praise and his thanksgiving.

Praise and giving thanks are the perfect expression of salvation. Evil is a prison and salvation deliverance. Envy is the guardian of this prison. It consists in being saddened over some good if others possess it, in enjoying a good on the condition of being able to enjoy it alone.

Freedom has an entirely different structure: praise rejoices about the good that others possess. Giving thanks recognizes in a good the gift that comes from another. That is why more than half of the Psalms have to do with praise and thanksgiving.

These truths need illustrations, and the Bible provides many of them.

1. The first is in a narrow relation to the Psalms, because it represents David and his conflict with Saul, the king whose crown he will wear. King Saul is a sad giant, prey to the attacks of a bad spirit; his destiny will lead him from failure to failure to suicide. Young David is a good warrior, speaking well, handsome, and a good musician (1 Samuel 16: 18). In order to bring peace to the king whose spirit is threatened by so much darkness, his acquaintances call for David:

> And whenever the evil spirit from God came upon Saul, David took the lyre and played it with his hand, and Saul would be relieved and feel better, and the evil spirit would depart from him. (1 Samuel 16: 23)

Let us note, so as to clarify the narrative, that the "evil spirit" is much the one that comes from God. This conception shocks us but it means, in the ideas of that time, that the cause of a sickness is more profound than all other possible explanations. Saul is someone who is oriented towards death. "... sorrow has destroyed many," says Ben Sira (Sirach 30: 23). We find that the only remedy for this sickness is David's harp, and the remedy is a good one. The person of David is the symbol or emblem of the entire Psalter. The narrative expresses in a marvelous manner that Davidic praises are a remedy against mortal sadness. These hymns heal the soul, fascinated by the sadness of death, just as the bird is fascinated by the gaze of the serpent. The stunned bird no longer sings and the bird that sings finds once again its wings of freedom.

In every man there is a Saul and there is a David. Saul experiences much affection for David (1 Samuel 16: 21), but when the remedy no longer works and the spirit of death once again takes hold of the king, this affection turns into a destructive envy. The story of the relation of these two men has no other force. When Saul throws his spear, he says, "'I will pin David to the wall.' But David eluded him twice" (1 Samuel 11). Jealous envy, which is death, wants to pin the good, which it loves, to one place and destroy it. By escaping, the good shows itself to be free, just like the bird.

12 Praise and Freedom

This is his victory, because David will never wish any harm to Saul and, even though the occasion might present itself, he will never take revenge.

The relation between this story and the Psalms was felt by the scribes, who placed the name of David many times at the head of each piece (see Pss. 3 to 41; 51-72; 86 ...). They even kept several episodes of his conflict with Saul (Pss. 18; 34; 52; 54; 57; 59; 63 ...). We can explain this by the messianic importance of the figure of David, prototype of the expected Messiah. In this figure, the hardships and travail of a David pursued by a death-wish are kept as an essential trait. That helps us understand, with images, the fight of death and freedom, of death and praise. For David is above all the symbol of praise.

2. The story of David continues and is prolonged with the story of Saul's daughter Michal, whom he marries. The fate of this unhappy daughter has it that, fallen in love with David, she becomes a trap for him (1 Samuel 18: 20-21). But David escapes once again. The crisis occurs at the height of the history of the new king, when he has taken the Ark of the Covenant back to Jerusalem. It is a time for exultation, and David dances before the Ark.

> David danced before the Lord with all his might; David was girded with a linen ephod. So David and all the house of Israel brought up the ark of the Lord with shouting, and with the sound of the trumpet (2 Samuel 6: 14-15)

This is also the moment when Michal, Saul's daughter, objects that David should show such exultation and share his jubilation with the young girls of Israel, who see him dancing. She thus reveals that her own spirit is not at all directed towards praise and thanksgiving. Quite the contrary. She thinks that David should not have made a sight of himself in front of the servant girls: she despises him for having joined the last ranks of the people. For this she is punished with sterility to the end of her days. The images of this scene again show, face to face, praise and the hostile force that resists it, the force of death marked by sterility.

3. The third illustration is in the Book of Daniel, and this under several forms. It has to do with the deliverance of believers. At one moment Daniel is taken unharmed from the lions' den "because he had trusted in his God" (Daniel 6: 24). Earlier young men of Israel are bound and thrown into the furnace and they sing hymns to God. It is then that Nebuchadnezzar, the king of Babylon, sees them "unbound,

walking in the middle of the fire, and they are not hurt ..." (Daniel 3: 25). And so the witnesses appear to us among all the symbols of evil; tied up, put into the pit, handed over to the mouth of lions, given up to death. The famous canticle of the three young men in the fiery furnace (The Prayer of Azariah and the Song of the Three Jews, Revised Standard Version) seems to be there in order for us to understand that praise and freedom are one and the same thing. The song of "eternal praise" is already a victory over chains and the fiery furnace. The canticle goes well beyond the present suffering: it invites all creatures to praise God, one by one.

The image of the three young men giving praise in the furnace will be taken up again from the very first days of Christian art, that is, at the time of the catacombs. One then wanted to do more than commemorate the heroes of the Book of Daniel: it was a question of proposing a transparent symbol, but one that was multiple. The group of the three young men announces the Christian community. Eucharistic prayer reunites it. The flames designate the martyrdom of Christ and that of his followers. If they have the force to praise in the flames of death, it is because God resurrects them. Their canticle beckons, at the same time, to the first and second creation, in order for all to reach together the end of everything: "... to the praise of his glorious grace" (Ephesians 1: 6).

Here we should remember that the Book of Daniel, which provides such beautiful images, does not do so gratuitously. It rests upon the experience of martyrs of Israel at the time of the Maccabees. The witness of these martyrs allows the author of the Book of Daniel to prophesy.

4. First visited by God, Mary then visits Elisabeth. Elisabeth praises Mary while congratulating her: "And blessed is she who believed ..." (Luke 1: 45). In this passage from Luke, we attend the birth of a song of praise, the *Magnificat*. The images of Christian art have expressed a thousand times the gesture of these two women face to face. This meeting, which makes one think of the disposition of a choir, is the foyer, the house and the hearth, where praise is born. Praise is a communion.

5. The fifth illustration comes from the miracles related by the Gospel of Luke. According to Luke, those who have been healed always render glory to God (Luke 5: 25; 7: 16; 13: 13; 17: 18; 18: 43). The same Evangelist tells us what the witnesses of these miracles do:

12 Praise and Freedom

... and all the people, when they saw it, praised God. (Luke 18: 43)

Again, according to Luke, the entrance of Jesus to Jerusalem, on Palm Sunday, gives a solemn conclusion to all the miracles of his life:

> ... the whole multitude of the disciples began to praise God joyfully with a loud voice for all the deeds of power that they had seen ... (Luke 19: 37)

But this summary does not exhaust all the gifts. Neither the wondrous deeds nor praise have come to an end. After Jesus Christ has manifested his resurrection we find all the disciples:

> ... and they were continually in the temple blessing God. (Luke 24: 53)

Those are the last words of the third gospel. But the series does not end. On Pentecost day the gift of the Spirit is recognized by the fact that its beneficiaries talk about the powerful deeds of God in all languages (Acts 2: 11). And Luke does not fail to describe the first community as being at once one of praise and one of salvation:

> ... they broke bread at home and ate their food with glad and generous hearts, praising God and having the goodwill of all the people. And day by day the Lord added to their number those who were being saved. (Acts 2: 46-47)

The salvation that permeates the Gospel of Christ, from miracles to the resurrection, is none other than victory over death. Its sign is praise. Those who are saved from death by Christ give thanks; they proclaim it to others so that they might praise in turn. Those who have seen him, filled with admiration, do likewise: they even invite those who have not seen to take part in praise. This schema is so invasive that we already find it in the birth narratives, in the telling of Christmas.

> The shepherds returned, glorifying and praising God for all they had heard and seen, as it had been told them. (Luke 2: 20)

The Psalms often speak of praising the Lord "always and everywhere." Sometimes the insistence is on "always:"

> O Lord my God, I will give thanks to you forever. (Ps. 30: 12)

> I will bless the Lord at all times;
> his praise shall continually be in my mouth. (Ps. 34: 1)

Sometimes, the extent, the number of brothers or the immensity of space is evoked:

> O magnify the Lord with me,
> and let us exalt his name together. (Ps. 34: 3)

Those who call to praise may be all of Israel and those who are invited to praise may be all the nations. Israel thus fulfills its role as witness:

> Praise the Lord, all you nations!
>   Extol him, all you peoples!
> For great is his steadfast love toward us,
>   And the faithfulness of the Lord endures forever.
> Praise the Lord! (Ps. 117: 1-2)

When just one witness invites a person to give praise, he represents an apostle. When an entire people invite other peoples to praise, they represent the entire Church, which communicates its joyous news to all the nations of the world. For us Psalm 117 signifies that Israel gives thanks for the good that it has received in Jesus Christ so that others might in turn praise God for this benefit. To proclaim the goodness that one has received oneself is to wish that others might receive it and not be envious. To rejoice over the benefit that others have received makes one capable of receiving it also.

If the texts of Luke frequently combine praise and the apostolate, there is a reason for this. The framework is the same for both: all the time of history, all the space of nations. The manner is also the same. It is well known. It is to proclaim and share joy and good news, and it announces even more than a birth since it proclaims, as already realized, victory over death.

13

BEGIN WITH PRAISE

There exists a kind of elementary grammar of prayer.
We shall keep two principles from it. The first is that praise is the beginning and the end of every prayer. The second is that praise and supplication are the two elements that suffice, by themselves, to describe the totality of prayer.

By showing that praise is the perfect expression of salvation, we have approached the first principle.

The second principle (praise with supplication forms a couple) is confirmed by several formulas of Saint Paul. Here are some of them:

> ... but in everything by prayer and supplication with thanksgiving let your requests be made known to God. (Philippians 4: 6)

> In our prayers for you we always thank God, the Father of our Lord Jesus Christ ... (Colossians 1: 3)

> ... pray without ceasing, give thanks in all circumstances... (1 Thessalonians 5: 17-18)

These two dimensions of prayer form a couple that we notice throughout the Psalter.

The second principle is already a practical rule: we should question whether our prayer is exclusively composed of requests. The opposite excess seems to be more rare; but we should also be concerned whether the miseries of life have not become a part of our prayer.

However, in order to attain a prayer that is true, it will not be enough to have the correct dose of praise and supplication. Prayer is something that is more alive. In the grammar of prayer, praise and supplication form an association as supple as the arrangement of words in a sentence. There is, between these two elements, a link that helps us to understand better what prayer is. Prayer is even transformed from this association and produces new forms.

Supplicants sometimes begin their prayer as soon as they open their mouth:

Answer me when I call, O God of my right! (Ps. 4: 1)

Give ear to my words, O Lord ... (Ps. 5: 1)

These are the first words of two Psalms that follow each other. But this is not the classical manner for asking. The beginning of Psalm 7 is, on the contrary, a more frequent model of prayer. Since we have spoken of grammar, we are going to analyze this model:

O Lord my Lord, in you I take refuge;
    save me from all my pursuers, and deliver me ... (Ps. 7: 1)

We shall first observe, in order to ward off all the intimidating effects of the word "analysis," that this request is perfectly natural and that nothing seems planned or forced. We are seeking rules, but may God preserve us from looking for and imposing some rigid framework on prayer! First of all there is language and then grammar. Likewise, there is first of all prayer and then its rules. Here, starting with our verse from Psalm 7, we shall distinguish four moments in prayer:

1. Nomination: Lord, my God,
2. Praise: You are my refuge,
3. List of concerns: They pursue me
4. Request: Save me!

This process of four times may seem to be long or complicated but, once again, the analysis gives the impression of a slow movie, whereas all is done, in life, with only one gesture, or like one sentence that grammar takes apart. In reality, it is because there is this series of phases that there is life. Life is a mobile articulation that animates, here, the giving of the name (1), the praise (2), the "list of concerns" (3)—what I thus call the description of the evil which motivates the request or petition (4). Were there only one phase, we would be a static reality or a dead one. And that is quite a reality when we know how to pronounce before God only the fourth element: "Save me." Having

13 Begin with Praise

only this note on our keyboard, we are condemned to repeat it, and this repetition does not make for music. It is then that we risk resembling pagans: "'When you are praying, do not heap up empty phrases as the Gentiles do ...'" (Matthew 6: 7). Elijah tells the priests of Baal: "'Cry aloud! Surely he is a god; either he is meditating, or he has wandered away, or he is on a journey, or perhaps he is asleep and must be awakened'" (1 Kings 18: 27).

Through the unfolding of this process, the request is restrained instead of being rushed. The request, already identified, had to let three elements precede it. And for that to happen the supplicant had to catch his breath. It is as though he was already detached from his sorrow. He already announces his liberation.

The supplicant begins by naming the one called upon. Strictly speaking, the naming only comprises the word Lord, what follows ("my God") being a transition between the naming and the praise. Lord translates the name par excellence, the name that is proper to God, the one from whom Israel received the revelation and which is written YHWH. The practice of not pronouncing this name has been maintained in late Judaism and, for reasons that are a bit different, in the Church. In canonical translations and even in modern liturgical texts, Lord replaces the revealed name. Here we are not entering into the secret of the name but we shall keep what is essential about it. The name of God must be treated with respect and this respect is already an entrance into prayer. That is why whoever has the name of God on his lips already stands at the threshold of prayer. To pray is to invoke.

The name rarely remains isolated. It is often followed by synonyms or words in apposition. In Psalm 7, there is "my God." Elsewhere we find other riches, but "my God" comprises them all. The enumeration of numerous titles of the interlocutor is, according to the cases, a plea or a caress through words. It is already a sign of love and of praise. Praise often takes the form of a litany, as in the Song of Solomon: "... my love, my fair one, ... my dove" (Song of Solomon 2: 13-14). We also find love and praise in this enumeration of Psalm 18:

> I love you, O Lord, my strength.
> The Lord is my rock, my fortress, and my deliverer,
>   my God, my rock in whom I take refuge,
>   my shield, and the horn of my
>   salvation, my stronghold. (Ps. 18: 1-2)

The personal pronoun my (with masculine and feminine forms in French, *mon* and *ma*, respectively, used above and in Psalm 7, 1) hides, in its simplicity, a secret comparable to that of the name. Everyone understands at once that it is a term of love. In addition, it takes on a particular relief in the biblical context. In reality the formula rests on terms that were used to proclaim the covenant: "I shall be your God and you will be my people." To utter "my God" is to recall: "YHWH is my God," a sentence which is a password of the covenant. For us, "my God" is filled with the reality of baptism, our covenant, which has given us the right to call upon God in telling him, "You are my God."

The rule of invocation thus teaches us that it is not good for man to call upon God without first recognizing him for what he is, and it is not worthy of a Christian to present his request to God without making to him an act of belonging and of love.

Between naming and praise, the descriptive litany effects a kind of transition. This descriptive litany is already praise. It is quite easy to understand how praise has its natural place in supplication, if we refer to a situation as natural as that of the Song of Solomon, chapter 5: 2. The order of the parts of the "sentence" is not quite the same as in that of our model from Psalm 7; the cards are shuffled in another way, but they are all there with some functions a bit changed, as in the case of number 1, where the invoked names the supplicant:

1. (nomination):   Listen! My beloved is knocking.
4. request: "Open to me, …
2. praise: my sister, my love, my dove, my perfect one
   (litany)
3. List of concerns: for my head is wet with dew …"
                                        (Song of Solomon 5: 2)

Two people are on each side of a door. Nothing is simpler, but nothing better evokes prayer. Even in forming a message as clear as "Open the door, I am drenched," it is necessary to exchange some signs of recognition: who is speaking to whom? And to ask what? And why to ask it? Without that, prayer is not a true exchange. There is a world in the simplest exchanges. Some people will say that tender words are used to soften someone up, that this is calculating. Yet others know that, in love, all is love, even the weapons and even trickery (to have been rained on is not the main reason why the supplicant wants to enter). So supplication is a fight in which the praise of love penetrates intimately.

One of the signs of love is really the distance that praise imposes in relation to the need, that is to say in relation to oneself. This distancing can be called recognition, a word charged with a richness of meaning. "To recognize" who God is. Recognition as the recall of belonging: "Our Father ..." "Recognition" finally in the memory of gratitude, which enumerates the benefits as gifts entitled to be loved, after having listed the "titles" of God. In its fullness, praise is at the origin of this distance that has the supplicant first recall the benefits from God: "You are my refuge." Often this praise-gratitude is much more prolonged and takes the form of a listing of the good deeds of history that is both individual and collective. This memory of a happy past is even a frequent trait in the prayers of request, in the Psalter and elsewhere. The great supplication of Jesus on the cross, Psalm 22, includes this remembrance:

Yet you are holy, enthroned on the praises of Israel. (Ps. 22: 3)

In Psalm 44, before saying to God, "Rouse yourself! Why do you sleep ...?" or "... wake up ... rise up" (verse 23), one first recognizes (the remembrance and praise) the past that is no more. In such misfortune, one then recalls the past: one takes it upon oneself to remember former times:

We have heard with our ears, O God, our ancestors have told us,
    what deeds you performed in their days,
        in the days of old ... (Ps. 44: 1)

This is the beginning of a grand cry of distress. Likewise, Psalm 89 is a grand supplication of Israel. Its king and people seem abandoned by God. Not only does this cry begin by the content but by the form of praise, as though the downtrodden had truly known how to forget their disgrace for a moment:

I will sing of your steadfast love, O Lord, forever;
    with my mouth I will proclaim your
        faithfulness to all generations. (Ps. 89: 1)

In Psalm 42 the supplicant, rather than giving thanks for the past, remembers that he did give thanks in the past:

> … how I went with the throng,
>   and led them in procession to the house of God,
> with glad shouts and songs of thanksgiving,
>   a multitude keeping festival. (Ps. 42: 4)

We can admire some nuances between one Psalm and the other; the grammar is living. The supplicant hesitates to describe past benefits. He thus gives proof, we have said, of love and forgetfulness of self. It is also true that he is arguing, that he is constructing his defense. "You have been good for us. Why have you stopped?" Why is a good term in arguing:

> … why have you forsaken me? (Ps. 22: 1)

But remembering a past good also serves to place the supplicant once more in hope. It provides some arguments in order to convince God, but it offers at least as many with which to nourish the hope of the Psalmist. The remedy may be bitter: it is hard to recall the best moments, when all departs in death, when all disappears.

In looking at it better, we see that the good has not disappeared. If I cry out, it is because I live and this life is a good for which I must give thanks.

I have to ask. But what good is it to ask if I do not look at what one has already given me? The more we think about it, the more we resemble children who, after having received what they wanted, throw it away. But the one who throws the good away is the one who asked for it badly, by repeating dead words.

To give thanks, yes. But before giving thanks, we have to recognize the good that we have and which we do not know how to see. We have to learn to find the good, quite simply, of existing in the most hidden recess of existing. We must praise before we ask, but in order to praise we must know what is good. So the first matter of every prayer is the rediscovery that the world is a good and that being in the world is a good, a secret good where we find God as Creator.

13 Begin with Praise

The summit of prayer is constructed with the same material: to praise God to give us life, at the very moment when he asks it of us.

14

Ending with Praise.—
But Now What?

"For the praise of his glory …" With these repeated words (Ephesians 1: 6, 12 and 14), Saint Paul indicates the end to which everything is called.

In the prayer of the Psalms requests are "finalized" by praise.

Since praise begins and ends everything, we may wonder for what purpose might there be a place between the beginning and the end. Praise in order to begin, praise with which to end—and this "now," which is neither the beginning nor the end, what color should it have if it is not that of praise? It does have another color. Now is often the moment of the cry and of supplication. It is with this moment, this present time that we began our first discussion. "Lord, we have been told about your great past acts. Today they have disappeared." What meaning should we give to the praise that precedes the cry of today? That question is what we have presented in the preceding chapter. In this one we shall see which meaning to give to praise that follows the cry if "now" is to be taken seriously.

In supplication, the promise of praise is often given like an argument in order to obtain what is requested. At first the argument functions under a negative form: "If you let me die, your name will not be blessed." It also functions in a positive form: "If you save my life, your name will be praised." In the first, negative, case, the supplicant then declares that his enemies will scoff at him:

> … and my enemy will say, 'I have prevailed',
> my foes will rejoice because I am shaken. (Ps. 13: 4)

> Do not let my treacherous enemies rejoice over me,
> or those who hate me without cause wink the eye. (Ps. 35: 19)

> By this I know that you are pleased with me;
> because my enemy has not triumphed over me. (Ps. 41: 11)

At times he declares that his friends will be weakened in their faith, or that he himself, finally, will have to stop praising God since he will be handed over to death and the dead do not praise (Ps. 6: 6). In the second, positive, case the supplicant stresses that, if he is answered, his enemies will have to be silent, and his friends will have a stronger faith (Pss. 35: 27; 40: 3-16). And he himself, especially, will begin a song of praise, inspiring others to praise God. This praise could arise from the entire world and, perhaps, even from his enemies. So there will be no praise if God does not hear the supplicant, and there will be if he is heard.

This helps give supplication the look of a plea. Some would even say that it hints at bargaining. But there would be bargaining only if one said: "I shall praise you on the condition that you grant my request." This is not the case, far from it. It is a fact in the eyes of the Ancients that the dead do not praise. The consequences of happiness or of misfortune on the friendly or hostile entourage are described in the Psalms for what they are, as a fact. This consideration has nothing petty about it. Yet it is true that it has an air of some kind of transaction in which there is not only an appeal to love or to goodness, but also to an interest in his glory or his name: "Save me and your name will be praised." Far from being shocked by this realism, I rather see in it a symptom of truth. To argue is a sign of passion. This reasoning sounds just. There is perhaps a double meaning: "I wish, by love for God, that his name be praised"—or—" I wish, by love for myself, that God be concerned about his name." But our relations with God are placed on a line that always penetrates several layers of meaning. It must be this way.

What is most important in all of this is, in the prayer between the supplicant and God, the introduction of a third party, or even of several people or of the entire world. This characteristic of biblical prayer is significant at the highest point. Being alone with God is not easily found in the Psalms. In praise we call upon what is near and far: "Come, praise the Lord with me." (Liturgists call this convocation the invitatory.) One speaks *to* others *about* God. In supplication, one speaks *about* others *to* God. "My enemies are winning and my friends are losing ground; all the earth sees my struggle." Whether there be

14 Ending with Praise.—But Now What?

praise or supplication, others are always present. We could say that the supplicant of the Psalms always occupies a strategic point in the world, and that all hangs upon his victory or his defeat. This surprises us, but it also teaches us. A correct meaning of the grandeur of the one God manifests itself in this: if the Creator of the world is interested in our condition, in the humble circumstances where it is played out, it is because our fate and that of the entire world are in solidarity. God remakes the world: that is what is at stake in our prayer.

That is what prepares us to understand this expansion of the soul of the supplicant when he gives such ample perspectives of praise to the finality of his cry.

This phenomenon, to which we can give a somewhat pedantic name of "hymnal expansion," is constant. The announced praise extends to the city:

> Be gracious to me, O Lord.
>   See what I suffer from those who hate me;
>   you are the one who lifts me up from the gates of death,
> so that I may recount all your praises,
>   and, in the gates of daughter Zion,
>   rejoice in your deliverance. (Ps. 9: 13-14)

God intervenes "for the honor of his name" and enemies see his triumph:

> You prepare a table before me
>   in the presence of my enemies ... (Ps. 23: 5)

God's response will be proclaimed: its echo will be heard faraway and will always last:

> ... you delivered me from the violent.
>
> For this I will extol you, O Lord, among the nations,
>   and sing praises to your name.
> Great triumphs he gives to his king,
>   and shows steadfast love to his anointed,
>   to David and his descendants forever. (Ps. 18: 48-50)

And so supplication finally ends in the contemplation of a future of divine glory. But, by evoking this future, one has already entered it.

Moreover, is it truly a future? It is also a past. In effect, before the moment that one cries out, before the door is going to open to death, praise already sounds out the benefits from God, as we have already pointed out:

> My mouth is filled with your praise,
>   and with your glory all day long. (Ps. 71: 8)

Now the supplicant promises that he will give thanks and will proclaim the justice of God in the grand assembly (Ps. 40: 10); the people cry out:

> Save us, O Lord our God,
>   and gather us from among the nations,
> that we may give thanks to your holy name ... (Ps. 106: 47)

But already, well before their misfortune:

> In God we have boasted continually,
>   and we will give thanks to your name forever. (Ps. 44: 8)

We understand that praise of God be given "from everlasting to everlasting" (Pss. 41: 13; 90: 2; 103: 17; 106: 48). We express it this way: "Now, and always, and forever and ever. Glory be ..."

So praise is folded in two like a sheet of paper. Distress with its cry is found in the middle, in the crease of the fold.

This brings up a big question. Let us use another image: supplication tears a continuous cloth, the praise that extends "from everlasting to everlasting." Is it enough, in order to understand the prayer of the Psalms, to say that God's response to supplication sews up this cloth? We might think so. Praise is a tradition: "We have heard with our ears, O God, our ancestors have told us, what deeds you performed" (Ps. 44: 1). As for me, Lord, I promise, when you will have saved me, to tell of all your works. The memory of the benefits from God is handed on from father to son not only through recitation but also by the witness of those who, from age to age, have begged to be saved and have been saved:

14 Ending with Praise.—But Now What?

> Yet you are holy,
> > enthroned on the praises of Israel.
> In you our ancestors trusted;
> > they trusted, and you delivered them. (Ps. 22: 4-5)

Yet here a question arises: does this tradition of praise put sorrow to sleep; is distress a "bad moment that we must go through?" This is truly a serious question which humanity asks with growing insistence: if praise belongs to the past and to the future, does our hope have, for its object, the "as before?" For some, is it the return to an original Paradise? For others, is it the return expected for centuries when "all went well?" If that is the case, man's hope, all at once, becomes slack and turns away from this objective. If the present is drowned in the indifference of identity, the hope of the future collapses.

Although they do it in a way that is still veiled, the Psalms do give an answer. Without stating it clearly, they leave a place for the one possible response, the one that dissipates our fear of being enclosed in repetition. "So we say, will 'after' be like 'before'?" For the person who pays attention, the Psalms rather suggest: "Before as after." It is the later that attracts the before, it is the future that is the model: the Psalms are a prophecy.

The indication of this call towards the future is found in the formula "new song:"

> Sing to him a new song … (Ps. 33: 3)

We know the expression (Pss. 40: 3; 96: 1; 98: 1; 144: 9; 149: 1). It can be connected to a cry of distress:

> He drew me up from the desolate pit,
> > out of the miry bog,
> and set my feet upon a rock,
> > making my steps secure.
> He put a new song in my mouth,
> > a song of praise to our God. (Ps. 40: 2-3)

And again, in the same context:

> Stretch out your hand from on high;

> set me free and rescue me from the
> > mighty waters ...
>
> I will sing a new song to you, O God ... (Ps. 144: 7 and 9)

When a man has gotten out of the depths his giving thanks will not be a simple repetition of the former song. To leave the depths is to be born. And every birth is newness. All salvation is new. The idea of salvation is associated with that of birth in Psalm 22:

> From you comes my praise in the great congregation ...
>
> Posterity will serve him;
> > future generations will be told about the Lord,
> and proclaim his deliverance to a
> > people yet unborn ... (Ps. 22: 25 and 30-31)

Is it only about the next generation or about a radical renewal with the coming of another race? The meaning opens towards the most unheard with the promises of restoration of Psalm 69: 36, and with the unbelievable amplitude of Psalm 102, where the nations will be affected through the renewed salvation of Israel:

> Let this be recorded for a generation to come,
> > so that a people yet unborn may praise the Lord:
> that he looked down from his holy height,
> > from heaven the Lord looked at the earth,
> to hear the groans of the prisoners,
> > to set free those who were doomed to die ... (Ps.102: 18-20)

The people delivered from death are again created and their song is new. This evokes much more than beginning all over again. It was worthwhile to lose everything in the ordeal; a different man comes out of it. The evil is between the two sheets, between the two wings of praise. But they do not come together; the scar does not close up "as though nothing had happened," which would horrify us.

If one thinks that all the earth and all men are convened, if one knows that hope desires a manifestation whereby God reveals himself

14 Ending with Praise.—But Now What?

entirely, the newness of salvation must teach us something about God who saves. The praise that sings of God must sing of him such as he is. The image of a praise that repeats itself does not do this.

Doubtless, God is eternal:

> ... but you are the same, and your years have no end. (Ps. 102: 27)

But the permanence of the praise "from everlasting to everlasting" is only an image of divine eternity. The repetition not only does not unveil, it can even hide what the true eternity of God is, for God is at once eternal and new, "new together as eternal" as the poet says ...[1]

In order for man to understand this, the ways of God lead him to lose, in suffering, the traces of eternal praise: "... your path, through the mighty waters; / yet your footprints were unseen" (Ps. 77: 19). Who will discover a new praise, a new song, if distress has not made him lose, for a moment, the traces of an old song? For a moment, but how heavy it is when it is the moment when we lose everything!

The marvel is that, in order to touch the veritable divine eternity, it is necessary to pass through what resembles it the least, through the instant, and more precisely through the moment of the vertiginously rapid loss of our being. But who, making this passage, has made it rather distant in order that a new song be born from it? Who, if not the one whom the Psalms await?

---

[1] The words are from the poem "Ève" by Charles Péguy (1873-1914): "Un Dieu nouveau lui-même ensemble qu'éternel / Regardait ce que c'est que jeune nouveau." Note of the translator.

15

TIME OF THE PSALMS

Eternity, an instant, each day, now ...
What is time? Such a question fascinates everyone. Any person who wants to enter into the meaning of the Christian faith feels himself especially concerned by the enigma of time once he has ever opened the Bible. "In the beginning, God created ..." Jesus Christ came "at the appointed time." And finally, ". ... Lord—how long?" (Ps. 6: 3). We could summarize the entire Book in this way.

That is normal: time is a frame that lets us say everything. "To find time long" is not to be happy; we say, "Time weighs me down." On the contrary, with the words, "I would have wanted it to last forever," we express the satisfaction that we have felt. Little sentences ("It is as though it were yesterday" or, inversely: "How distant that is!") let us distinguish what remains and what passes in our everyday lives.

Time is life, "the good time." But we also evoke "counted time," or those times we have known: "... at the time," that is to say, then, many years ago. We say more things in talking about time than in simply talking about life, because time is at once life and death.

Permanence, recurrence and return are part of happiness. And praise is an especially beautiful expression of happiness. The entire Book of Psalms, in Hebrew, has as its title *Tehillim*, that is, "Praises." In it, however, we have found praises, strictly speaking, and supplications. But praise includes supplication; it precedes it and follows it. It is therefore precise to call the Psalter "Book of Praises."

Whoever does not understand praise understands absolutely nothing about the Bible. The door is closed to him and this door opens onto what is essential, since "praise" is a word that stands for "love." It is not quite a synonym, to the extent that praise does not perhaps say everything but does underline a particular aspect of love. Particular, but essential. In effect, praise again reinforces, if it is possible, the disinterested side of love, forgetfulness of self. Impossible to love God without praising him, impossible to praise God if we do not love him:

we would find neither the words nor the breath for it. But to love him while praising him is to love him while leaving ourselves.

If someone has disposed us to believe in God, it is because men have known how to praise him. Praise affects us more than affirmation does. We affirm, and it is over. But when we praise, we are no longer allowed to stop. We have to praise all the time. We cannot possibly continue if we do not always have a reason to praise. It is a fact that men have had this reason and this breath in order that their praise might continue. We therefore call the hymns of the Bible—we call the Book of Psalms—a witness. Some men, who have certainly experienced throughout history the same misfortunes as we, have not let this flame of praise go out.

Today, even, we glorify the Trinity by saying: "Now and always and forever and ever. Amen!" This means that praise lasts all the time:

> O Lord my God, I will give thanks to you forever. (Ps. 30: 12)

And if praise is uninterrupted, it is daily prayer:

> Then my tongue shall tell of your righteousness
> and of your praise all day long. (Ps. 35: 28)

In the course of a day, praise invades the rhythm of the hours. Whoever wants to sing, play hymns, seizes the day at sunrise:

> Awake, O harp and lyre! I will awake the dawn. (Ps. 57: 8)

The name of the Lord is praised (Ps. 113: 3) in space as well, from the rising to the setting of the sun in time, from the rising to the setting of the same star:

> All day long my tongue will talk of your righteous help. (Ps. 71: 24)

Throughout the day ... that extends to all of life (Pss. 104: 33; 146:1 ... .). But one life forms a chain with all lives: "... from age to age," according to the formula that is so often repeated. "... our ancestors have told us ... we will tell to the coming generation..." (Ps. 78: 3-4). And the chain goes back to creation itself. The continuity of days and nights is itself a witness that proclaims the glory of God:

15 Time of the Psalms

Day to day pours forth speech,
 and night to night declares knowledge. (Ps. 19: 2)

So we have just encountered, in praise, the articulation of two opposing features. In order to praise, it is indispensable to have a reason for praising strong enough to give it some effort. That can only come from experience: admiration is what each person, all alone, experiences when faced with what he or she encounters. At the same time, and contrary to this, we also praise because of others: those who have praised for a long time have witnessed to that fact. So I do not only praise because of what I have seen. If I need a witness, it is because I have not seen. Or, finally, what I have seen is precisely others who have witnessed. And I praise because of that, because others praise.

In the manner of a poet who goes further than appearances and feels pushed to contradict them, the author of Psalm 19 (because of this we say that he is "inspired") says that day and night tell us something, whereas no one has ever heard them utter a sound. According to him, by this voice that is not one they relate what we have not seen: this morning and this evening tell us about the first morning and the first evening, the first day and the first night. And it will be the same tomorrow.

The message of the day and of the night is very much an extreme example, or a perfect figure, of the admirable relationship which links praise and witness. If one praises only because of what one has seen, why would the Psalmist tell others to praise. See for yourselves, to convince yourselves, how many times the Psalmist uses this plural form of the imperative mood in French, a form which, in the liturgy, has received the name of invitatory, because a man invites his neighbor to give praise:

Rejoice in the Lord, O you righteous. (Ps. 33: 1)

We can say that, in doing this, the Psalmist imitates the linking of day to night. Like them, he "passes the word on," he fulfills the office of a link, he links the tradition of praise. But there is a difference, as soon as there is a question of now, not of day and night, but of man living now. We expect more initiative. The Psalmist does not only link; he breaks into song. It is often clear that he gives witness. He is the one who has touched, received, and seen something marvelous in his flesh and he "invites" others to praise on his word. A man has been saved and he says before the assembly: "Give thanks to the Lord: he has saved me!" This is the subject matter of Psalm 118 and of many others. A soloist intones praise and starts with only his salvation. Also, Israel might assume the figure of a soloist by witnessing as only one person before all the nations:

> Praise the Lord, all you nations!
>   Extol him, all you peoples!
> For great is his steadfast love toward us,
>   and the faithfulness of the Lord endures forever. (Ps. 117)

The words "toward us" refer to Israel, which is not the nations, but which speaks to the nations. Praise has for content an event announced by Israel, proclaimed outside of Israel. Here Israel praises, Israel witnesses.

In order to speak of an event, we say that something is going on. The expression fits very well here. A man has been saved: he has seen and touched in himself this salvation. He has received it in his body. He passes it on to others, by passing on the word: he passes on to the ears of all what the eyes of a few have seen; he passes on in a long period of time what took place in an instant. That is what "passing on" is: the transmutation of a local and brief fact into a word that is propagated in time and in space. So the person who intones praise, because he changes his experience into a word-for-another, requests that we believe him and that, believing him, we also praise.

Our conclusion will be that to praise is to believe.

So praise is not the easy conversation of naivete since it is the victory of faith. We shall say that the soloist, the man who intones praise, is someone who has seen. But we must not forget that, in the Psalms, the soloist is the one who has crossed through the mortal ordeal. In the depths of that ordeal he has cried out. His supplication was the cry of his faith:

> I kept my faith, even when I said,
>   "I am greatly afflicted"...
>
> What shall I return to the Lord
>   for all his bounty to me?

15 *Time of the Psalms*

> I will lift up the cup of salvation
> and call on the name of the Lord,
> I will pay my vows to the Lord
> in the presence of all his people. (Ps. 116: 10, 12-14)

The tradition of praise thus links supplication and praise, the faith of supplication to the faith of giving thanks, expressed by the cup that the saved man holds up while invoking the name of the Lord before all his people. The chain of praise is the chain of faith to faith, which goes from mouth to ear.

Does this chain make us a slave to monotonous repetition? I do not think so, since one often calls praise, in the Psalms, a "new song." Each soloist renews this song; if praise has been able to continue, this is because it has been able to renew itself. But, in order to end our conclusion, we must remember how Jesus Christ is the soloist par excellence, because of his way of intoning praise. We must ask ourselves why his song is newer than all the new songs, and what is the ordeal that it follows.

16

Praise Night and Day

Our third part has followed the path of praise.

1. Chapter 12. Praise perfectly expresses salvation and freedom. It is the opposite of envy; it illustrates that the good is communicative. To praise and to announce to others the good news are two quite related approaches.

2. Chapter 13. Praise is the beginning of prayer. Here we already notice supplication: every request, in effect, must be based on the love of God, especially on the love that God has already shown us; we must begin by thanking and praising.

3. Chapter 14. Praise is also the end of prayer. But if it is the beginning and the end, is there not anything new? On the contrary, a new canticle results from the mortal ordeal. Praise is here completely transformed through supplication.

4. Chapter 15. Supplication is a rupture. This helps us understand the interruptions of praise and its character of witnessing, which does not let us attend the event; praise is an act of faith.

In praise, it is the night of supplication itself that becomes light, as in the resurrection. We are thus invited to participate in the true now of Christ.

There is always a night, an ordeal of praise. I have said that to praise is to believe. Even if praise is certainty and joy, we see constructed in it the place for an ordeal. At the heart of praise, a lodging, one that is quite prepared, opens up for the ordeal, for suffering, for darkness.

Praise overwhelms us. The password is given to us by "Day to day ... and night to night" (Ps. 19: 2); praise proclaims that life, the good, and salvation are from God since they always endure. They are from God because they are everywhere. But these two words, "always" and "everywhere," are quite apt for indicating the time and place where I am not: I, I am not always and I am not everywhere. The word of praise tells a truth from which, for a great part, I am necessarily absent. I cannot directly touch all those who say: "One has always said it," "Everyone says it ..." I could not hear as much; I have lived so little. In the tradition of praise there is a space, a hollow; it is what separated me from those who praised yesterday, or what separates me from all those who praise far away.

The word of praise is on the side of day, the side of light. There is a dark side, a night side, in praise itself. In other words, there is in the word of praise its feature of being a word. But there is also its feature of silence, where what escapes is going to reside and what I cannot touch. Psalm 19 is an illustration of this contrast. It shows poetically the extent of praise. It begins at creation. It goes everywhere. It is like the sun, which makes one think of the beginning of creation and which sheds light on all space:

> Its rising is from the end of the heavens,
> and its circuit to the end of them,
> and nothing is hid from its heat. (Ps.19: 6)

But it is a silent word, a narrative which is transmitted since the beginning, and nevertheless:

> There is no speech, nor are there words;
> their voice is not heard ... (Ps.19: 3)

Let us try another way to say the same thing: praise is, on earth, what most resembles eternity. That is why it overwhelms us: it is a word that says that life goes beyond man, a word that comes from God and which carries God.

> ... yet their voice goes out through all the earth,
> and their words to the end of the world. (Ps. 19: 4)

That is why one says, "From you comes my praise in the great congregation ..." (Ps. 22: 5). One tells God this. But a terrible distance is formed between this word and man. Praise is what most resembles eternity and, because of that, it is the word of God. But it happens that man is what least resembles eternity. He passes on, he passes on very quickly and, while he lives, he already carries his death; and he does it so well that the question is asked in these terms: how can praise, the word of God eternal, become the true word of man who is dying? True word, not only learned and repeated!

We see that praise needs testing.

There is an emptiness and a pause in the continuous line of praise. Whoever occupies this hollowness and this space occupies the place of an ordeal.

" ... day speaks to day," but, between the two, there is the night! The word is transmitted, but between the words, in the heart of the words, there is silence. The one who passes through this night and this silence occupies the time of the ordeal.

What is empty, blank, silent—the space of the ordeal of praise—is still the space of praise. To experience is also to verify. A word that is experienced is also a true word, verified, and confirmed:

> The promises of the Lord are promises that are pure,
>   silver refined in a furnace on the ground,
>   purified seven times. (Ps. 12: 6)

Men, generations of men, give the word of praise. Praise, because it is handed on and circulates, carries with it the sign of life. When something is exchanged, there is a moment when we are not sure whether the first has let go of it and whether the second has taken it. That is a moment of confidence. It is the same for the word. That has to be the case for the word to circulate, for it to run its course like the sun of Psalm 19, the sun that

> ... comes out like a bridegroom from
>   his wedding canopy ... (Ps. 19: 5)

There is a moment when the word seems to rest on nothing. The person who is subject to the test is chosen for this time. He is chosen in order for the word to be reborn again, to live again.

The "day to day" transmits praise. But this is also true of "night to night."

In the Psalms we see quite well this place that is constructed where the ordeal will occur. Praise names itself "always." The place of the ordeal is named "now."

This does not mean that every time we say "now" we think of an ordeal. But, beyond any ordeal, we do not see that now is truly different.

We have what we had yesterday, without even realizing that we have it. There is truly no time. We also believe that everyone is like us; we think that here and elsewhere are not different. This indifference is a manner of living a false eternity, a kind of false image of God. This is an idol, a non-living image of a living God. When the ordeal arrives, here and now take on a harsh relief. The Psalmist remembers the narratives of the past, those that he heard from the mouth of his ancestors:

> ... what deeds you performed in their days,
>   in the days of old ... (Ps. 44:1)

What one says about the deeds of God is what makes the obscurity and abandonment of today bitter:

Yet you have rejected us and abased us ... (Ps. 44: 9)

"Now" is no longer as "in their time"! And yet, he says, it is not our fault:

> All this has come upon us,
>   yet we have not forgotten you,
>   or been false to your covenant ...
> For we sink down to the dust;
>   our bodies cling to the ground.
> Rise up, come to our help. (Ps. 44: 18 and 25-26)

It is truly a question of a "now:" the proof for this is that God must act quickly, before it is too late.

However, a fullness is missing in this "now" of the Psalms. What can it lack since it is the "now" of salvation? It is true that the hand of God is here, in order to give even plenitude to a "now" that is passing on. But it is still a "now" which is passing on. Therefore, it is a salvation that passes on. It is not complete.

Whether it be a question of a liberation, of a healing, or of a victory, the one who sings it has always finished by knowing death and by disappearing. His praise has not yet quite filled this hollowness, this emptiness. He passes the word on without completing the meaning of the word.

Even the miracles that Jesus made in the Gospels bear this hollowness. The eyes of the healed blind men, without exception, did one day finally close. Lazarus had to taste death a second time. To the extent that the "now" of their salvation was an act of God, it was not a "now" like the others. But to the extent that it was followed by other moments, it showed itself to be a "now" like the others; not truly full. A "now-before," a "now-not-yet" …

However, these moments of praise were already resplendent. What is strange and very beautiful is that it was not only or especially by the goodness that they received that they shone forth. No, they were beautiful because of the good deed that they had one hope for and which was not yet accomplished. They were beautiful as signs, as an anticipation of the perfect "now." The one who was saved at the time of the Psalms and before the death of Jesus was already touched by the resurrection of Jesus.

To be saved from death before death is not a perfect "now," because it is still directed towards death. Yet the one who is saved from death when death touches him lives a perfect "now." More a "now-before," a "now-not-yet." But it is also an eternity, which is also not after something, because its true name is "now."

But that person does not speak in the world. He has filled up the hollowness of praise:

> So, now, Father, glorify me in your own presence with the glory that
> I had in your presence before the world existed. (John 17: 5)

Only Christ can give true praise, only he can verify it by going to the very end in death. He does not speak in the world. But he does speak at the heart of words, at the heart of imperfect words and imperfect signs: "… their voice is not heard …" is what we just read but also these words: "… yet their voice goes out through all the earth …" (Ps. 19: 3 and 4, respectively). Christ occupies the depths of the words of the Psalms; his suffering has won him this place, where the truth of praise is hidden.

It is the "now" of true salvation in the shadow of salvation that we know, since he has opened the true "now." He is the true salvation of our joys that pass, and he now calls on our night to disappear.

That is the good news, the word of praise that we pass on to others.

PART FOUR

PROMISE

17

Response

Prayers of supplication, prayers of praise and exultation: the Psalter is thus traversed by a very lively contrast. Does any unity between these two prayers exist? We cannot do without either one. But we cannot remain either in one or the other. Praise says that it is forever, but it is interrupted. Neither can supplication always last; that would mean that it would always remain without an answer. Praise and supplication can alternate, a kind of law of life. But if they alternate in order to attenuate each other, if man praises with less joy because he must also cry, if he begs with less ardor because praise puts him to sleep, the result of the two forces will rather be a kind of erosion; a rather dull mid-point between laughter and tears; or even an average that is falling, whose meaning is finally death. That is probably a possible outcome of the crisis, which can lead our voice in descent from laughter, in descent from tears into this "Sheol" of the Psalms, where nothing resonates.

But there is another possibility. If it is realized, we shall see in the Psalms a text coming from God. Perhaps praise and supplication attract each other. This attraction is made possible and plausible by the fact that praise and supplication are ordinarily found within each poem. The majority of the Psalms are composites. But if praise and supplication attract each other, they do not weaken one another. On the contrary, laughter and tears reinforce each other mutually instead of having both become neutral; this mutual attraction of opposites is much the secret of the Psalms.

Several conditions are needed in order to sustain this contrast. Force was first needed, the force that God gave to the just of Israel. The force to hold on up to the point where life and death, without giving in, fight the decisive battle; the force to hold on until the very day and hour when God will place the Just One of the just, alone able to sustain this struggle. And it was also necessary, as a condition for Israel to have this force, that God answer the prayers of Israel. The Psalms witness to this: men say that God has answered them.

The response of God is thus, with praise and supplication, the third moment in praying the Psalms. In a first consideration, we shall find out whether this moment is recognizable. Then, in chapter 18, we shall ask whether it organizes the relationship of praise and supplication in a different way. Only then shall we have answered this question: do praise and supplication find their unity?

In reality, many Psalms are attestations of a response from God: praise and supplication then form a framework in order to capture this significant moment. This feature of witnessing is not the easiest one to explore, because rituals frame lived reality and because we are not very familiar with the rituals of prayer in the ancient world. But we are able to verify that a Psalm is often more than words for prayer that are communicated to readers. It is frequently the memorial of a particular act of prayer, the *ex voto* of a supplicant who has been heard. "I have prayed to God," the supplicant says, "and he heard me, and I praise him here as I had promised him I would." If that is the way it is, we do not receive with the Book of Psalms words which are taken to be excellent in sincerity, adapted for their purpose, inspiring, or beautiful and, in this way, capable of competing with other compositions endowed with better or lesser qualities. We are invited to enter into a chain of acts of salvation, and this is something all together different. It would be necessary to explain how we are invited to share, in making it our own, a prayer which is meant to witness to a particular moment of grace (Ps. 69: 13; 102: 13). We shall try to do this in the following chapter. Yet, for the time being, we can identify this particular mark and observe this general communication that has reached us. This is already enough to get our attention. With the Psalter the Bible does not depart from one of its merits called "historicity:" even the most universal prayer has the stamp of moments that cannot be exchanged, which have happened only once.

17 Response

Often the poem of the Psalmist is the memory of a journey towards the Temple where he finds solace in its presence, like the memory of a pilgrimage undertaken in order to obtain something good or to give thanks for it. In such a case, it was not unusual to spend the night in the sanctuary, as Jacob had done in Bethel (Genesis 28: 11-18) or Solomon in Gibeon (1 Kings 3: 5-15). God had answered both through a dream. This is because man, when asleep, loses the defenses that often keep him from understanding, and we wonder whether God needs our sleepy moments in order to meet us when, decidedly, it is impossible to reach us in our sharpest reflections.

Ancestors left their businesses, their homes, their spouses, and their families in order to beg within the walls of the sanctuary at the end of the day. The leave-taking was probably accompanied by corporal and interior acts of purification and, quite frequently, by a vow (1 Samuel 1: 11). The supplicants let night speak (Ps. 16: 7) and ended up by allowing their own forces give way to sleep:

> I cry aloud to the Lord,
>   and he answers me from his holy hill.
>
> I lie down and sleep;
>   I wake again, for the Lord sustains me. (Ps. 3:4-5)
>
> .... I will sing aloud of your steadfast love
>   in the morning. (Ps. 59: 16)
>
> O Lord, in the morning you hear my voice ... (Ps. 5: 3)
>
> If you try my heart, if you visit me by night ...
>   ... when I awake I shall be satisfied,
>   beholding your likeness. (Ps. 17: 3 and 15)

We would like to know how much time these kinds of retreatants insisted on in order to obtain the divine response, what help they received from priests and others familiar with the holy place. But we only have a few details at our disposal, even though they are important. Already without any official function, the priest of Shiloh who takes the desolation of Hannah to be drunkenness still succeeds in confirming her prayer (1 Samuel 1: 17), just as he informs Samuel how to listen to a God whom he himself does not know how to hear. Isaiah serves as an intermediary between the king, attacked or sick, and his God; but this king does not believe himself to be dispensed by this prophetic help from going to the Temple every time (Isaiah 37-38). A Psalmist relates that he once fulfilled the rites of prayer—fasting and penance—for friends who were seriously ill (Ps. 35: 13-14). So one did not always pray alone and the composition of a Psalm for a supplicant, whether he was or was not yet heard, must have been a part of these helpful means and accompaniments that fell to inspired or consecrated men and, for this reason, went well beyond the formal competence of a simple public writer.

The Psalms thus bear the recognizable traces of a spiritual ministry exercised within the Temple area. This space had been recognized for a long time:

So I have looked upon you in the sanctuary,
    beholding your power and glory.

… when I think of you on my bed,
    and meditate on you in the watches of the night;
for you have been my help,
    and in the shadow of your wings I sing for joy. (Ps. 63: 2, 6-7)

The ministry, be it that of Levites or some inspired person, is not less important. We read in the books that the priests pronounced an oracle as a response to prayer, a ritual that seems quite distant to us, because the habits of other societies, especially when they are reported to us in our style, disorient us. However, even among ourselves, everyone acknowledges that someone else can effectively help us to hear the word of God. And the story of Samuel's mother seems to us as subtle as it is reasonable: sent home with some banal encouragement, Hannah feels her heart transformed by joy.

Aspects of an oracle of the Lord that interrupt the course of prayer are rather direct. This oracle may just be solicited:

… say to my soul, "I am your salvation." (Ps. 35: 3)

But it is often noticed:

17 Response

God has promised in his sanctuary … (Ps. 60: 7)

Once God has spoken; twice have I heard this … (Ps. 62: 11)

Let me hear what God the Lord will speak,
for he will speak peace to his people … (Ps. 85: 8)

There are texts which are more indirect but which, in some ways, are more striking where it seems that the supplicant, all at once, completely changes his tone. He hardly says why: "Now I know…" (Pss. 20: 6; 56: 9). With a few words he declares that he has been "heard" (Pss.6: 8; 28: 6; 61: 5; 86: 7).

I hear a voice I had not known … (Ps. 81: 5)

In the text that I just quoted, the text of an oracle follows its proclamation. Yet, it happens rather often, in order that all readers of the Psalms become used to it, that the movement from tears to joy is brusque and without any apparent cause:

Save me, O God, by your name …
But surely, God is my helper … (Ps. 54: 1 and 4)

Psalm 22 is an exemplary case of this absence of a transition.

There was something enigmatic in the abrupt succession that goes from supplication to praise in the same Psalm. We have tried to explain it, since the phenomenon is repeated. The intervention—let us say irruption—of an answer from God gives a coherence that is expressed in three terms that are connected by the middle one: request, answer, thanksgiving. That we might not be able to explain immediately that God answers us should not surprise us, as long as we are in our right mind. We have only to remember that the intrepid faith in the fact that God answers prayers is expressed often in the mouth of Jesus and of his first witnesses: this certainty is one of the principal traits of the New Testament, but here we are touching upon some of its roots. Let us be certain that the supplicants of the Psalms, in order for God to hear them, did more than just pronounce some beautiful utterances; they purified their soul in their actions. The place for the response of God remains like an empty place, something beyond the text, a blank space. With just a few exceptions, we only recognize it by a kind of scar. God's response occurs intermittently.

At this distance where we read these texts, this characteristic relates the placement of the divine response in the Psalms to that of death in our lives. A place which opens onto a definitive response to all our cries or which is the only possible one for such a response. A place to which the Letter to the Hebrews leads us by the manner with which it reads the resolution of the story of Jesus: "In the days of his flesh, Jesus offered up prayers and supplications, with loud cries and tears, to the one who was able to save him from death, and he was heard" and became "the source of eternal salvation for all ..." (Hebrews 5: 7). Had we truly understood that Jesus had begged to be delivered from death? Had we truly understood that in saying that he was resurrected, we were saying that his Father had answered him? This verse is one of those texts that allow us the most strongly to read the fate of Jesus as the Psalms present it. And this all the more since, if our Psalms are the memorial of a moment of grace, always impossible to confuse with others, then the Letter to the Hebrews describes the ordeal of Jesus as that moment which comes about "now, once for all, at the end of time" (Hebrews 9: 26-28). This is why we are not the first to hear passed on the news of the Gospel, when we read in the Paschal light:

I lie down and sleep;
 I wake again, for the Lord sustains me. (Ps. 3: 5)

18

Memorial

Praise and supplication come together in several ways, but we must begin with the most simple, which is often the one that we think about last of all. They come together on the page. They are together because we read them together, because a Psalm is a written text, intended for readings and re-readings after which all its parts are interpreted in the mind.

A grand discovery, one will say. We have known that the Psalms are a book, but we wanted to go further back than this form, still an artificial one.

The difficulty is that, in going much further back, we still find a book. On the first day of the composition of a Psalm, even while a cantor composed it, the work was already distant from this event of salvation for which it was raising a monument, the memorial. We read:

... the waters have come up to my neck. (Ps. 69: 1)

But the one who is drowning is not writing and the one who writes is not drowning. We must conclude from this that he writes before being in the waters, or after having been there. This is also the case for the person condemned to death and led to his punishment or for the sick person who senses that his end is near.

If the written word is truly a memorial, if it is composed after the event of salvation, we are not surprised that it includes the giving of thanks on the part of the man pulled out of the waters. What we have to explain is the presence of supplication: why beg when one is already saved? The story of King Hezekiah can enlighten us on this point. The prophet Isaiah, we read in 2 Kings 20, gives him the response of God to the supplication that he has just made to him at the highest point of his sickness: "'... I will heal you; on the third day you shall go up to the house of the Lord ...'" (2 Kings 20: 5). Let us note in passing that this oracle is not judged to be incompatible (and why would it be) with the application of a poultice (2 Kings 20: 7). Let us especially keep, in this collection of Isaiah, the word "writing" by which the psalmist's poem is designated and composed for the thanksgiving by the king, probably at the time of this visit to the Temple that followed his cure (Isaiah 38: 9-20). It might seem that this text would have been enough for composing this thanksgiving. Besides that, we find in it, as though consigned by archival documents, supplication. Such supplication, which an agonizing person would not have been able to write, is introduced by the words "I said ...," which places it in the past (Isaiah 38: 10). This supplication probably ends at verse 16. Such introductions are also found in the Psalter (Ps. 30: 8; 32: 5; 41: 4) but the same remembering can take place without an introduction. In fact, the process is quite natural.

Many popular *ex votos* placed in small country chapels under the image of the Virgin Mary or of a saint have the form of a picture which naively represents some misfortune: a fall, a collision or a shipwreck. Here, distance does not imply anything that is artificial on insensitive. To be far from evil is at once to be saved and to be able to relate. It is not a question of going back in time. The narrative, in words or in painting, by which I tell of my mortal ordeal becomes the most timely, the most tangible and, finally, the most joyful sign that I have taken from it, I who was, precisely, supposed to stay behind. On the contrary, it is my misfortune that goes ahead and becomes life with myself, when I talk about it. But then what happens, if not a transmutation of supplication into thanksgiving without changing the words?

Although he is not subject to arguments or exegetes, young Alyocha, a main character of *The Brothers Karamazov* by Dostoevsky, understands all that:

> "Karamazov," cried Kolya, "can it be true what's taught us in religion, that we shall all rise again from the dead and shall live and see each other again, all, Ilyushechka too?"
>
> "Certainly we shall rise again, certainly we shall see each other and shall tell each other with joy and gladness all that has happened!" ... [1]

---

[1] Fyodor Dostoevsky, *The Brothers Karamazov*. The Constance Garnett Translation, Revised by Ralph E. Matlaw. *Backgrounds and Sources. Essays in Criticism*. Edited by Ralph E. Matlaw, University of Chicago. W.W. Norton & Company, Inc., 1976, p. 735. (Note of the translator.)

18 Memorial

"To tell again ..." Nothing makes one understand better how salvation, and in particular this form of salvation that our faith calls resurrection, differs from an enchanted operation, from a spectacle of forgetfulness. To be saved forever is to become forever the one whom God snatches from death and from the evils that have preceded it. It is not to forget, not to be forgotten.

The written word is thus not a stepping away from the warmth of the event; it belongs to the event because the written word has something to do with this transmutation of supplication. It is the remedy for forgetfulness but its status is richer. If the written text is a component or, as modern criticism says so well, an "attribute" of the event, the writer is more than a notary. The one who composes the Psalm is usually someone other than the supplicant himself, but this other is a true mediator. That is why these Psalmists who do not write for themselves but for the king or for others were, in the eyes of ancestors, consecrated and are, in our eyes, inspired. These are qualities that suppose a participation of the writer in what he writes. He participates in the misfortune of the supplicant, but he also turns this same misfortune towards the entire community and exposes it.

But how shall I receive what is turned towards me? As a right hand accepts a right hand: by directing itself towards the other side of his own. The supplication that has become, without changing words, thanksgiving will become supplication for me. But since these words would never have been preserved if their author had not been saved, it is as though I entered, in putting on a garment of tears, in a garment of joy and salvation. I learn the cries that God has heard and, quite specially, I learn the clamor that God has heard once for all. Writing is probably thus an artifice. We can call it, like the instrument of the potter, a wheel. But it is a wheel of the wisdom of God.

It is by this wheel that the unity of praise and supplication is accomplished because, at the same time and in order to complete everything, the one who in this way puts on the request of another also puts on his giving of thanks, and it is well before being saved that he pronounces this second one, thanksgiving.

Thus have the same texts functioned on several fronts and new functions have produced new texts during the long period when our Psalms were composed. It would be naïve to reduce them all to one type, and I must resist the desire to describe here more numerous varieties. We shall have at least cleared a path towards the principle of these varieties from a reduced number of cases, especially to the extent that we can hope that our prayer and our life find themselves enlightened by them.

From this point, if we do not know how to explain, at least we shall not be too surprised that, by the inverse movement of the one we have just described, supplicants afford so much place to thanks and to praise before they have obtained anything. Lazarus is still in the tomb and has not even been called to come out by the voice of Jesus, who gives thanks to the Father for having answered him (John 11: 41). This feature is not altogether new. Three texts of the last periods of the Old Testament shed light on it. The Wisdom of Solomon relates that even before having been saved from Egypt and death, during the first night of the Passover, the children of Israel, full of faith, "already … were singing the praises of the ancestors" (Wisdom of Solomon 18: 9). On what day? At Passover, the main time of salvation.

In the Book of Chronicles we read that the Levites, (among whom there is a family mentioned several times at the beginning of the Psalms) having been assured by an oracle about the defeat of the enemies, also intone Psalms of praise before battle (2 Chronicles 20-22). There is something analogous in the story from the Book of Daniel about the young men thrown into the furnace: God answers their prayer by sending coolness and an angel to them in the midst of flames, but they are not taken out of the furnace when they sing their hymns of praise. Coolness in the flames (see The Prayer of Azariah and The Song of the Three Jews, verse 27), a symbol taken up again by the Book of Wisdom (Wisdom of Solomon 16: 17-23), speaks better than all the rest. It describes how praise and supplication are united. It also says how the death of the just person is changed into life and his ordeals into joy.

In the situation where thanksgiving precedes salvation, the writing was also able to play a role. As it is still practiced in many areas of the world, the supplicant was able to indicate his request on a manuscript, but he accompanied it with an anticipated thanks that he committed himself to perform through a vow that was to be completed when he would be satisfied. This is what Jacob does at Bethel (Genesis 28): in the morning he recognizes the nocturnal answer of God by marking the stone where he has slept. Although he does not recite a hymn, he prepares himself for the "recognition" of the place where he commits himself through a vow to return in order to pay the tithe. Promising

18 Memorial

with a vow intervenes in numerous Psalms and it is reasonable to think that it was often done in writing, with the beginning of praise. Jesus did not leave any writings, but he made an analogous gesture by instituting, before being saved, a memorial of thanksgiving that he will complete when he will drink with us the fruit of the vine in the Kingdom of Heaven.

Jesus could not leave any writing once all of Scripture was accomplished around the time of his death. His cross is his writing. Before the cross, by his gesture; after the cross, by our own. The Eucharist is our life.

In the memorial of the Eucharist, which is, according to the liturgical disposition of our church, the central point of every song of the Psalms, praise and supplication are united more than anywhere else, because passion and resurrection are not separated there. The unity that we were seeking is thus found at the same time as bread.

If so many Psalms were not to be read as a memorial, they would be less near our Eucharistic memorial. These are the presuppositions of what is going to follow. Praise and supplication are at times so intimately intertwined that one will be able to speak of a new kind of prayer, the Psalm of confidence, which we could also call the Psalm of the pathway. It is easy for a Christian to formulate this newness. The superior unity of joy and tears is the substance of the resurrection that is already communicated to us, with the bread or "viaticum" of our route. What unites joy and tears also unites the before and the after or what precedes and what follows. There is no resurrection beyond our death if it does not invade our death; and the Church does not bring us anything else, with baptism, but the entrance into resurrection at the beginning of our lives; nothing else with the bread of life but the entrance in resurrection on each day of our lives.

And so it is in the atmosphere of the Psalms of confidence that we enter the path of promise. Here are the stages that we shall cross:

Chapter 19. The desire of the Psalmist awakens our hope.

Chapter 20. The man of the Old Testament gets our attention by his refusal to cross the line of death in his imagination.

Chapter 21. The reading of the "terms" of the Bible is a journey and crossing through our entire history. The crossing within a word is called its "meaning."

Chapter 22. We perceive the movement of the Psalms if we are ourselves on the "path" towards the promise.

19

Desire

The most frequently mentioned characteristic of men that is expressed in the Psalms is their desire for life. It is also the most striking. This makes them seem very different from the men of our society. At the same time, this intensity of desire makes us envious and awakens us.

We are sensitive to it because the meaning of the word "life," in the Psalter, is simple: it has to do with what everyone still understands today by this word. There are several ways for saying it in Hebrew. But here is a significant case: the word "néféch," for example, is quite near to that of "life." It denotes the principle of breath, but also the personality ("me," that is my "néféch"), but also the throat. That is what hunger and thirst make dry, what food satisfies, what anxiety compresses. But there is not another word for saying "soul." When they thought about what we mean by "soul," these men evoked the main conduit that receives life. And when the Christian reader of the Psalms realizes that Christ proposes life and himself under the form of bread and wine, not only is he not surprised but he is faced by the evidence of the solidarity between Christ and man, the one who, in the Psalms, speaks in our name.

The will to live is there, from the moment that life begins, under the form of confidence:

> Yet it was you who took me from the womb;
>   you kept me safe on my mother's breast.
> On you I was cast from my birth,
>   and since my mother bore me you have been my God.
> Do not be far from me, for trouble is near
>   and there is no one to help. (Ps. 22: 9-11)

And so the hope that is tested during the ordeal is fused with the hope that was received with life:

> For you, O Lord, are my hope,
>   my trust, O Lord, from my youth.
> Upon you I have leaned from my birth;
>   it was you who took me from my mother's womb.
> My praise is continually of you. (Ps. 71: 5-6)

But the will to live, confidence, and hope have a strange characteristic. If I think of a comparison, I think of the wings of a large airplane; few things in the world, thank God, are as solid as it. However, they do oscillate a little bit during flight; a certain elasticity is a part of their resistance. Hope, which has us live just as wings carry a plane, is still more supple. The hope for life is living and flexible. A hope and a desire to live that is too rigid, as those that one at times preaches, have something conventional and false about them ... and too fragile. What we read in the Psalms is quite the opposite. It is only on the face of a child that we can find the alternation of an exuberant smile and tears comparable to the one that the prayers of the Bible offer. We have the impression that hope, like the grand flapping of wings, always leans on some emptiness or vacuum, which should cause its fall.

> Even though I walk through the darkest valley, I fear no evil;
> for you are with me; your rod and staff—they comfort me. (Ps. 23: 4)

> Though I walk in the midst of trouble,
>   you preserve me against the wrath of my enemies ... (Ps. 138: 7)

> Trouble and anguish have come upon me,
>   but your commandments are my delight. (Ps. 119: 143)

The crises that hope traverses are given with the tone of a proverb, as a present reality.

> Many are the afflictions of the righteous,
>   but the Lord rescues them from them all. (Ps. 34: 19)

The teaching of such a proverb can always be contested from an objective point of view. But its second part is valuable only if it is a witness. Given by a man who lives the first part, he hardly has an illusion as to what awaits the just person. But have we not encountered the most beautiful hope among those who were the most tested? For them, hope is a risk, a dangerous wager, a true spending of life for life. This is what we also encounter in the Bible. The Old Testament does not seem to know stoicism. Either one suffers, cries out and falls, or one lives, and cries out in hope when life itself is threatened. Man does not multiply protections against the attacks of suffering. The only one that he knows, hope, is what makes him vulnerable at the same time. There would not be so many cries in the Psalter without that.

Hope is first of all the desire to live, and what makes it vulnerable is, in biblical prayer, what simply puts life at risk. These texts do not give much place to diffuse worries or fears brought about by worrying about distant evils. The danger is always quite precise. It touches this place that we were invoking earlier, this "self" that is not the coexistence of soul and body, but a soul body, soul flesh. This manner of understanding man is imposed on the entire Psalter. It surprises many Christians. However, it does not reduce man. On the contrary, the more the soul descends into the body, the more one sees that it is a soul; the body is made in order for it to appear. In the Book of Job, Satan tells God, "... But stretch out your hand now and touch his bone and his flesh, and he will curse you to your face" (Job 2: 5). Satan is mistaken as to the result that he is counting on but he is not mistaken when he designates the place where hope is active. By exposing his body, Christ very much gave the demonstration of his hope for our life.

The oscillation of biblical hope goes from everything to nothing, from life to death. Through our daily joys it is the all of life that is touched. Bread and wine are not just means for living; rather they are the symbol for it. Inversely, privations that are not absolute are received as the symbol of death. The more these joys and privations are close to the corporal level, the more they take on a symbolic character, because the body is the symbol of the soul. That is why, in the texts offered for our prayer, there is so often this matter of harvests, vineyards, family, houses, running water, and dirty water. We find readers of the Psalter who are surprised about what they believe to be a materiality of the biblical man, and who miss the point. There is a materiality of the Gospel, of Jesus who is so concerned with the body and whose first manifestation shows him being reborn from living water. The first explanation of Jesus with Satan begins on the day when he was hungry (Matthew 4: 2). But it is also the lesson of daily life, when we do not always see that the things which pass from our hands to those of another and from those of another to our own—food, clothing, medicine—are symbols of life and of death, and not only means. Hope plays out in our most simple actions. We can refuse symbolically what one gives materially, and life is no longer received.

Elijah stops in the desert: "He asked that he might die: 'It is enough; now, O Lord, take away my life ...'" (1 Kings 19: 4). God appears to him and gives him some bread. Hannah, the mother of Samuel, cried and did not eat. Then we saw her pray in the sanctuary and receive an answer through the priest. Later "the woman went to her quarters, ate and drank with her husband, and her countenance was sad no longer" (1 Samuel 1: 18). This also happens to wicked people: Ahab, deprived of the vineyard of Naboth, "lay down on his bed, turned away his face, and would not eat" (1 Kings 21: 4). This vineyard had been promised to him in these terms: "... Get up, eat some food, and be cheerful ..." (1 Kings 21: 7). He does not wait in order to relive: hope gives him back his appetite. Here this is a bad hope and the promise does not come from God. But man is always man, whether good or bad, and our prayer starts at this level, which is common to all.

Here is an example that will take us further.

In the shipwreck narrated in the Acts of the Apostles, it is the life of many men, good or bad, which is at peril. One of them, Saint Paul, speaks to all: "'... Paul urged all of them to take some food ... After he had said this, he took bread; and giving thanks to God in the presence of all, he broke it and began to eat. Then all of them were encouraged and took food for themselves" (Acts 27: 33, 35-36). The remainder of the story tells about the good ending of the voyage. What gets our attention in the prayer of Saint Paul and especially in his gesture is that it is difficult not to think of the Eucharist when we read this narrative. On the one hand, the relationship between danger, hope, prayer and bread places us in the ambience of the prayer of the Psalms. On the other hand, taking bread and breaking it while giving thanks to God reminds us of the Eucharist. Indeed, the prayer of the Psalms and of the Eucharist have the same source and have always been together since the time of the First Supper. This is what I am going to explain.

Saint Paul's gesture, related by the Acts of the Apostles, is certainly a ritual. Saint Paul does not only want to refresh himself in order to whet the appetite of the scared people who surround him. The solemnity of the tone and the religious meaning of the words of the text indicate it rather clearly: Saint Paul blesses the bread according to a

19 Desire

custom of his people. This suggests a rite of supplication that probably expressed their confidence through thanksgiving before any answer would be given as to the anticipated health, security, and salvation. This ritual was significant; one still hoped for the gift of life and this confidence was expressed through the gestures of a meal. At the same time, this meal was an anticipation. The prayer had cleared the throat (the "néféch"); while giving it the promise that the gift of life would continue, it had made this throat capable, once again, of receiving food. One celebrated, while receiving life through bread, the promise of receiving it again. One anticipated the meal of thanksgiving that would be celebrated, once the threat of death had been visibly put aside. This is what Saint Paul did.

There are reasons to believe that this is what Jesus also did, by celebrating a meal of thanksgiving before his death in order to anticipate the definitive meal of thanksgiving. His anticipated giving of thanks tells of his confidence and it is also his supplication before the ordeal-limit of hope, faced with the destruction of his body. Jesus then drinks and eats the Passover: "'I have eagerly desired to eat this Passover with you before I suffer; for I tell you, I will not eat it until it is fulfilled in the kingdom of God.' Then he took a cup, and after giving thanks he said, 'Take this and divide it among yourselves; for I tell you that from now on I will not drink of the fruit of the vine until the kingdom of God comes'" (Luke 22: 14-19). The Eucharistic giving of thanks anticipates the salvation of his body. This saved body is a source of life; he already gives it, he already gives his body. The Father is also present to him as he is present to the Father, and the life that comes from the Father passes on, through this bread, which is the body of Christ, to all men.

Biblical surprises, movement from the nearly elementary to the nearly inaccessible, set the rhythm of the prayer of the Psalms! ... I have just described the mystery of the Eucharist as being "nearly inaccessible," and it is true that it contains what is most elevated, everything of Christian initiation. What is still true is that God makes himself accessible in it. Nearly alone among pagans on the sea, Saint Paul probably did not celebrate this mystery. But Luke thinks about it while relating it, he thinks about it as a promise exposed on the infinity of the world that then opens up to the Gospel. Today, while reading the Psalms, we have a place for understanding how the mystery of life is truly a gift that wants to reach us.

The Psalms are the prayer of men threatened by the shipwreck of their life, and we hardly see one case (with the exception of Psalm 88) when, addressing prayers of supplication to God, men do not also express praise. We know that there is no supplication more perfect than praise: "They walked around in the midst of the flames, singing hymns to God and blessing the Lord" (The Prayer of Azariah and the Song of the Three Jews, Revised Standard Version, verse 1). Under these conditions, thanksgiving helps one to entreat, just as supplication also serves to express gratitude. All the Psalms thus lend themselves to be recited before some peril and after it. Is that not our life, always after some hurt and before another? But before being saved from death and unable to escape its approaches, we are able to anticipate the song of thanksgiving of true life. Thus has Christ, at the same time, made the prayer of the Psalms his own and confirmed it by exposing himself to death even more completely than the three young men in the fiery furnace. It is in the same Psalm that we read:

Why have you forsaken me? (Ps. 22: 2)

and that we formulate the promise:

> ... my vows I will pay before those who fear him.
> The poor shall eat and be satisfied ... (Ps. 22: 25-26)

In the Eucharist and in all of our life, Jesus anticipates the promise through this sharing of bread and he invites us to do likewise.

20

Promise of life

"For you have delivered my soul from death ..." (Ps. 56 13). These words are nearly a refrain of the Psalms, even if the terms change a little from one page to the other. Death is also called "the abyss," "the chasm," "corruption," "the Pit."

> For you do not give me up to Sheol,
> or let your faithful one see the Pit. (Ps. 16: 10).

> O Lord, you brought up my soul from Sheol,
> restored me to life from among those
> gone down to the Pit. (Ps. 30: 3)

The Hebrews called Sheol the place that gave asylum to the personality of the dead. A kind of underground pocket, this sojourn was characterized by a pale sadness, not by torments or punishments. The principal cause of this sadness is rather clear: regarding the state of dead people, one remembered especially silence, the end of all expression, be it a cry towards salvation or a song of joy directed to God.

> "What profit is there in my death,
> if I go down to the Pit?
> Will the dust praise you?
> Will it tell of your faithfulness? ..." (Ps. 30: 9)

As extraordinary as that might seem to us, it was thought that the relation of man with God dwindled after death, to the point of becoming insignificant. Such certitude is present in the Psalm itself; to express these words that cry, praise, and plead is to proclaim that one is alive. The living person is the one who prays the prayer of the Psalms, whatever the misfortune that he might have to face. On the other hand, putting an end to the flow of this prayer is enough to designate perfectly the place of death:

> The dead do not praise the Lord,
> nor do any that go down into silence.
> But we will bless the Lord ... (Ps. 115: 17-18)

To murmur these words of complaint and gratitude throughout one's days is to live. Life asks to be maintained; the word asks to continue:

> For in death there is no remembrance of you;
> in Sheol who can give you praise? (Ps. 6: 5)

At the heart of our experience of time, man understands how the life of God can be a life which is a gift without completely satisfying one. He praises God and prays in order to be able to praise him again:

> Hope in God; for I shall again praise him ... (Ps. 42: 5)

It is in the disappearance of his own mortal life that the Psalmist understands who God is.

The one who is mortal "thirsts for God, for the living God" (Ps. 42: 2). The Psalmist receives all from God all the more avidly since God lives forever whereas man lives for a moment. The faithful of that time either ignored or did not dare affirm that God gave man this aspect, this line of eternity that is attached to the human soul from the moment of birth. It is evident that this manner of seeing, though we find it often and clearly expressed in the Old Testament, is not the one that we have learned. These texts were written a very long time ago and other principles have come to light, here and there, shortly before the Christian era. But, for the believers of the Old Testament in general, everything happens to man before his death and nothing after it, nothing—at least—about which one might speak with certitude or profit.

Or rather, and only this matters, ignorance was greatly beneficial for these believers. Paradox, their manner of seeing, even if we find it little enlightened, is quite apt for correcting our own habits and for serving as a remedy. The least refined is an indispensable help to the most developed; let us receive that from the Psalms. In effect, the Psalms

20 Promise of Life

only perceived, for the beyond, shade. The result is that they so valued the friendship of God during this mortal life, which seemed to them rather like a "brief encounter" with God, that they did not want to lose it. They needed to warm this earthly life in the sun of God, because it goes by quickly and they did not imagine how God could keep up a relationship with a man after he died. One must hasten to love God (or to praise him: it is all he same) because one would not meet him again! That is the conclusion that these men of prayer took from the little they knew about the future. More clarity does not always lead to anything better than that.

We could imagine that a man might calculate his fate in this way; he would renounce his estate that he loves in order to find God in the next world, and this would not be because he loves God, but because in the next world his property would no longer exist. God being the only good which is then offered after death, we would prepare ourselves for God to the extent that there is no other choice. Such a calculation could hardly tempt believers of the Old Testament; they were preserved from this by the silence of their religion regarding all future and invisible realities. Since God for them was the God of the living, they desired to meet him before their death:

> My soul thirsts for God, for the living God.
> When shall I come and behold the face of God? (Ps. 42: 2)

This request, at the time of the Psalms, hardly envisages to be heard elsewhere but here.

Moreover, which calculation would be possible between the one who lives at all times, God, and the one who will die at any moment, man?

> For he knows how we were made;
> he remembers that we are dust.
>
> As for mortals, their days are like grass;
> they flourish like a flower of the field;
> for the wind passes over it, and it is gone,
> and its place knows it no more. (Ps. 103: 14-16)

This memory of the human condition may distance us by its austerity or because we know it only too well. But we should look more closely at the text. It is not always to man that it is said, "Remember..." or "Remember that you are dust." Here, God is invited to remember through man: "For he knows how we were made:/ he remembers that we are dust" (Ps. 103: 14). Instead of making it cold, this cry has our blood flow in biblical prayer. It will soon be too late, and tardiness is incurable after death. The God of the Psalms does not have eternity in order to save a man:

> To you, O Lord, I call;
> my rock, do not refuse to hear me,
> for if you are silent to me,
> I shall be like those who go down to the Pit. (Ps. 28: 1)

> Do not let the flood sweep over me,
> or the deep swallow me up ...
> for I am in distress—make haste to
> answer me. (Ps. 69: 15 and 17)

> Answer me quickly, O Lord;
> my spirit fails. (Ps. 143: 7)

Urgency whets the utterances of the Psalms. It animates the experience of God with a shiver: life passes. The dialogue is exposed to all that is tragic. Because so little time is left for God to give an answer, we can foresee strong anguish and ordeals that then turn into joy if God answers. A hope of this type must always come to terms with verifiable reality.

What comes to us with the Bible is the fact that such a hope has not disappeared. It is handed on from mouth to mouth and from age to age. The Psalms, composed during several centuries, tell of this.

> He drew me up from the desolate pit,
> out of the miry bog ...
> He put a new song in my mouth ... (Ps. 40: 2-3)

> ... you have delivered my soul from the
> depths of Sheol. (Ps. 86: 13)

> For you have delivered my soul from death,
> my eyes from tears,
> my feet from stumbling. (Ps. 116: 8)

God has nurtured hope every time and has allowed it to continue: "I shall not die, but I shall live ..." (Ps. 118: 17). As light as a stream of water, the flow of this utterance of hope, which is life itself, has come even to us in these words.

Christians are the sons of this prayer: from the prayer of the Psalms to the prayer of Christ, there is a relationship, a transformation, and a new birth. The prayer of the Psalms needs the light of Christianity, and the inverse is also true. More clearly than the Psalmists, we have learned from faith that God conquers our death. But through their prayer we know and we also believe that our life now is true and that it is in God.

The definitive victory of Christ over death is only attractive if it does not invade our lives; the victory is not reserved for our life beyond. It crosses the barrier toward our life now. Without seeing clearly regarding the resurrection, the men who sang the Psalms believed that God was active in their daily lives. If, while believing in the resurrection of Christ, we thought that it touches us only in the aftermath of our lives, we would be less advanced than the believers of the Old Testament.

On the contrary, through faith, a life that has already conquered death transforms us as of today. We understand this better in recalling that Jesus Christ was the bearer of the hope that we have just described with the words of the Psalms, and that he himself cried out for his salvation and for that of others. He experienced the misery of those who, most tested, were taken to him "in the evening" so that he might deliver them from the spirits who tormented them:

> This was to fulfill what had been spoken through the prophet Isaiah, "He took our infirmities and bore our diseases" (Matthew 8: 16-17).

These healings, which bring joy, announce the passion, which takes God closer to our death. The compassion of Christ, which introduces God into the suffering of man, announces his resurrection and our own. Jesus Christ, resurrected, proclaims not only that death will be vanquished but will be vanquished today.

21

True Bread

"I am the Lord your God,
 who brought you up out of the land of
  Egypt.
Open your mouth wide and I will fill it ...
O that my people would listen to me...
I would feed you with the finest of the wheat,
 and with honey from the rock I would
  satisfy you." (Ps. 81: 10, 13, and 16)

With what is God going to fill this mouth that he wants to see open? What are the "finest of the wheat" and this "honey from the rock"? To ask this question is to ask a very ancient question, the very classical question about the meanings of Scripture. In order to answer it we shall have to talk a little bit about theory, which concerns any reader of the Bible.

Some will be relieved to learn that it was thought that Scripture had several meanings. That is a guarantee of freedom. One probably had to review these meanings according to an itinerary ruled by reason, but this did not decrease one's freedom. Two meanings were distinguished. First of all, a quite natural and corporal one: the verses that we have quoted say that people are hungry and that God promises to give them something to eat. This is the best food, if the people open their ears and their mouths. Is this not, in effect, what everyone understands? Then there is a spiritual meaning, generally more difficult to agree upon. God gives to his own either divine life, which is at this very moment true nourishment, or the Eucharist. Or better still, he promises divine life in absolute fullness, such as it will be given at the end of time.

This will perhaps upset other readers of the Bible. It would be simpler for them to have only one meaning. And, when positive science made its grand conquests, around the beginning of the twentieth century, some readers saw in it the promise and the means for simplification. It would supremely establish for the Bible one meaning. The situation of this period was even able to invite one to go further, to declare as the one and only true meaning the corporal sense, which even became at times a material meaning. One would then be able to replace Psalm 81: 11-17 with these words: "I present myself," says God, "as the provider of food composed of grains of good quality" ("finest of the wheat") "and of glucides, under the form of this 'honey from the rock,' whose properties remain to be established by the naturalists." Let us imagine that, from this point, from this legitimate and scholarly language, were we to reject the former plurality of meanings, we would lose something in the reading of the Bible.

Someone will retort: why come back to these debates, for readers whom these arguments never divided? Indeed, it would be quite advantageous to forget them, if there were men capable of deciding, in such matters, without any hesitation. If there was a problem in the past, there is generally an obstacle today. And if we are able to find a simpler path today, it is generally thanks to the itinerary that others took in the past. A glance backwards teaches us also to be wary of certain solutions that are too simple.

Let us begin again with these expressions that are analogous to those that we quoted from Psalm 81. How numerous they are in the Psalms!

> May our barns be filled,
>   with produce of every kind;
> may our sheep increase by thousands,
>   by tens of thousands in our fields ... (Ps. 144: 13)

Or this:

> For he satisfies the thirsty,
>   and the hungry he fills with good things. (Ps. 107: 9)

Or this:

21 True Bread

> You open your hand,
> satisfying the desire of every living thing. (Ps. 145: 16)

Food, hunger and thirst, satisfaction, the best nourishment, promise on the condition that the mouth be open; what is this all about?

I answer that it is about what everyone desires in hearing these words. This is a simple answer but perhaps not so massively simple, not so exaggerated for all that. Because it signifies that it is truly not about a material object! Need can be directed to some material object and be satisfied by it. But we must distinguish between need and desire. Need does not need words. But desire is a function as essentially human as intelligence. Human, that is to say, essentially oriented towards God. As soon as the utterance is formed, it comes forth as a function of desire. And God is in every desire.

We would not be forcing the meaning of Psalm 81: 11-16, if we gave it these words: "God said, 'Desire only, and I am there, with this nourishment which signifies me.'" We can talk of a spiritual meaning, on the condition of beginning with the spiritual that is present, without any magic, in every human utterance. Man cannot desire bread without being implied in the spiritual. This keeps us from introducing bad divisions, from founding the plurality of meanings on deadly divisions between meanings. The past has not always avoided this drawback. Let us continue.

Man can only desire God, whether he realizes this or not. But no man can abstract himself from the position of his body in the world when he seeks God. God is the Good, signified in everything that is good, and we understand by "desire" the movement which goes towards a good, at once for itself and to the extent that it signifies God. Man, image of God, is attracted towards God not only in an exceptional way but everyday, during the week as on Sunday, morning and evening. His desire is at once unique, because it is desire of the unique (God), and complex, because he desires the unique in the plurality of things. This is the law of a movement, of a story. If man who desires bread is implied, by the very fact, in the spiritual—how much true this will be of the human being who desires the human being! It is the very movement of desire which, in the individual story, with more or less success, passes from the desire for nourishment to sexual desire. It is the same movement, always spiritual and always divine, by which all humanity desires itself in political society, in the city.

Knowing that there are not two desires is a great joy, because we understand that the spiritual begins at the root of the body, at the most extreme beginning of our being.

Even if it is a bit unexpected, this clarifies all at once many passages of the Bible. We were surprised, also! We were surprised that God should promise so many visible and material goods! So it was necessary either to understand in their true meaning our so-called earthly desires or to censor many passages of Scripture. Faced with this alternative, let us not make the bad choice!

> I walk before the Lord
> in the land of the living. (Ps. 116: 9)

> I cry to you, O Lord;
> I say, "You are my refuge,
> my portion in the land of the living." (Ps. 142: 5)

Such is the language of the Psalms. It provides us with everything that is colored, sunny, tangible and warm, like bread coming out of the oven. Here "land of the living" means what every man desires when hearing these words! This interpretation does not err by excess of simplicity because no man knows quite exactly what he desires. That is what desire is. But this interpretation is not hazy, because, all the same, we know how to desire. This interpretation teaches us one thing: it is necessary to desire when one reads these biblical texts; one must read them with one's desire. One must read one's desire in them. That is prayer.

With this established, can we still say that Psalm 81: verses 11-16 has some relationship to the Eucharist, with the life of God that God himself gives through grace, with the life which shall have conquered our death? Is it the life that our ancestors called eternal life? Is the "land of the living" the one that has an encounter with all who have died?

The gift of eternal life in the bread that is the body of Christ is what the Gospel proclaims; it is the Revelation. The desire of man is like a milieu of resonance outside of which the Gospel cannot be heard. And it is always possible to muffle or stifle a resonance.

So there is a milieu of resonance, our desire, and there is the trumpet sound of revelation. What resonation does the trumpet make?

21 True Bread

We learn that God gives us a bread that is his body, that God gives a new world where death is conquered by Jesus Christ, that Jesus Christ unites, in the love of a new nuptial, all humanity and has it reborn together. The reasons for calling it revelation are quite clear. No one can say, while hearing it, "I know it." But only: "I believe it."

But we may say, "I desired it." "I desired it, but I did not know what I desired." Because man does not know too well what he desires. How could it be otherwise? Desire is a movement towards an Other, whom one cannot invent, and desire is a movement towards a gift that one cannot give to oneself.

When the Other comes and when the gift is present, then everything changes. It is then revealed that we desired this Other and this gift and that this Other had made us with this desire in order to fulfill us. The Gospel thus teaches us that those who wrote the Psalms already desired, in their condition that was similar to our own, what God proclaims and reveals today. The Gospel reveals that this "finest of the wheat" of Psalm 81: verse 16, is this bread that begins with our bread and ends in a divine life that is stronger than death, and passes through our Eucharist.

There are several meanings of this bread, because this bread has a history. It is a history that no one could make in advance. But this history has one movement that the Gospel reveals to us.

The Gospel teaches us how this bread is baked: it passes through the cross of Christ, the true place of its transformation. All the senses which call our desire towards what our desire does not know pass through the sensory matrix of the cross of Christ, the "*sensible de la croix.*" It is there that all appearances disappear in order to announce the message of the Gospel.

22

Path

The Psalms answer one another and this coherence is a sign, not of rigidity, but of life. However, we know that this life is not always perceived.

A center of gravity is still necessary in order for us to better grasp this entity. We need to find a point from which all can be colored and animated.

What is necessary for a man to be pursued by "envy," a sign of evil, and for him to live under the threat of death? What is necessary for there to be, all about him, the noise and furor that fill the Psalms? What is necessary for there to be praise, supplication, and confidence?

This only happens to the man who is in movement, who walks about, who is on the move. The Psalms are like a painting in the center of which we find the Psalmist. If we place a Psalmist in the center and have him be immobile, all around him will be pale and immobile. There will be no incline that allows for the possibility and fear of slipping, no noisy chasms, no wicked people who slander. Nor, consequently, would there be a paschal gesture by which God saves while giving wings. On the contrary, make the Psalmist move and all begins to move: false witnesses plot death, the mouth of the tomb roars in order to make one afraid and become paralyzed. Given this, God sends his angel and his providence.

The Psalms praise for the wonders of Providence or bemoan their absence. But there is no Providence for the man who remains seated. Providence only knows the man who walks.

Walking is a term that the Psalter uses constantly, to the point of satiation. In order to walk, there must be a path, and the theme of the path is also one of the most frequent in the Psalter, to such an extent that we do not pay it much attention. In a more solemn vocabulary, paths are called ways, "ways of God," and ways of the just man or of the ungodly. Be they paths or ways, we must be reborn to the truth of these images, if we want to make biblical prayer our own. This should be easy, because they speak to what is closest to our soul, to our body.

A path has what is at once solid and mobile. It must be a solid support, like the earth and rock. But it must be free of any obstacle and invite one to movement. The path has to do with the ground because it is stable and with the sky because one moves ahead on it "as though one had wings," when one walks towards a very desired destination. Everything that happens to the Psalmist happens to him when he changes place between one point and another:

> The Lord will keep
>   your going out and your coming in ... (Ps. 121: 8)

> He leads me in right paths ...
> Even though I walk through the darkest valley,
>   I fear no evil ... (Ps. 23: 3 and 4)

The text of these prayers gives much place to the body but, because it is a question of walking, much detail is always given to the feet. Limbs for movement can be captured by the net that immobilizes (Ps. 9: 15; 25: 15), stopped by the obstacle that makes one stumble. Thus does God keep the feet from a fall or from slipping (Pss. 56: 13; 66: 9; 121: 3):

> When I thought, "My foot is slipping,"
>   your steadfast love, O Lord, held me up. (Ps. 94: 18)

Man needs ground that welcomes and supports his foot, and he needs a winged foot in order for the path to be open to him and to take him to his goal. This gift is described and desired as a grace of the Lord:

> ... make your way straight before me. (Ps. 5: 8)

> You gave me a wide place for my steps under me,
>   and my feet did not slip. (Ps. 18: 36)

> My foot stands on level ground ... (Ps. 26: 12)

22 Path

We often represent the man who prays as looking up, whereas the man of the Bible always has his gaze turned in the opposite direction, towards his feet. However, it is not only a question of the ground, and not only of the sky. The path resembles its end or destination, which is the mountain, the elevated rock. At once solid and free, the path must present the qualities of the peak, solid and aerial, safe and free. Desire soars towards the peak:

Lead me to the rock that is higher than I ... (Ps. 61: 2)

In the memory of Israel, a fundamental situation gathers all these images together. This is the Exodus. Leaving Egypt, the people escape the chasm, when the sea changes into a path:

He turned the sea into dry land;
  they passed through the river on foot ...
... who has kept us among the living,
  and has not let our feet slip. (Ps. 66: 6 and 9)

The people are called towards a place by their desire. The place is the mountain of God and the promised land, often compared to a mountain. According to certain traditions, they are carried "on eagles' wings" (Exodus 19: 4; Deuteronomy 32: 11-12). But other traditions remember that the people used their legs, and the help of God, in these traditions, takes on as marvelous a form, all the while remaining more on the land: "... your feet did not swell these forty years" of walking in the desert, between the sea of Reeds and the promised land (Deuteronomy 8: 4).

What does this insistence on the safe and quick march mean, on the ground that is as elevated as Mount Zion?

Happy are those whose strength is in you,
  in whose heart are the highways to Zion ...
They go from strength to strength;
  the God of gods will be seen in Zion. (Ps. 84: 5 and 7)

These images describe the place where our desire must tend. The landscape of the Psalms, we have said, remains inanimate if the Psalmist himself is immobile. On the contrary, his movement gets everything going. But how do we advance if we are not called by some desire? Finally, how can we desire if nothing presents itself that is made for us? Thus does a chain of associations connect, in the themes of the Psalms, path, walking, land and, finally, the promise of land:

> ... he led them by a straight way,
> until they reached an inhabited town. (Ps. 107: 7)

Just as a river cuts through the city of God (Ps. 46:4), and just as the mountain is the place where streams begin to flow, so the desire of man is only called towards the realities where the Spirit is present. Desire itself, when it is true, has its source in the Spirit.

Only desire that is in us is able to give a meaning to the words of the Psalms, and this to the extent that it sets us in motion where we find ourselves in our daily reality in order to have us go towards the end. God calls us to himself by calling us towards the new world that he promises. So he does not call us to leave this world according to our likes but to traverse it according to the path that we must find, each his own. To find this path is a frequent request (Ps. 25: 4 and 9; 27: 11; 139: 24; 143: 8).

Why would one speak of a path if it were a question of entering directly into eternal life? For that one would rather talk about an immediate jump into the absolute. But we speak about a path because, in order to go towards God, it is always necessary to go through the actions of this world, everyday acts, and earthly encounters. By desiring God we desire always, at the same time, what leads us towards him. If Christ came to earth, if God became man in this world, we are not going to fly away to find him. And if we pretended to do that, we would be lying to ourselves.

There are, in this world, places that are different for each of us, that each must cross, and there are faces to meet and complex tasks that are difficult to perform. All this forms the path: we shall advance on it only if "our heart is in it." Prayer is the moment for putting one's heart on this road. When we pray, we should probably not think all the time about these tasks of the day. But if what our heart wishes when we do not pray is truly something else when it does pray, what true prayer will be possible? Prayer must transform the desire of the heart, but the desire of the heart must nurture prayer. "Make me know your path," but also: "...help me to advance on the path where I am."

22 Path

The term, the finality, of our desire, the world of our prayer, bears a name: it is the Kingdom of God. As the Gospel describes it, it is made through many displacements, corporal actions, encounters where one does not only exchange words but visible objects. And if we do not flee from these conditions, the Kingdom of God comes about through many ordeals. The Kingdom of God is this unity that comprises God, his Christ and those whom he gives to us and promises as brothers, the entire world that Christ transforms. Scripture should teach us to make our prayer the prayer of the Kingdom. We shall then pray in, with, and for the entire world: "… thy kingdom come …"

But we shall also pray in the moment where we find ourselves and with the risks that our faith requires of us in this world. Our life will be questioned and we shall ask for "our daily bread." Our enemies will be ready for action and we shall need to be "delivered from evil." We pray because we walk and we walk because we pray. That is the path of the Kingdom.

We can well desire a new earth, since we ask that "His will be done on earth as in heaven" and since Christ said that "the meek shall possess the earth." He was quoting Psalm 37:

> Trust in the Lord, and do good;
>   so you will live in the land … (v. 3)

> Commit your way to the Lord;
>   trust in him, and he will act … (v. 5)

> … but those who wait for the Lord shall
>   inherit the land … (v. 9)

> But the meek shall inherit the land … (v. 11)

> Our steps are made firm by the Lord,
>   when he delights in our way … (v. 23)

> Wait for the Lord, and keep to his way,
>   and he will exalt you to inherit the land;
>   you will look on the destruction of the wicked. (v. 34)

PART FIVE

THE PSALMS AND THE WORLD

The exposition of biblical themes, of their coherence and resonance, can ordinarily be read without difficulty, as the author who writes the exposition is also the one who regulates and arranges the linking of ideas for the reader. We have approached the Psalms, up to this point, according to this method.

Now we shall adopt an approach that is a bit different, because we are going to take one Psalm per chapter. We shall then keep closely to the arrangement of the given Psalm. This task is more laborious since the commentator is less the master of the developments to be followed and then because the originality of the developments that a Psalm offers us makes them difficult to foresee and even to discover. For each new Psalm there is a new path to follow. It is different every time, like another face, or another city … But that is not all. A man who lived in the Jerusalem of yesteryear or in some other city of Israel before our era gave his words a certain nuance and turn of phrase, a style which is not our own. To become accustomed to this is one of the greatest joys that exegesis offers. But this joy requires some patience.

In any case, the commentator has us read two texts at once: the one that he comments on and the one that he writes. This first requires more effort.

The transition from the exposition to a kind of commentary of a text is a change in method. But at the same time we are going to take up a fifth and last aspect of the Psalms, which is a change of subject. The title "The Psalms and the World" reminds us that the prayer of the Psalms does not concern the individual. It goes very far in the opposite direction, to judge by the number of cases where it is the prayer of a city, of a people, and more largely still, the prayer of all creation or for all creation. "Creation" is much the most universal term, since it designates all that is not God.

"I believe in one God, the Father almighty, creator of heaven and earth." Among all the paths that this affirmation of faith has taken, that of the Psalms is one of the most attractive. Probably because it is not more rectilinear than a mountain path. To go over and over again, to turn at a sharp angle, but always to be climbing is what would be necessary to do while discovering that the reality of the creative act is at once:

A. the closest to ourselves, a creation that is near (chapters 23-26).

B. the farthest because it embraces everything, a distant creation (chapters 27 and 28).

C. the most desirable because it also designates our future, creation to come (chapter 29).

The Psalter will lead us in the same direction as does our Credo, towards the world to come.

The path comprises some turns in the road. I shall even say that the detour is an aspect inherent to the meditation of God Creator, a detour since we are led to ourselves and to God by considering what is neither God nor ourselves. As far as meditation leads us into the cosmos, creation always puts into play a particular aspect of our personal relation with God. I shall call this aspect the point of creation. But in order to find it, we must make the detour of the entire world. We then come back to the point of creation by a kind of curving of the itinerary. And this itinerary is obligatory: the distant and the near are necessary in order to enter into the truth of the creative act. All thought about creation is in this coming-and-going that, as we shall see, Psalm 139 describes:

> Such knowledge is too wonderful for me:
>   it is so high that I cannot attain it. (Ps. 139: 6)

We shall first see how we are led towards the nearest and the least visible.

A. Near Creation

23

Psalm 8

1   O Lord, our Sovereign,
     how majestic is your name in all the earth!

     You have set your glory above the heavens.
2   Out of the mouths of babes and infants
     you have founded a bulwark because of your foes,
     to silence the enemy and the avenger.

3   When I look at your heavens, the work
       of your fingers,
     the moon and the stars that you have established;
4   what are human beings that you are mindful of them,
     mortals that you care for them?

5   Yet you have made them a little lower than God,
     and crowned them with glory and honor.
6   You have given the dominion over the works of your hands;
     you have put all things under their feet,
7   all sheep and oxen,
     and also the beasts of the field,
8   the birds of the air, and the fish of the sea,
     whatever passes along the paths of the seas.

9   O Lord, our Sovereign,
     how majestic is your name in all the earth!

The Psalms invite us to pray to God the Creator and this seduces us. We willingly choose to introduce stars and rivers in our face-to-face encounter with God, rather than to pray "with our head in our hands." Others will say that more maturity and more ordeals keep them from leaving their inner life; after all, that is where the greatest tragedies have their last effect. It is outside that humanity lives its dramas; it is within that it recalls them. The name Auschwitz teaches us that, were this interiority of man to be closed up, the forgotten victims died for no one.

But biblical prayer overcomes this opposition of the exterior and the interior; the prayer of the heart is a prayer of the body. The heart perceives nothing without the outside, but the outside leads us to the heart, the seat of presence. It is only from this place that creation appears what it is; intimate, secret, and the ultimate action of God. A discrete word: only such a murmur made in the night can be heard as the proclamation of a divine victory over death.

Everything begins with an experience of the senses, with the eyes:

When I look at your heavens, the work of your fingers,
   the moon and the stars that you have established ... (Ps. 8: 3)

But this line is quickly crossed by another. We think of the words of Pascal: "... nothing is simple which is presented to the soul, and the soul never presents itself simply to any object."[1] Creation is a contrast and it refers back to the contrast in man. The view of the cosmos, of the extraterrestrial world, makes it difficult to believe that man is so important:

... what are human beings that you are
   mindful of them ... (Ps. 8: 4)

Our gaze is thus taken from the stars to man, who
seems to be so insignificant:

---

[1] "*Inconstancy*—Things have different qualities, and the soul different inclinations; for nothing is simple which is presented to the soul, and the soul never presents itself simply to any object. Hence it comes that we weep and laugh at the same thing" (Blaise Pascal, *The Thoughts of Blaise Pascal*. Westport, Connecticut: Greenwood Press: 1978). Note of the translator.

23 A. Near Creation: Psalm 8

Yet you have made them a little lower than God ...
... you have put all things under their feet ... (Ps. 8: 5 and 6)

Dominated and dominating, frightened then crowned "with glory and honor" (Ps. 8: 5), man is, in the cosmos, a point of disequilibrium, frailty held back on the edge of an abyss. It is exactly on this point that all thought of creation is concentrated; it is here that it is born. It is on this edge that man loses heart, and where he recoups his courage. A gaze that would remain on the distant circle of things would not have one look toward a Creator God; he finds him only by looking back on himself.

A new surprise: crowned above "everything," man—in literal reality—has power only over animals:

... you have put all things under their feet,
all sheep and oxen,
   and also the beasts of the field,
the birds of the air, and the fish of the sea,
   whatever passes along the paths of the seas. (Ps. 8: 6-9)

Dominated by stars, dominating animals—biblical wisdom places man on this very fine, median line. Modern wisdom would find very little in this having to do with glory and honor, and would not see much that is royal in this position. However, the Bible insists on this. The first chapter of Genesis stays with it: deprived of power over the stars, man will know how to conquer the earth because he will command herbivorous animals. Nothing more is suggested, beyond this empire judged to be rather glorious. (The reader might want to verify it for himself by turning to Genesis 1, 28: man cannot multiply himself, fill the earth and submit it to himself if he does not command the animals which, like himself, multiply and fill the earth. The second task is a condition of the first.) For humanity that has now walked on a star, the message does not go very far.

But we can walk on a star and not have a finely tuned ear to hear the message of an ancestor. He has us understand, in Genesis, that man is in the image of God and, in Psalm 8, that he is almost a god (verse 5). The two texts are in agreement in teaching that the divine image is situated in what differentiates man from an animal. Here again, the thought of relation takes us back not only to man but to what, in man, is not the most visible.

However, are not this difference and this royalty of man over animals quite clear? Our ancestor has an answer for us: "Animals," our ancestor remarks, "devour one another and men also; so their difference is not so evident. Animals, according to the narrative of creation in Genesis (1, 30) are only herbivorous by the commandment of God, and this restriction is not due to their nature. In order to dominate this nature, man relays God in the post of commander, through the effect of his delegated word (it is true, and rather astonishing, that one speaks to animals). Animals refrain from devouring each other. But after Cain kills Abel and, since then, men devour one another, as they do from Cain to the deluge, their word loses all power to impose meekness upon animals. If today men imitate animals that devour each other by nature, it is proof that they do not dominate them. Because men imitate animals, they resemble them. And if they resemble animals, it is the evident sign that they have lost their divine resemblance, on which their power was founded. They will probably dominate them again, but this time by force and terror; man will have power over the lion by the means that the lion has over the lamb. He no longer commands by the word. After man sank into violence, God adapted his word for him: 'The fear and dread of you shall rest on every animal of the earth …' (Genesis 9: 2). Since then, the state of war has also reigned between animals, between man and animals, between man and man. It is only on the day when God will have healed man that 'the calf and the lion' will lie down and eat together because they will be reconciled and, if that is the case, it is because 'a little child shall lead them' when the time for the end of wars arrives (Isaiah 11: 1-9; see also 2: 4). — And so," our ancestor concludes, "the power over animals which seems to you to be so little is what you, walking on a star, do not have. Perhaps you have it less than ever."

The more we go back in time, the more we find in our ancestors this ability to read a mystery through the letter or the fable of a text. Once retraced according to their rules, their angle connects with us; the man nearest the stars might have made himself the most similar to animals. Having put his feet there, he is not less alarmed than the Psalmist to be nearly a god, since the war of today lets him know that he possesses the power to "uncreate" the world. And so, meditating on creation does not distance us too much from our own dramas.

23 A. Near Creation: Psalm 8

The man who is at war snarls and hardens his skin. He remakes himself in the image of the shark, of predatory birds, of a big cat. His force is violence. The only one in the image of God is the one stronger than his own force. Meekness is more than non-violence. Regarding this, Jesus confirms Psalm 37: the meek are called to possess the land, just like the child in Isaiah.

So here we are, from gazing at the stars, called towards what is not the most visible in man, towards the image of the meekness of God. This conversion, this turning or detour, is a law of all biblical thought about creation. It was probably necessary for us to interpret human royalty, in noting its limits, according to Genesis 1 and what followed. This detour should not surprise us if we remember how the triangle which joins man to the stars and to the animals was familiar, through all the zodiacs and related systems, to ancient thought, which did not venture down these paths in order to discover trivialities.

But, come to this point, Psalm 8 does not abandon us. Creation is very much a tour de force and victory where "the enemy and the avenger" are reduced to silence (Ps. 8: 2). But the context helps us to believe that violence is the enemy and that force is meekness or even weakness. One cannot have it understood better than by saying:

> You have set your glory above the heavens.
>   Out of the mouths of babes and infants,
> you have founded a bulwark because of your foes ... (Ps. 8: 2).

At the most archaic level, the image was formed in a mythological figure of divine babies or twin gods. Whatever its origin, this portrayal of the newborn, described in their powerlessness as being the most apt to sing the victory of God, has not been lost. According to Matthew 21: 16, Jesus notes this. He had come in order to accomplish the mission of this child who reconciles ferocious beasts through the meekness of God.

24

Psalm 19

1 The heavens are telling the glory of God;
    and the firmament proclaims his handiwork.
2 Day to day pours forth speech,
    and night to night declares knowledge.
3 There is no speech, nor are there words;
    their voice is not heard;
4 yet their voice goes out through all the earth,
    and their words to the end of the world.

   In the heavens he has set a tent for the sun,
5 which comes out like a bridegroom from
        his wedding canopy,
    and like a strong man runs its course with joy.
6 Its rising is from the end of the heavens,
    and its circuit to the end of them;
    and nothing is hid from its heat.

7 The law of the Lord is perfect,
    reviving the soul;
  the decrees of the Lord are sure,
    making wise the simple;
8 the precepts of the Lord are right,
    rejoicing the heart;
  the commandment of the Lord is clear,
    enlightening the eyes;
9 the fear of the Lord is pure,
    enduring forever;
  the ordinances of the Lord are true
    and righteous altogether.
10 More to be desired are they than gold,
    even much fine gold;

sweeter also than honey,
    and drippings of the honeycomb.

11 Moreover by them is your servant warned;
    in keeping them there is great reward.
12 But who can detect their errors?
    Clear me from hidden faults.
13 Keep back your servant also from the insolent;
    do not let them have dominion over me.
    Then I shall be blameless,
    and innocent of great transgression.

14 Let the words of my mouth and the
    meditation of my heart
    be acceptable to you,
    O Lord, my rock and my redeemer.

The Psalm begins with these words:

The heavens are telling the glory of God…

They were the most known and quoted words of the entire Psalter (*coeli ennarant gloriam Dei*). If they were quoted so often, it is because they impressed. But every quotation resembles a marker left in a book; it signifies that an encounter is set for this passage. It is not that one has misunderstood it, nor is it that one did understand it so completely that another reading might be useless. A marker left in a book means that the words are still with us and that it is calling us back to them. And so I shall start to talk again about Psalm 19.

The words have touched us and they surprise us. The reader who is the most apt to be surprised is the best reader, and a more banal text would never be quoted. With words such as "the spectacle, the sight of the heavens raises us …" or something like "the heavens are an image of … ," all surprise would disappear. The idea that the heavens "speak" is an idea that does surprise and get our attention. The idea surprises because, if the heavens are silent, we know only their silence. The idea, however, strikes us. Why?

Silence is not without some relation to the ear. Silence visits the ear, invests it, and awakens it. It is not foolish to have the ear be attentive

24 A. Near Creation: Psalm 19

to the celestial firmament, to orient our tympanum towards the tympanum of the heavens. We would say that it hears, that all the words of the world continuously impress its surface and that it sends them back to us. All the words ... but the totality that gathers the words cannot strike the ear; it is only present beneath all the audible words. Only multiple words strike the ear, but the meaning, which unifies the words, does not strike it. However, we say that the meaning is "heard." We call "understanding" what perceives the meaning of the words in the silence of their unity, a silence that is all the more great as this unity is total.

Thus does God speak to men by many words, those of the Bible and of other books, those of the servants of God and of Jesus of Nazareth. But what makes the unity, the meaning of all these words, must be one like God himself. This is the Word of God and this Word does not make any tympanum vibrate; it is not pronounced and is heard only in silence. In diverse testimonies, multiplicity speaks. Between testimonies and in order to connect them, unity becomes silent, the Word becomes silent. God addresses the silence of the Word "to the good listener:"

> ... and the firmament proclaims his handiwork.
> Day to day pours forth speech,
>   and night to night declares knowledge. (Ps. 19: 1-2)

A way by which the cosmos speaks to us is by having it perceived as ancient and identical to itself. Oldness and meaning go together; identity, which allows one to name, is what endures. To be is to remain oneself. But, and this is strange, no identity would be perceived if there were no movement. We only know the identity of day to day and the identity of night to night thanks to the fact that these two times alternate. We see them return; we recognize them; the "speech" or the "knowledge" that they transmit is at first the manifestation of their respective essence. If they were confused in the immobility of only one, they would not come back. They would not return and who would recognize them?

So this Psalm verifies the law of "rerouting" in the creation narratives. God creates things but, through this detour, he leads us back elsewhere: God especially creates meaning. Creation is "his handiwork," but his entire action is "speech" and "knowledge." It bathes in the utterance. The great work of God, the inaugural act of creation according to Genesis 1, is to have separated light from darkness, the heavens above from the heavens below. One is right to say that it is a question of separating in order to organize. But one first separates in order to make known. Knowledge and utterance are narrowly connected. One organizes only by instituting the sayable. God says: let there be separation, and he named the firmament "heavens" (see Genesis 1: 6-8). To create is to make meaning. To speak is to make meaning. God creates by speaking. Creative separation, like the creative utterance, is seen in the duration, the permanent movement of the cosmos.

God creates by speaking. The idea that his Word is not a word among all those that make noise did not await the critical spirit of recent times in order to be formed. The alternation of separated day and night gives us the word of the Word. However:

There is no speech, nor are there words;
   their voice is not heard;
yet their voice goes out through all the earth
   and their words to the end of the world.

There exists a system of non-sonorous signs that are only visual, distinct and repeated. The effectiveness of this system that transmits words depends greatly upon duration. Here I am referring to writing, which sends us back through time or times to the beginning original mark of its author. Thus do several exegetes understand that the repeated movement of the stars in the heavens emits silent noise comparable to that of the page of a book (since the term translated by "voice" more often means "line"); the cosmos would then be the first model of a written law. Others observe that the Greek version understood "sound," as a hymn of Qumran will later do (col. 1;29). It is at the same time on these two paths that Saint Paul, in the Letter to the Romans, encounters our Psalm.

This message that extends to the ends of the world is, for Saint Paul, nothing other than the preaching of the Gospel. Here is what he writes in the Letter to the Romans: "So faith comes from what is heard, and what is heard comes through the word of Christ. But I ask, have they not heard? Indeed they have; for 'Their voice has gone out to all the earth,/ and their words to the ends of the world'" (Letter to the Romans, 10: 17-18). If there exists, in the dwellings of God, a heavenly chamber where we can place all the smiles of superiority that this use of the Psalms has inspired among commentators for about the last hundred years, then this room would be quite large. Many have thought that Saint Paul does not respect the meaning of the Psalm very much. Several seem to have thought that the Apostle quoted Scripture only to ornament his erudition. However, it is certain that Saint Paul thought that he had come upon the secret of the text that he was quoting.

In the context of the Letter to the Romans, the preaching of the Gospel appears well in light of the Law, such as Deuteronomy, according to the tradition of Wisdom, understands it. The Law has the dimensions of heaven and earth, and it crosses them, as the Hokhmâ or "Sophia" do, because it is greater than heaven and earth. The Law and Sophia talk about origins, a tradition that day transmits to day and night to night. But the world is not their true seat. Deuteronomy asks and, after it, Saint Paul: Where is the Law, where is Wisdom … ? The answer comes in all its force; it is the utterance in your mouth and in your heart. It is you, man, who says the Law. In effect, Deuteronomy does not just grant an immense place to the mediation of Moses, defining the Law as what Moses said (under the dictation of God). Every man in Israel must write and pronounce the Law as soon as it has left the mouth of Moses. And yet this Law loses nothing of its character to be as wide and as old as the world.

According to the Letter to the Romans, the preaching of the Gospel takes the Law as its model and occupies its place. The word of the Gospel posits an act the fullness of which corresponds exactly to the fullness of the act posited by the word of creation. The act of this word has the same character, at once total and intimate, and it is only known if it crosses the entire world as the sun traverses all of space from one end to the other.

A certain stupor penetrates the text of Saint Paul. The story, the proclamation, the message—identified with the word of creation such as we apprehend it in the very silence of the Word—are suddenly found to resonate in his own mouth, as in that of everyone who proclaims the Gospel. Man does not recite the word of God. The word of God is in the mouth of man.

This is what the news consists in, the news which has crossed Deuteronomy and reached us. Here Saint Paul interprets a Psalm of creation according to the biblical logic of a detour proper to these texts. They tell us that God is speaking, but it is man who says it. In this, man recognizes that his word comes from God. In reality, when God, by his word, makes his image, he makes a speaker. The image is not God but only a resemblance. When man speaks, he makes noise, unlike God. But God is in his image and that is why the word of God is in the silence emitted by the meanings of the words of man. The heart of every creation narrative is an act of faith in the truth that the silent word of God confers upon the word of man. The Gospel is the extreme moment, in Jesus Christ, of this act of faith.

Under these conditions, the objection raised by modern exegetes (that man, in the creation narratives, is in reality relating himself and placing his own words in the mouth of God) is at once honored and overcome. In effect, the biblical authors place, every time, different words, their own words, in the mouth of God the Creator. There are several creation narratives: Genesis 1, Genesis 2-3, some Psalms, and some prophetic texts ... Between these texts, in the space that separates writings or authors, the Word is silent and always inspires new texts. The Word traverses and goes beyond texts and our words, just as it traverses and goes beyond heaven. To read, to understand, and to write is to traverse:

> In the heavens he has set a tent for the sun,
> which comes out like a bridegroom from
>   his wedding canopy,
> and like a strong man runs its course with joy.
> Its rising is from the end of the heavens,
>   and its circuit to the end of them ... (Ps. 19: 4-6)

The man who talks about creation has God talk, it is said, and that is true. But by what other detour or turning could he understand and have us understand that God speaks in him, makes him capable of speaking, and has him speak?

How do we know if the Psalmist is telling us the truth? Our faith answers that, if God makes him speak, God can have us understand himself through this poet's words. The sign for this will be that we shall be touched somehow by this fire, warmth, "and ardor" that the Word of God, like the sun, communicates:

> Its rising is from the end of the heavens,

24 A. Near Creation: Psalm 19

and its circuit to the end of them;
and nothing is hid from its heat. (Ps. 19: 6)

Let us note that at first God creates light. The eye is the sense to which perception of the totality is reserved, the sense that the sun traverses. But what would creation of the totality make me if I were forgotten in it and if the Creator did not find me there? In order to signify presence, touch does much better than the eye; "heat," warmth, penetrates deeper than light.

Having sung creation as a chain of tradition, as a silent clamor similar to what the page of a book has one hear or even like some precise horizons that the infinite traverses, the Psalmist is able to praise the Law of Moses, such as the best in Israel have received it, the Law that is limpid, pure, and flavorful; life, gold, and honey.

Is living according to the Law not to live according to appearances? The Psalmist answers that justice delves more deeply than any surface:

But who can detect their errors?
Clear me from hidden faults. (Ps. 19: 12)

The repetition of the word "hidden" (in verses 6 and 12) is intentional. The sun penetrates, by its warmth, as far as the invisible. Likewise, the truth of the Law is only complete if it reaches the hidden zones of man. Some will say that, thanks to the Law, I can see all at once all my faults and all my good deeds. The Psalmist does not use this mirror language where a surface (that of the page) reflects a surface (that of man). The true light of the law must traverse everything in order that nothing escape it; this request could pass for an obsessive scruple to be perfect. In the harmony of the totality, it is better to understand something else. Since the meaning of an utterance is not in the words, but in the silence initiated by good listening, so true justice is not in any particular observance. The seat of justice is rather in the invisible center of man. Man does not even have access to it if he is left to his own devices. Only God can "clear" him of faults (Ps. 19: 12).

The sign, moreover, that we remain on the surface of the Law is that we take pride in it. That is true, be it of the utterances of Moses or of those of Jesus Christ. So, admire that a prayer to observe the Law ends by imploring that one not fall into the greatest trap that it has set:

> Keep back your servant also from the insolent;
>   do not let them have dominion over me.
> Then I shall be blameless,
>   and innocent of great transgression. (Ps. 19: 13)

Far from the surface of creation, far from the surface of the Law, the greatest secret of both is hidden. It is humility. Creation and Law are fulfilled in what is most hidden, completed in humility. This praise had to overwhelm with joy the first disciples of Jesus when they found themselves to be depositories of what is transmitted "from day to day" and "from night to night" since the beginning of the world.

25

Psalm 104

1 Bless the Lord, O my soul.
     O Lord my God, you are very great.
    You are clothed with honor and majesty,
2   wrapped in light as with a garment.
    You stretch out the heavens like a tent,
3   you set the beams of your chambers on the waters,
    you make the clouds your chariot,
     you ride on the wings of the wind,
4 you make the winds your messengers,
     fire and flame your ministers.

5 You set the earth on its foundations,
     so that it shall never be shaken.
6 You cover it with the deep as with a garment;
     the waters stood above the mountains.
7 At your rebuke they flee;
     at the sound of your thunder they take to flight.
8 They rose up to the mountains, ran down to the valleys
     to the place that you appointed for them.
9 You set a boundary that they may not pass,
     so that they might not again cover the earth.

10 You make springs gush forth in the valleys;
     they flow between the hills,
11 giving drink to every wild animal;
     the wild asses quench their thirst.
12 By the streams the birds of the air have their habitation;
     they sing among the branches.
13 From your lofty abode you water the mountains;
     the earth is satisfied with the fruit of your work.

14 You cause the grass to grow for the cattle,
   and plants for people to use, to bring forth food from the earth,
15 and wine to gladden the human heart,
   oil to make the face shine,
   and bread to strengthen the human heart.
16 The trees of the Lord are watered abundantly,
   the cedars of Lebanon that he planted.
17 In them the birds build their nests;
   the stork has its home in the fir trees.
18 The high mountains are for the wild goats;
   the rocks are a refuge for the coneys.
19 You have made the moon to mark the seasons;
   the sun knows its time for setting.
20 You make darkness, and it is night,
   when all the animals of the forest come creeping out.
21 The young lions roar for their prey,
   seeking their food from God.
22 When the sun rises, they withdraw
   and lie down in their dens.
23 People go out to their work
   and to their labor until the evening.

24 O Lord, how manifold are your works!
   In wisdom you have made them all;
   the earth is full of your creatures.
25 Yonder is the seat, great and wide,
   creeping things innumerable are there,
   living things both small and great.
26 There go the ships and Leviathan
   that you formed to sport in it.

27 These all look to you
   to give them their food in due season;
28 when you give to them, they gather it up;
   when you open your hand, they are filled with good things.
29 When you hide your face, they are dismayed;
   when you take away their breath, they die
   and return to their dust.
30 When you send forth your spirit, they are created;

25. A. Near Creation: Psalm 104

and you renew the face of the ground.

31 May the glory of the Lord endure forever;
    may the Lord rejoice in his works—
32 who looks on the earth and it trembles,
    who touches the mountains and they smoke.
33 I will sing to the Lord as long as I live;
    I will sing praise to my God while I have being.
34 May my meditation be pleasing to him,
    for I rejoice in the Lord.
35 Let sinners be consumed from the earth,
    and let the wicked be no more.
    Bless the Lord, O my soul.
    Praise the Lord!

The text of Psalm 104 is richer than that of Psalm 19 and becomes clear once we sense its composition. This Psalm reviews the work of God in the cosmos, part by part, in an order that is similar to the one that the most famous of the narratives on beginnings uses to talk about the first days of the world (Genesis 1: 1).

> You are clothed with honor and majesty,
>   wrapped in light as with a garment. (Ps. 104 1-2)

These words begin the Psalm, whereas Genesis begins by describing the breath of God that "swept over the face of the waters" (Genesis 1: 2). Here, the breath (or winds, it is the same word) only intervenes a bit later (Ps. 104: 3 and 4). But this privileged place given to light has us remember the first day of the world. God unfolds the heavens as though they were a covering: "You stretch out the heavens like a tent …" and he has the waters positioned "above the mountains" (Ps. 104: 2 and 6). With the earth firmly established, he then has the waters flow down to their place:

> They rose up to the mountains, ran down to the valleys
>   to the place you appointed for them. (Ps. 104: 8)

Next leaves, prairies, wheat, vines, cedar and fir trees appear (verses 12-18). According to Genesis, this is the work of the third day of creation. In the place that corresponds to the text of the fourth day, God put the same objects as those in Genesis: the moon and the sun.

> You have made the moon to mark the seasons;
>   the sun knows its time for setting. (Ps. 104: 19)

In both texts, the fifth day talks about the birds and the fish. On the sixth day, finally, God gives nourishment (Genesis 1: 29-31):

> These all look to you
>   to give them their food in due season;
> when you give to them, they gather it up;
> when you open your hand, they are
>   filled with good things. (Ps. 104: 27-28)

This parallel order should not have us think that this Psalm is talking about creation. To relate or discuss is one thing, and to describe is another. Here creation is not related but described. The author of Genesis 1 stops at each work in order to make each day precise. He already records the grand interval that counts out time, he relates and he dates. There is nothing like this in our poem. Rather it describes what now is. This is confirmed by an important divergence that separates the Psalm from the narrative; animals and people do not show up, in the Psalm, as in the narrative. They do not appear at the end. They were already there from the moment that the first elements were described. While the animals of Genesis appear when all the rest is in place, here the water is already drunk by the onagers (or wild asses, verse 11) as soon as it runs down the hills. We only see the trees full of birds; the separation of day and night, the work of the fourth day, allows men and wild animals not to meet each other when they go out since night time is reserved for wild beasts:

> When the sun rises, they withdraw
>   and lie down in their dens.
> People go out to their work
>   and to their labor until the evening. (Ps. 104: 22-23)

The sea carries Leviathan (see Genesis 1: 21: the large dragons) as well as boats and their crew; animals and men are everywhere.

25. A. Near Creation: Psalm 104

The first chapter of Genesis, with its same frame, is the narrative band of the furthest past, of the first week. Our poem suppresses the vertical bars that separate the frame (let us say days); it keeps the order of the elements of creation, but it disseminates the living beings in the midst of them, throughout the narrative band. It is no longer a narrative band; it is no longer the first week of the past that we see. Thanks to the superimposition of the daily spectacle on the narrative band of Genesis 1, we are before the creative act such as it is visible today. It is not yesterday that the waters below flowed towards the place that God prepared for them; they even flow there now—let us look at them run down the sides of the mountains.

Water flows and its mobility, which animates the entire poem, is also the best symbol of what it means. If creation unfolds in the past, we tend to forget that it is an act and we are inclined to represent its results. The results of the oldest of all acts appear to us naturally as the most immobile, like the great masses of the cosmos. Here, it is the contrary; in the present mobility, we do not see the result or the effect of the act but the act itself, and we see it in the present. We are used to hearing that God created and the formula keeps all its meaning. But the Psalm reminds us, in the present, that God creates. He creates our present, which is mobile. If attention concentrates on the mobile present, instead of on the immobile past, it will follow that the most present or the most mobile will be seized as the object par excellence of the creative act of God. What is more present and more mobile than the living being? That is why it appears here that, more than anything, God is the Creator of the living.

We have underlined that, in comparison with the tradition of the "narrative of creation" (Genesis 1), the living being carries in this poem the principal variant; it is in function of the living being that the entire composition is recast. The condition of the living being is the backbone of the text. It is not only a question of the ideas; the use of the words themselves (what counts, in poetry) confirms this organization. The word "created" was written, in all and for all, only once in this poem, and it is in order to express the act which makes the living being exist, by this I mean the act of giving it spirit, of giving it breath (verse 30).

Nothing is frail like breath. But frailty is inseparable from the condition of the living. It is its manner—extreme—of being present. The extremely frail is extremely present. What is solid and immobile, probably, is also qualified as being of the present, like the great masses of the cosmos. But the very solid is not only present; it is something else, being also past and future; it was and will be, as much as it is. Present, past and future ... these three essences share, in that which is solid and massive, the place that the essence of the present occupies alone in what is fragile, in the rose or in the insect. Such is the quality of the living being: to depend upon nourishment and breath, in the most pure essence of the present, the instant. Who says "now" says the "maintenance of an instant."

> ... when you give to them, they gather it up;
> when you open your hand, they are filled with good things.
> When you hide your face, they are dismayed;
> when you take away their breath, they die
> and return to their dust. (Ps. 104: 28-29)

Thus, to be near the essence of the present is to be near the essence of God. This proximity of essence is the status of the image, which is not essence, but which cannot be absolutely far from it. In the entire world, only the living being is the image of the "living God." But how do we explain that the nearest to God in creation is also the most precarious? In effect, creation is not finished when God created meaning. After having inscribed high and low, with the grand acts of separation, on the volume of the world, there was still the need to mention this feature of fragility. Were we not saying that it is exactly on this point of fragility that the act of creation is to be grasped? We are thus led on a slope, like it or not, as it often happens to the reader of the Bible; in us the present is the image of the pure essence of God, but we only experience the present in the fact that it ... passes. And this is how our transience, our very mortality, finds itself as intimately bound to our condition as creatures created in the image of God, as it is bound to its opposite. God makes his image as a fleeting present, because God is God and because his image can only subsist by receiving itself from God. There is no image of God if it is received from itself; the image of God is only a lie if God is not present to it, if God does not love it. To live as a maintained precariousness is the only possible status of the image. It is to live by the love of God, because there is no image of God without love or no image of God outside of God. This connection between frailty and the essence of the image is expressed in the fact that

25. A. Near Creation: Psalm 104

breath, which is fragility itself, is also the essential divine, if it is true that life is breath of God:

> When you send forth your spirit, they are created;
> and you renew the face of the ground. (Ps. 104: 30)

By the breath, by the spirit, the face of God and the image of God (the living one), do more than just resemble each other: they touch each other. It is forbidden for them to stop at this resemblance, which does not remove the distance and which could have one believe that God can be imitated or multiplied. Because God is one and not two, the face suppresses the distance by attracting to itself its image; he touches it by the breath of his love.

But let us contain the movement that carries every Christian, led by his liturgy, towards these regions of promise: *emitte spiritum tuum et creabuntur*. Send forth your Spirit and they are created. Let us return to the times that preceded Christ. That the face of the Earth would be renewed signifies, within the horizon of our song, this: though the living can be killed nearly everyday, God still sends his breath, his spirit, to others. "Creation" is manifested by the fact that there are always living beings, life having this power to renew itself. "… are created" are the words reserved here (since this is the only time that this verb is used) for this power of maintaining newness of life on earth, days that are always new, living beings that are always new. Let us go back to this horizon in order to share the joy that frail man maintains in its limits, but that he also takes from these limits:

> I will sing to the Lord as long as I live;
> I will sing praise to my God while I have being. (Ps. 104: 33)

Was it necessary to control our enthusiasm, whereas we received a greater hope with the Gospel, and was it necessary to recoil when faced with this one? It was indeed necessary because we shall meet on this path many of our contemporaries who, without having our hope, are able to love God and love him truly. It was also necessary in order for our hope to remain hope and not be transformed into a knowledge that is at times satisfied, at times staggering. That said, we need not blush if we read our hope in this Psalm and we should not let ourselves be intimidated by the pedantic scruple of those who would like the meaning of the text to be reduced to verifiable certainties that it is supposed to communicate. In fact, well before the time of the Gospel, Psalm 104 must have effectively communicated, whether the author wanted it or not, some hope that was similar to our own. He talks only about the living and, in this way, underlines what the condition of animals and of men have in common. This is a community that, we know, fascinates biblical man. But we had certainly already read that only man, not the animal, was the image of God or, at least, that God had approached only man, and no animal, in order to breathe "into his nostrils the breath of life …" (Genesis 2: 7). It is on this difference that hope could be based, the hope that, by offering God his entire frailty at the very moment of rendering his last breath, man might be attracted to the pure essence of the present such as it is in God. This is the only truly "new" creation, escaping the repetition of the chain of the living.

26

Psalm 139

1 O Lord, you have searched me and known me.
2 You know when I sit down and when I rise up;
    you discern my thoughts from far away.
3 You search out my path and my lying down,
    and are acquainted with all my ways.
4 Even before a word is on my tongue,
    O Lord, you know it completely.
5 You hem me in, behind and before,
    and lay your hand upon me.
6 Such knowledge is too wonderful for me;
    it is so high that I cannot attain it.

7 Where can I go from your spirit?
    Or where can I flee from your presence?
8 If I ascend to heaven, you are there,
    if I make my bed in Sheol, you are there.
9 If I take the wings of the morning
    and settle at the farthest limits of the sea,
10 even there your hand shall lead me,
    and your right hand shall hold me fast.
11 If I say, "Surely the darkness shall cover me,
    and the light around me become night,"
12 even the darkness is not dark to you;
    the night is as bright as the day,
    for darkness is as light to you.

13 For it was you who formed my inward parts;
    you knit me together in my mother's womb.
14 I praise you, for I am fearfully and
        wonderfully made.
    Wonderful are your works;

that I know very well.
15 My frame was not hidden from you,
when I was being made in secret,
intricately woven in the depths of the earth.
16 Your eyes beheld my unformed substance.
In your book were written
all the days that were formed for me,
when none of them as yet existed.
17 How weighty to me are your thoughts, O God!
How vast is the sum of them!
18 I try to count them—they are more than the sand;
I come to the end—I am still with you.

19 O that you would kill the wicked, O God,
and that the bloodthirsty would depart from me—
20 those who speak of you maliciously,
and lift themselves up against you for evil!
21 Do I not hate those who hate you, O Lord?
And do I not loathe those who rise up against you?
22 I hate them with perfect hatred;
I count them my enemies.
23 Search me, O God, and know my heart;
test me and know my thoughts.
24 See if there is any wicked way in me,
and lead me in the way everlasting.

Psalm 139 takes us, as does the interior of an immense theatre, fully into the volume of space, with its cosmic dimensions—a kind of empty and closed field where but one alternative is offered, to flee God in vain since he seizes man, or to be seized by God without fleeing from him.

You hem me in, behind and before,
and lay your hand upon me.
Such knowledge is too wonderful for me;
it is so high that I cannot attain it.

Where can I go from your spirit?
Or where can I flee from your presence?

26. A. Near Creation: Psalm 139

If I ascend to heaven, you are there,
if I make my bed in Sheol, you are there. (Ps. 139: 5-8)

This frame already includes important correctives to several automatisms of thought.

At first, the contrast between Psalm 104, where space is filled and furnished, and this one where only height, depth, and the distant, completed in the night of a space without any objects, shows that cosmic vision, in the Bible, is something other than continually positive. Already, when the heavens relate the glory of God, they do so by their silence. Here space is not only empty, but negative. It is indeed there and does not let itself be forgotten, but it seems to be made of nothing other than the distance to traverse, than the separation that must be overcome in order for God and man to meet each other. Distances become greater or less along several lines that mark all space. Man is pursued and goes his way; he avoids and he finds. In this space that is crossed in all directions, the classic affirmation "God is everywhere" changes meaning: space contains nothing, it is only the possibility of an encounter with/flight from God. This image might well cause us some anxiety, but not an anxiety that is purely without any object. It is more about the message of alarm sent by reality to whoever distances himself too much from it. So this is neither a positive vision of space nor simple fear. We are not to choose between a religion of naivete and one of distress:

If I take the wings of the morning
 and settle at the farthest limits of the sea,
even there your hand shall lead me,
 and your right hand shall hold me fast. (Ps. 139: 9-10)

Then, we shall improve our idea about the presence of God. This is often represented by the image of God as Eye. The ubiquity of the divine eye is an adequate symbol of human anxiety before the divinity. The eye is the function of space, but it is at the same time the function of absence. One only sees the part of space where one is not; this negative mark strongly colors vision, if it remains isolated from the other senses by a kind of antagonism between the eye and the seen. There is aggression by the divine eye. There must be something that is intolerably and radically wrong in the image of God as Eye (once it is known that God cannot be visualized in an image) since he then becomes the image of visualization. I know quite well that, God not being seen, God sees; these are the terms of the Bible itself. That does not have me change my mind, because the one who sees is not Eye. He uses two eyes, a necessary condition in order to see the contours and thus guide movement, in order to meet and to touch: "… your hand shall lead me." Binocular vision is what already makes an alliance with the rest of the body and with touch, a sense towards which the entire Psalm leads us. Let us remember that the oldest iconography represents God by a hand.

(On the contrary, the one who, with his hand, gouges out one of his eyes in order to dilate the other beyond measure, this is the damned person of the Last Judgment according to Michelangelo; that eye stares at the vision of absence.)

In this Psalm, God knows, and this is quite different than seeing. "… you have searched me … ," the first utterance of the poem, designates this type of vision that goes beyond vision by cutting through surfaces. God searches and penetrates, he runs, he breathes and his hand shakes, leads, and grasps. Let us repeat: it is necessary that the face of God touch his image, for the image says only the universal and only touch says what is concrete. Such is the movement of the Psalm, towards a central point.

It is from this point, called the "point of creation," as one says "vanishing point" or "point of view," that the Psalm is constructed, in a fine opposition between an expanse, a disseminated space that is the outside of the encounter or the place of the negative action of God—and the warm ball of the embryo in the night of the womb of his mother, where God acts positively:

> For it was you who formed my inward parts;
>   you knit me together in my mother's womb.
> I praise you, for I am fearfully and
>   wonderfully made.
>   Wonderful are your works;
> that I know very well.
>   my frame was not hidden from you,
> when I was being made in secret,
>   intricately woven in the depths of the earth.
> Your eyes beheld my unformed substance. (Ps. 139: 13-15)

26. A. Near Creation: Psalm 139

If there is a text where the natural movement of man falls back towards an internal point from where it is only possible to express all that it means to be created, it is this one. Space appears as the element from which God chases man outside the void. But God does not hunt man outside this void in order to lead him towards some super space. Through the cosmos, stripped by night, God leads man towards fullness, towards the blind embryo that God sees:

> If I say, "Surely the darkness shall cover me,
>   and the light around me become night,"
> even the darkness is no dark to you;
>   the night is as bright as the day,
>   for darkness is as light to you. (Ps. 139: 11-12)

The vision that was able to traverse every obscurity is no longer the vision about which we were just talking; it has united itself to the darkness. Light is another light; it is no longer only the opposite of night, when God is there. It has found presence.

God is not in space, such as the beginning of the Psalm represents it. The eye of man, eye for which God is only invisible, rightly apprehends, in space, the absence of God. But vision changes during the night. It withdraws itself from space into the nocturnal center, up to the "point of creation." In this "point of creation," we also find, after our reading, a kind of point of condensation for several of our Psalms. Psalm 8 contemplated the stars, but it led us towards the image of the newborn. Psalm 19 went from the heavenly firmament to the most hidden point that the sun warms, and to what is most hidden in man subject to the Law. Psalm 104 delved into the secret of the frail living being. Here Psalm 139 ends its spatial journey with a new departure taken from the prenatal element, where the nearly born occupies the most hidden center of the world, in the germination of the living being. God sees him there with a vision that is different from man's own.

This vision of God setting his eyes on the embryo is enough to end our meditation. We have known that our body is situated in the world. But there is quite a path from the surfaces where the eye bruises itself to this body which is already, by itself, an interior and therefore the opposite of a surface, but which was yet more foreign to every gaze when it had not come to light. We also knew that God sees more deeply than we do, but the biblical manner to say it is more concrete and more simple: before my consciousness, my body is found; before my body, my embryonic being in the womb of my mother, and it is there that God sees me. For the "I" who speaks in this poem that is composed in the first person, the center of the prenatal body, is at once the center of the earth and that of divine presence:

> ... when I was being made in secret,
>   intricately woven in the depths of the
>   earth. (Ps. 139: 15)

It is striking that the oldest Jewish commentary of the Psalms called *midrash Tehillim* has attributed this poem to Adam, born of the earth, although it gives different motifs for that, motifs which are not taken from this verse.

The same commentary introduces us into the space of a speaking silence that connects texts to texts just as it connects constellations to constellations, when it talks about the embryo and the vision of God. But, to do this, it chooses another Psalm, Psalm 8, verse 3, regarding "babes and infants." We read that when Israel was at Sinai to make an alliance with God, " the womb of the pregnant women became as transparent as glass, in such a way that the embryos were able to see God and converse with him." In a more indirect manner, Jesus teaches, regarding the "little ones," that "their angels continually see the face of my Father in heaven" (Matthew 18: 10).

When the Psalmist circulates in cosmic space, he seems to be aware of death and, when he discovers the prenatal space, he finds the departure from life. In this scene we attend a struggle between death and life. At first there is the fitful flight of a nocturnal insect that gets caught in the light; he is destroying himself. Then his rest comes when the light goes out, for night is his light:

> "... and the light around me become night ..." (Ps. 139: 11)

The same drama is the strength of many other texts. Not only in Psalm 139, but several times in Scripture, we find the map of what we could call the absolute path; the highest, the deepest abyss, the most distant horizon. When the scene is thus set up, it is ready for us to see death appear in it, or for us only to get a glimpse of it, a form of appearance that is even more expressive when it is a question of death.

26. A. Near Creation: Psalm 139

For example, chapter 28 of the Book of Job describes the cursus that wisdom takes in all the dimensions of the cosmic axes, and to the very end. This end is death, a subject that concerns all the characters in the Book of Job in all their conversations and that is touched upon very closely. In the New Testament, Saint Paul (Romans 10; Ephesians 4: 8-10) has us read the same cursus (while appealing to Deuteronomy 30: 11-14) as being that of Christ raised to the heights, lowered to the very depths of the abyss, and found by the Father in the womb of death.

We owe the Book of Jonah for the colorful edition of an analogous schema, but more particularly similar to the one in Psalm 139. This prophet could have said, "… where can I flee from your presence?" (Ps. 139: 7). He flees beyond the seas, and then he descends into the deepest parts, into the darkness of the stomach where he begs for help. Restored to life, he is able to speak about God, but he is not yet able to understand him, since Jonah desires death for the men of Nineveh. He will also find his "point of creation." Jonah has crossed space and the abyss, but God becomes present to him through a worm of the earth and by the leaves of a tree: they suddenly dry up when the worm attacks the tree and Jonah is deprived of their shade. Then God tells him: "You are concerned about the bush, for which you did not labor and which you did not grow; it came into being in a night and perished in a night. And should I not be concerned about Nineveh, that great city, in which there are more than a hundred and twenty thousand persons who do not know their right hand from their left, and also many animals?" (Jonah 4: 10-11). So here is yet another meditation on creation that ends with what is most fragile in the living being.

The vision of God, being presence, is also a touch. God acts upon this near-born. He proclaims his word and his path. His path no longer bumps into the murderous walls of the world, but is recentered from the "point of creation":

> See if there is any wicked way in me,
> and lead me in the way everlasting. (Ps. 139: 24)

He also proclaims his word, and it is the Psalmist who says it:

> Even before a word is on my tongue,
> O Lord, you know it completely. (Ps. 139: 4)

It is with much joy that I quote the commentary of the *midrash*. For him, the Psalmist wants to say: "No Psalm, no chant, no meditation that I must still compose is now unknown to you." And so, in the act of saying a Psalm, the origin of his utterance in the divine creative utterance is revealed to the Psalmist. Stated otherwise, the place of the divine creative utterance is that of the Psalmist.

For the Jewish commentary, it is clear that the Psalmist was talking about himself, since he says "I." It is also clear, since he represented Adam to himself, that the Psalmist was talking for all men. The *midrash* has noted that, with this return at night, the Psalmist's gaze encompassed both death and birth. The Jewish commentary returns several times to the resurrection. It concludes with some questioning on the following verse:

In your book were written
   all the days that were formed for me,
   when none of them as yet existed. (Ps. 139: 16)

Here is the commentary: "This means that on the day when God fashioned Adam, he wrote in his book the name of all those to whom he wanted to give being, from the time of Adam to the time of the resurrection of the dead. Thus did God read to Adam the names of each generation and of its preachers, of each generation and of its leaders, of each generation and of its wise men, of each generation and of its prophets, of each generation and of its scribes and scholars to the time of the resurrection of the dead."

Christians must then feel themselves close to the ancient Jewish commentator, when they find, in their "Roman missal," these words for the second opening antiphon for Easter day:

I am risen and I am again with you.

This is a slightly recast translation of the *surrexi et adhuc tecum sum* that suggests the idea of resurrection in the Psalter of the Vulgate, but also translates word for word:

I come to the end—I am still with you. (Ps. 139: 18)

26. A. Near Creation: Psalm 139

Who could limit the enchantment of this verse to just one evocation? It is a birth that snatches us from the night every morning; a kind of leave-taking from the darkness of prayer with a response from God. It is also a perfect formula of nuptial exultation, which connects us (another symbol of resurrection) to the hymn of the sun according to Psalm 19:

> ... which comes out like a bridegroom from his wedding canopy, and like a strong man runs its course with joy. (Ps. 19: 5)

Just as this solar circuit leads us towards most secret places, so does our faith in the Resurrection, which has been able to suffer from being too exposed to the sun, find it helpful to follow the paths of the Psalmist that offer more shade.

B. DISTANT CREATION

With another series of Psalms we are able to meditate on creation under a different angle.

In the preceding series (let us call it "series A"), creation appeared as a daily action, permanent and renewed: God creates. He creates now. This can only be understood and said from a certain stance of freshness and keen experience: creation that is seen close up can only be expressed by a poet, who speaks in his name, in the first person. "When I look at your heavens ..." (Ps. 8: 3, according to the Hebrew); "Clear me ... " (Ps. 19, see v. 12-14); "...as long as I live" (Ps. 104: 33); "O Lord, you have searched me and known me" (Ps. 139: 1). Let us summarize in two words the characteristics of the series: creation is near; it is described or sung by an individual witness.

In the series that we shall exam from this moment on (let us call it "series B"), creation is a distant and old action. It is related to the collective experience of a people.

Just as series A was coherent, near-individual and formed a pair that is well connected, series B likewise, with its distant-collectivity, forms a solid unit. In effect, the identity of the individual rests on a near past, whereas the identity of the collectivity rests on a distant past. This past is the object of a narrative that is called history. Such a narrative tends to be constituted according to a complete form; this form requires then that the narrative fill up the totality of time. In this case, the beginning of the narrative is the beginning of time, a place that the act of creation occupies. That is why we shall say that "creation" is distant when "history" is constituted, hence the pair creation/history. It forms the structure of many biblical units.

When distant creation is associated with history, it tends to take on the form of a narrative, whereas near creation was expressed in a poem. We shall say, provisionally, that a near poem thus opposes itself to a distant narrative. In this case, creation becomes the oldest of all narratives; having become a narrative of the beginning, it is still a narrative:

narrative   history

creation

This form plays a privileged role and even a principal one in the Christian world, because of the place that it gives to certain texts. The first pages of the Bible are perhaps poorly or hardly known; their position of honor in the Psalter has it that they are still the most known of all the Scriptures. The celebrity of the narrative of the seven days and of the narrative about the creation of Adam and Eve and their drama in the earthly Paradise explains why representation of distant creation occupies nearly all the place in the collective imaginary of the Christian world.

We have contrasted two types of texts, two series that we cannot nor desire to separate completely. And we have only distinguished their elements so as to better appreciate the richness of their combinations. This richness allows us to propose yet other categories. Certain texts can belong to several categories at once. And we must not see only differences between categories. In this regard, the most important thing is to know that all the texts of creation have a common point; they concern what is going on. This makes us correct a bit the helpful opposition that we underlined provisionally earlier: the nearest is not only near, and the most distant is not only distant.

Creation as a "near poem" (series A), is concentrated, it is true, on what is most intimate and most minute; But it is by means of a detour through the most distant space, the space of the stars, of the entire cosmos.

Creation as a "distant narrative" (series B) takes us up to a time which seems inaccessible. But this time is not quite foreign to our own, since it suffices to count, starting with that time, the days of our own history. No one relates or listens to the grand narrative of the history of the world without wondering where he is in relation to it. It is still a question of the present, but of a more collective present. It is not less real nor less lived, since we experience in it the fragility of monuments, of institutions, of the city, of the entire people, of humanity. The more the human frame is ample, from the city to all of humanity, the more creation is pushed back to a distant limit in time. It is therefore in order to rejoin and think present events within its most collective form that we

B. Distant Creation

make a detour by the most distant time. If I think about my creation, I do not need a long chronology; if I think about the creation of all humanity, I need a universal chronology. This one may seem to push creation into an abstraction. But universal creation is only thought starting with the dramas of universal humanity and these dramas can deprive me of life and of the meaning of life. That is why distant creation is not thought of in cold terms. To say it another way: it is also in its place, in the element of the poem. It is also sung and that is why we find it in the Psalter. But we shall have to distinguish between the poetry of series A, which we shall call lyric, because it sings about the pains and joys of one man, and the poetry of series B, which we shall call epic: it sings of the destiny of a people, who never forget their misfortune, when it is a question of a complaint, and who celebrate their good fortune when it is a question of a hymn. In the "epic" series, we shall say "we" rather than "I."

27

Psalm 136

1 O give thanks to the Lord, for he is good,
   for his steadfast love endures forever.
2 O give thanks to the God of gods,
   for his steadfast love endures forever
3 O give thanks to the Lord of lords,
   for his steadfast love endures forever;

4 who alone does great wonders,
   for his steadfast love endures forever;
5 who by understanding made the heavens,
   for his steadfast love endures forever;
6 who spread out the earth on the waters,
   for his steadfast love endures forever;
7 who made the great lights,
   for his steadfast love endures forever;
8 the sun to rule over the day,
   for his steadfast love endures forever;
9 the moon and stars to rule over the night,
   for his steadfast love endures forever;

10 who struck Egypt through their firstborn,
   for his steadfast love endures forever;
11 and brought Israel out from among them,
   for his steadfast love endures forever;
12 with a strong hand and an outstretched arm,
   for his steadfast love endures forever;
13 who divided the Red Sea in two,
   for his steadfast love endures forever;
14 and made Israel pass through the midst of it,

for his steadfast love endures forever;
15 but overthrew Pharaoh and his army in the Red Sea,
   for his steadfast love endures forever;
16 who led his people through the wilderness,
   for his steadfast love endures forever;
17 who struck down great kings,
   for his steadfast love endures forever;
18 and killed famous kings,
   for his steadfast love endures forever;
19 Sihon, king of the Amorites,
   for his steadfast love endures forever;
20 and Og, king of Bashan,
   for his steadfast love endures forever;
21 and gave their land as a heritage,
   for his steadfast love endures forever;
22 a heritage to his servant Israel,
   for his steadfast love endures forever.

23 It is he who remembered us in our low estate,
   for his steadfast love endures forever;
24 and rescued us from our foes,
   for his steadfast love endures forever;
25 who gives food to all flesh,
   for his steadfast love endures forever;

26 O give thanks to the God of heaven,
   for his steadfast love endures forever.

We know quite well Psalm 136. We often repeat these lines from it:

... his steadfast love endures forever ...

We repeat it twenty-six times. This refrain follows every phrase. So, for twenty-six phrases, there are twenty-six refrains.

Why do we always repeat the same thing? The simplest reason for this is that it is always the same thing. "Forever." Not to change it is a way of signifying this word "forever," of committing oneself to its meaning. A repetition will always be monotonous, but it can also give pleasure. That is often the case in praise; to praise is not to be tired of

27. B. Distant Creation: Psalm 136

saying what gives us pleasure in what we praise "now, always, and forever." Is it because the good that is present before us is truly good, that we feel no need to change it? This is the case regarding the good that our translations call "his love." The Hebrew word does not perfectly correspond to any word in French. It would be necessary to translate it with a periphrase such as "promised love," or "sworn love" or "bond with love." In short the word evokes the covenant and, by that very fact, it also evokes duration, stability, and finally (when it is a question of God) even eternity. Being in an alliance where the love of God for us always endures, we do not tire of talking about the good that we receive from it:

> O give thanks to the Lord, for he is good,
>   for his steadfast love endures forever.
> O give thanks to the God of gods,
>   for his steadfast love endures forever.
> O give thanks to the Lord of lords,
>   for his steadfast love endures forever ... (Ps.136: 1-3)

We do not get tired ... Or rather we would risk falling asleep if the twenty-six other sentences were not, each one, different. In the first lines, which I have just quoted, there is a bit less variety. Only the name of God changes a little, because it is a question of getting some momentum with this Name that the cantor of the Psalms has on his lips and savors. What the name of God means, what the name of God contains, that is the subject matter of this Psalm.

For twenty-six repetitions of the refrain there are twenty-six phrases, and each one is different. Why this change? Because the content of the Psalm is a narrative, and to relate and repeat are two actions that are difficult to reconcile. In effect, something always happens in a story. Every narrative is necessarily divided into episodes and there can be an episode only if, each time, a new fact is related. That is why, at least from verse 5 up to verse 23, each verse number represents a particular scene, except when the content is only a proclamation of what follows (verse 7) or a continuation of what precedes (verses 12, 18, 22). Verses 23 and 24 are a summary.

Here are the different episodes in the order in which they appear; the making of the heavens, the placement of the earth on the waters, the making of the sun, then of the moon and the stars, the extermination of the first-born of Egypt, the flight from Israel, the opening of the waters of the sea, the crossing and drowning of the pursuers, the march in the desert, the defeat of the kings who barred the road to the Promised Land, and the entry into the Promised Land. Except for a few details, all these episodes are listed in the order that the other grand books of the Bible have used. So it is almost a summary of the Bible from the Book of Genesis to Joshua.

This grouping or, as it is said, this narrative content, is divided into two parts. The first is the "creation narrative" and the second is the "history narrative." But with that, it is as though we have no narrative, and this has us make an important observation. To relate is in effect to introduce some connections, a kind of continuous flow that gives pleasure. Here, however, the refrain separates like scissors cutting all the episodes that form the narrative band. Let us analyze the produced effect. Each episode is cut up, isolated as in a medallion or niche. By this we understand that it is not caused by what precedes but, each time, by the fact that God wants this episode. For example, Israel would have been able to cross the Sea of Reeds, but its pursuer would have been able to do the same, had it not been for the will of God. Israel would have been able to come to the desert, but to die there, to cross it but to go no further than the doors of the Promised Land. The process has one sense that that every episode is new. The refrain sings what is eternal. The message of the lines that are grouped two by two throughout the poem is that, when it is a question of the actions of God, it is always the same thing and always new.

The combination of the new and the eternal have something divine about them, which escapes man. What is eternal reminds us that we are not here forever; the oldest monuments or the mountains remind us that we pass on more quickly than they, but we would not like to be eternal while being as immobile. The pleasure of newness is indispensable to us. One of the most frequent ways of finding it is to hear a story told, whose renewals are maintained for the time it takes. But all stories end and many are tragic. Man does not know why tragic narratives give him such pleasure and that, everywhere on earth, the most tragic ones are also those that are most repeated. The most probable reason for this is that every narrative, finally, is a game with death and asks the question whether we are alive or dead. Every narrative puts newness into play in order to ask the question about eternity. Newness, by definition, passes on, and to pass on is to die. The continuity that is proper

27. B. Distant Creation: Psalm 136

to narrative is able to hide this interruption from us for a time, but it cannot hide it indefinitely. The interruption can only be suspended because every narrative must be interrupted at least when it finishes. To suspend is to relate. The end is necessary because, if it were not necessary to hide the end, no narrative would exist. Is not the end of every narrative productive, rather than destructive?

The way by which the narrator keeps us attentive to his words, what keeps us spellbound is our secret; the place where the eternal and the new are one does not depend on anything in this world since it is this oneness that supports this world, and that is why it is necessary to surrender everything in order to know it.

Psalm 136 tries to define in its way the secret of man by talking about the things of this world, for the secret of man invests the entire world: the new and the eternal seek each other throughout this world by the work of the presence of God. We have said that the content of the Psalm was divided into two parts. The first part, which is creation, presents us especially the eternal side, and the second part, which is history, presents us especially the new. The same thing can be said in another way, if we note that creation is suggested to us by the space that, for man, expresses more the eternal, whereas history concerns time, and it is in time that the new can be produced. The Psalm couples these two values, the new and the eternal, in its most material arrangement (26 + 26). But the same effect is obtained by a more internal work.

At least by approximation or through an image that is constantly accessible, creation presents us the eternal aspect, because of the grand duration of its effects:

> ... who by understanding made the heavens,
>   for his steadfast love endures forever;
> who spread out the earth on the waters,
>   for his steadfast love endures forever;
> who made the great lights,
>   for his steadfast love endures forever;
> the sun to rule over the day,
>   for his steadfast love endures forever;
> the moon and stars to rule over the night,
>   for his steadfast love endures forever ... (Ps. 136: 5-9)

The expressions and the choice of words in these verses show that the Psalmist was familiar with a tradition that was quite close to that of the beginning of Genesis; he thus reproduces a "narrative program" and that is why the reader who is familiar with this program through Genesis 1: 1-24 finds himself surprised that he has been left in the lurch, that is to say (see verse 9) after what corresponds to the fourth day of the week, during which the stars were created. For the Psalmist, would creation be finished on Wednesday evening, after the clock of the heavenly bodies has been set forever? In any case, the model of the seven days seems to have been abandoned in our Psalm, and we should try to find the reason for this.

The reason exists, and it is simple. Everything that is kept in the list of the poet is of the same nature; only the unchangeable parts—we might say the "buildings"—of creation, everything that is a sign of the eternal, and only that, occupies verses 5 through 9. But everything that is omitted also forms a homogeneous unit; it is a question of the "furniture" with which the "buildings" are filled: plants, animals, men—in a word, the precarious living being, everything that is a sign of newness is absent from the list of creation in this Psalm. But what is omitted is replaced. The sphere of the living is replaced by the sphere of history, in which the drama of newness is signified and played out on the collective plane and even on the universal level. It is probably significant that the movement of history starts at verse 10 once the astral movement has been set up. It allows one to measure the time of humanity through the displacement of these intermediary heavenly bodies found between the eternal and the ephemeral because their movement is unchanging. Measures of time inscribed in space, the stars accomplish some periods that are comparable by their scope to the fullness of the narrative of human history. Having thus placed such markers, the narrative of creation founds a kind of eternal contract: why would God begin to act in order to interrupt himself later? To the extent that every narrative implies a contract, creation is the preface to the narrative of history; history is a test of the promises of creation. The movement from the eternal to the new is presented as a danger; Israel does nothing other than risk its existence in it.

At this point of our reading, since the eternal is signified by what corresponds to the content of the four first days of creation (verses 4-9) and the new (as a test of the eternal) by the memory of history (verses 10-22), we still need to know how the unity of the eternal and

27. B. Distant Creation: Psalm 136

the new is signified (other than by the alternation of twenty-six lines for twenty-six refrains), without which God would not be able to be expressed, and how this unity finds a place in the dénouement, if the narrative truly has one.

The sign is given at the level of the composition. Biblical men have this in common with the most modern of the moderns; they think by groups. It is impossible to think about the beginning of the narrative of the seven days of creation without thinking about its end. It is impossible to think about the beginning of the narrative of the foundational history of Israel without thinking about its end. The end is the same for the narrative of creation and for the narrative of the history, for the narrative of the first week and for the narrative of the founding years. Of course there exists in the Bible different narratives and even multiple ones either about creation or history. But these narratives can be grouped according to their types or models, and we know which models our Psalm follows: the narrative of the first week and foundational narratives (particularly used in the texts of the covenant), which relate the entrance into the Promised Land, precisely this Land that the covenant promises. These two different models have the same end: in the model-narrative of creation, the last benefit introduced by the words "God said" at the end of the narrative of Genesis is the gift of nourishment. In the model-narrative of the foundational history, the statement is that God gives bread to his people (the generic term for all that has one live) and it is bread that comes from the land where he has them settle.

But, in Psalm 136, there are not two mentions of nourishment. There is only one. The line of creation and the line of history, the line of the eternal and the line of the new encounter one another in the one finale:

... who gives food to all flesh,
    for his steadfast love endures forever;

O give thanks to the God of heaven,
    for his steadfast love endures forever. (verses 25-26)

It is difficult to imagine any bread bearing a heavier weight of meaning and life. Because it signifies the encounter of the eternal and the new, this bread signifies God and gives God. With this bread, the

Psalmist has found his "point of creation," but the path towards this point takes, as usual, long detours.

God Creator maintains fragile life. We know this action. We are familiar with it. But by a modification that has a great impact, this point of creation is also a point "of universal history." In order for this bread to be on the table, creation was certainly necessary, but also the sufferings and this historic liberation of an oppressed people through the defeat of their oppressors. A judgment of all humanity was necessary … So we should not think of this Psalm as a narrative that ends with the mention of bread. It is however what it is, to go no further. But in a more concrete understanding, the Psalm begins with bread. All is said in order to give thanks (verse 26) for the bread that is on the table before the Psalm, which is then defined as the recitation of thanksgiving over the bread. In order to give thanks we should recall what we only know by hearsay, "to call up the memory," the sufferings of the ancestors. To remember the history of a bread is what theologians, liturgists and others call "anamnesis."

But it was necessary that "near creation" fall very far back, under the influence of the narrative of history, in order that the bread be, on this table, a meeting of universal history. And so we do not only read that he gives food "to Israel …" but that he gives it "to all flesh … ." He gives food; he gives bread. In the history that has unfolded, what was at stake and signified for all ages was the justice rendered to the poor, or the injustice exercised through the harshness of the powerful, the "famous" and the "great" (verses 17-18). No one should fall asleep thinking that the bread on the table represents an immediate relation with the creative God. Thus conceived, "near" creation would only be near according to the intimacy of a pure dream, if one forgot that bread is the result of a relation with men inscribed in historic conditions of work, thus political ones. The bread here is that of a free man, taken out of slavery. "Distant" creation is an indispensable concept in order to encounter universal humanity. The bread that Israel eats comes from God only on conditions of justice; and it is truly for all men on the same conditions. The Psalmist testifies, by his hymn, that he has not forgotten that his table is called to be a sign of justice.

Given that, are the promises of eternity that the narrative of creation contains kept? Biblical history, as the Bible sees it, is summarized in verses 23-24:

27. B. Distant Creation: Psalm 136

> It is he who remembered us in our low estate,
>   for his steadfast love endures forever;
> and rescued us from our foes,
>   for his steadfast love endures forever ...

And so the man who gives thanks for the bread of the universal encounter is the man snatched from the hand that gives death. Such is the dénouement. The ordeal and the promise of eternity are concentrated on the same bread. Strengthened by this bread, the man who has experienced the ordeals of the narrative advances towards the test that will end the narrative. But, while waiting, man, with each day of his life in suspense, has to find his bread. The bread is neither eternal nor historical; it is daily bread. Victory over death must be renewed every day. But to renew it is also to put off the decisive moment, which is on its way. The witness of Jesus Christ, who takes these words from the Psalms as he goes to his own death, allows us to say that they are promises of eternity.

The Evangelist Matthew reports that Jesus, having shared bread and wine, headed to his Passion "after they had sung the hymn" (Matthew 26: 30). He particularly refers us back to Psalm 136 because, with other Psalms, it closes the Passover meal. If we answer the invitation of Matthew, the Psalm helps us to find Christ nearer to us. But, while reading in the Psalm that Jesus Christ gives us the bread of God, a renewal stronger than the death that he himself traversed, then the Psalmist seems to be closer to us, because he is also attracted by the mystery towards which we ourselves approach.

28

Psalm 74 and Psalm 89

In Psalm 74 as in Psalm 89, two themes come together. I am only going to quote the passages that most concern us, as they are too long to be reproduced in their entirety. The poet meditates on the destiny of a people caught in the drama of all humanity; the poet meditates on the narrative of creation, on the distant origins of the world. The narrative is called an epic, because creation is related as a heroic action of the primordial age. Here, this action is a war:

> Yet God my King is from of old,
>   working salvation in the earth.
> You divided the sea by your might;
>   you broke the heads of the dragon in the waters.
> You crushed the heads of Leviathan;
>   you gave him as food for the creatures of the wilderness.
> You cut openings for springs and torrents;
>   you dried up ever-flowing streams. (Ps. 74: 12-15)

Here God is called "King" because royalty is illustrated, confirmed, and merited through singular actions in war. The Creator takes on this kind of action by struggling against the sea, and the sea is animated, even personified, because it is a symbol of the undetermined chaos that wants to keep good and evil together. To speak about the dragon is to personify the sea, especially if one gives the dragon a proper name: Leviathan.

Psalm 89 says the same thing in other terms; it calls upon God in this way:

> You crushed Rahab like a carcass;
>   you scattered your enemies with your mighty arm.
> The heavens are yours, the earth also is yours,

the world and all that is in it—you have founded them.
The north and the south—you created them ... (Ps. 89: 10-12)

In the preceding Psalm, the aquatic animal called Leviathan now receives the name Rahab that, for the readers of the time, had one think of Egypt, but it is the same animal. Victory over the monster is related in the past ("crushed"): it is the distant act of creation. The mastery that calms the sea is told in the present: it is the near act. In effect, for each of us, it is near and may even be renewed daily near the sea; on every beach, a sound and a breath are perceived by the ear and the skin, at the same time that waves give the eyes the image of a project which always fails, since they make the indefinitely thwarted and repeated movement to advance in order to cover the land. Ancient narratives of creation attributed to the word and breath of God the power to hold the oceanic deluge at bay, as a monster is kept on a leash:

You set a boundary that they may not pass,
 so that they might not again cover the earth. (Ps. 104: 9)

In the epic narratives of creation, God appears like a warrior who has at first made the invader fall back by conquering him in a grand battle but without exterminating him and, then, this conqueror succeeds in containing the enemy on the other side of the border. The initial action is maintained by a permanent one. Initial (distant), or permanent (near), the divine action is painted under images of war. To repel or to contain is always the use of force.

The same characteristic is found outside the Psalms. Isaiah talks about the Lord: "On that day the Lord with his cruel and great and strong sword will punish Leviathan the fleeing serpent, Leviathan the twisting serpent, and he will kill the dragon that is in the sea" (Isaiah 27: 1). Deutero-Isaiah implores God to wake up, as he did "in days of old ... Was it not you who cut Rahab in pieces, who pierced the dragon?" (Isaiah 51:9). The Book of Job relates that God, by his force, calmed the Sea and, by his intelligence, crushed Rahab, cleared the skies by his breath and, with his hand, pierced the fleeing serpent (Job 26: 12).

These descriptions are colorful and, consequently, are sometimes called "primitive:" they also resemble those that pagans drew about the exploits of their gods; the Leviathan that Isaiah 27: 1 mentions had

28. B. Distant Creation: Psalm 74 and Psalm 89

already been painted with the same attributes in a Canaanite poem older than Moses. Some texts that have the same Canaanite origin relate how the god Baal was stronger than "Yam," a word that means the sea. A great Mesopotamian poem tells how the king-god Marduk, among other feats, is able to cut to pieces the monster Tiamat. This Yam corresponds to the biblical "Tehôm," which is the aquatic abyss divided by God into the waters above from those below, which are themselves separated from the land. The biblical schema, as early as the narrative of the beginning of Genesis, is not without some resemblance to the Mesopotamian model according to which Marduk "divides the monstrous flesh" of Tiamat in order to make several parts of the world with some pieces of his body. The God of the Bible wants to maintain the limits of the sea just as, in the pagan poem, Marduk imposes his law: "He pulled on the latch, appointed a porter, and ordered them not to let the waters out" (in the poem *Enuma Elish*; see Psalm 104: 9, quoted earlier).

The Psalms and the Bible in general offer many surprises, unless the reader has become too numb to be surprised or has found some infallible way to become quickly calm. It is as though, in this kind of text, we are dealing only with images that poets used in order to get our attention. It is also like saying that these texts, since they come from or are borrowed from non-biblical mythologies, lose for this very reason any value for carrying a message and are thus reduced to a residual state which could disappear without any loss for the Bible or ourselves. But the Bible has delved much more often and much wider than we think in the great fund of pagan beliefs. It does so, each time, in order to deliver to us the utterance which is hidden in them and which is meant for everyone.

The path of biblical surprises attracts us because astonishment is the sign of childhood. Why is the child given as a model? It is not because he believes everything, because he does not believe everything. But different from the adult, he neither admires nor becomes indignant for ready-made reasons, reasons that are already programmed. The child is surprised and asks to understand. If we adults have not willingly become numb to being astonished and had earned patience, we would be able to bear the length and the detours of the biblical path.

God creates while speaking ... God creates while being silent ... God creates now ... God creates in the beginning ... God creates the most delicate fibers of the living being ... God creates for a promise against death ... God creates some mortals without making their nature stronger than death ... And now we read that God creates in a victorious hand-to-hand fight during which chaos is vanquished. The Bible states, regarding creation, now one utterance, now another, but these words form a path, which the style of the narrator cannot quite describe. Still, we have to pursue this path.

Perhaps these warrior images prevent us from advancing. We are at ease with a more refined style, which we also find in the Bible, for example in the passages that the poet Racine chose in order to adapt them for classical French taste:

> Tu dis. Et les Cieux parurent,
> Et tous les Astres coururent
> Dans leur ordre se placer.

> You spoke, and the heavens appeared
> And all the stars ran
> In order to their place.

In these beautiful verses, we find no weapon that cuts up a monster and no arm to hold it. God creates without using his hands. But I believe that the child, to whom we referred some lines above, is not put off by a tragic version of creation. He listens attentively and remains so if he hears the weapons of the narrative clashing against each other. This is because the drama of existence dwells in him and there takes on an intensity that is superior to what all the television screens will ever be able to offer him with their images of violence. The young child knows where such a drama has been able to take place, where a mortal danger has been barely overcome; everything that talks to him about drama reminds him of his own birth. God creates the frail; nothing is as fragile as the body; frailty is at first experienced in the first victories of life, always won over its opposite, its adversary.

The drama of birth does not last for only a moment. We are always threatened by what does not want us to be born, outside of us, in us. What does not want to let us be born ... what name shall we give it? We can identify it under the traits of Leviathan, Rahab, Dragon of the ocean Abyss, Tehôm, daily bellowing at our interior frontiers. However, Leviathan and other powers are not Satan, the absolute evil. It is, nevertheless, a question of his instrument, since what keeps us

28. B. Distant Creation: Psalm 74 and Psalm 89

from being born is often our own desire, and at times it is those close to us, our world, everything which can organize, with the help of the good, some form of slavery. Everything that, in us and outside of us, hardens against us. As a retort, the Psalm raises the protestation of the child who wants to be born.

The truth of creation has often taken us to a point of fragility. This is the first time that this point of fragility declares itself so visibly as being death:

> Do not deliver the soul of your dove to the wild animals;
> do not forget the life of your poor forever. (Ps. 74: 19)

Or even:

> Remember how short my time is— ... (Ps. 89: 47)

A kind of equilibrium is set within Psalm 74 as in Psalm 89. The imminent end, already tasted with its savor of death, has the beginning and its violent taste of birth rise up. If the beginning was a war, a hand-to-hand struggle with death, and if the war never ended since then, will the fight at the end be a birth? The memory of the absolute beginning, which is the memory of creation, is never so strong as when the absolute end approaches, that is to say, death.

This combination of creation and death is something new in the series of Psalms that we have seen.

It is not completely new, because Psalm 104 already led us to the moment when God renewed the earth and Psalm 106 contrasted the loss of self in the cosmos to birth as a work of God the Creator. But, in our series at least, Psalm 74 and Psalm 89 are alone in expressing the anxiety of an imminent death and in finding the outcome of recalling in their cry the act of the Creator.

This relation is not the only newness of Psalms 74 and 89. Our two Psalms express the cry of a people and not that of an individual or of a child. But, in this regard, a difference separates the two Psalms. Psalm 74 is the cry of the people about their misfortune. Psalm 89 is still the cry of the people, but it is about the misfortune of the individual who represents it, namely the king, the humiliated successor of David. In both cases, since it is a question of the people, under one form or another, the misfortune has one remember the past. Everything is lost; one remembers all that was had; and one remembers that one possessed it by virtue of the promise of God, through the covenant. Remembering the promise, remembering the covenant and its consequences is history, a distant history when it is a question of a people:

> Remember your congregation, which you acquired long ago,
> which you redeemed to be the tribe of your heritage.
> Remember Mount Zion, where you came to dwell. (Ps. 74: 2)

Likewise, in Psalm 89, the people remind God that he once promised David a posterity that was supposed to continue in the centuries to come. It is by following, in each poem, the traces of the distant and collective history that the thought of the Psalmist bears upon the origin. The origin is the point where, at the same time, history and creation begin. "In the beginning," according to the consecrated formula, history and creation come together, and this appears in the passages which describe the distant and initial divine action, the primordial action. Since it is a question of a junction, we shall have to consider two points of view in order to understand it. First of all, in effect, creation receives aspects of history and salvation but, secondly, history and salvation receive aspects of creation.

1) In his epic victory, the divinity cut up the body of the Beast of the Abyss. This initial action is an image of creation, because God creates while placing meaning, high and low, right and left, in order that man orient himself. How does one come to some meaning through the epic struggle with the Beast? The beast Leviathan or Tehôm, the chaos of the abyss is the place where everything remains mixed. The stomach of the abyss, the personified abyss, keeps everything in an obscure confusion, in the "tohu bohu." These two words have come into our language from Hebrew. In effect, Genesis 1: 2 uses them. For the Bible, to create is to place "meaning," to place in light and in order. And so one says that God creates by his Wisdom (Ps. 104: 24, regarding the stars). But, to put something in order, it is necessary to separate what is mixed, by way of an act, no longer one of wisdom but by force. In order to separate, a blade is necessary. But, in God, Wisdom and power are one and the same reality. Different from soldiers who think too little and from thinkers who do nothing, the one who has created us through an utterance that is a sword places the burst of force in the very place where he puts the light of meaning. What happens when God has "cut

28. B. Distant Creation: Psalm 74 and Psalm 89

the monstrous flesh?" A glance at Psalm 74 shows us that, hardly has the sea been divided, hardly has Leviathan been crushed, that the stars have been set in place to guide caravans and boats, to give calendars their references (see Psalm 74: 14). In Psalm 89, the God who has just subdued Rahab immediately creates the cardinal points:

The north and the south—you created them ... (Ps. 89: 12)

To create is thus to make it possible that a geographic map helps men to cover several times the same route and so meet one another. God essentially creates the necessary conditions for the existence of a human community. We consequently find in the primordial schema of creation all the characteristics of an action that saves, this in several ways. First of all this is because God saves by means of victories, and because creation itself is conceived according to this model of an armed event. Secondly, because all through history, God saves what is basically a collectivity, a people, and creation is much more than the mere efficient cause of the appearance of one or several beings; it is the establishment of the conditions of their "being-together" in body and in reason. It offers men the power to be together and even this union of force and meaning called "love." That is why creation resembles salvation. This notion is now familiar to modern commentators. In it they have found the advantage of rendering to life a representation of creation which had made it seem distant for a longtime, almost absent or even imaginary. But, up to now, this success has kept us from making a further step in going ahead, this time, on another incline.

2) Salvation is also an act of creation, as though it received in exchange the qualities of creation because it had infused it with its own. That is why several descriptions of the primordial act of war may be read like these figures formed with cubes whose corners appear, willingly, either curved or raised. The act is painted, willingly, either as creation, or as an act of salvation in history. In effect, to master, to divide, to drain the sea and, with the same gesture, conquer the enemy is an image of salvation in history which we recognize immediately: for a long time after the beginning of Genesis, Exodus and Passover, acts of salvation par excellence, are related on the model of a victory won at once over Pharaoh and the sea. The Exodus, like Creation, divides the sea. By this we understand that, if creation was related as an epic victory, historic salvation ... was, for its part, represented by the images

of a creation. It transforms the sea and, as was the case on the third day of the creation of the world, it has the dry land suddenly appear amidst the separated waters. But, like creation itself, the Exodus takes on a kind of permanent characteristic. It is inscribed forever: "there is Exodus" at every return of Passover, just as there is a set time for high tides and the stars. A moment has passed, but a world has come forward; words, commemorative texts, and rituals have it that the Exodus is here today. It surrounds me. My history has become my body. Just as each week and each sabbath make the creation of the world present, each Easter makes the Exodus present with its salvation. More widely still, each first-born of the people is like a daily and living effect of the Paschal salvation of yesteryear, through which God spared the first-born. Finally, as the manna was by nature a divine word which established that man did not live by bread alone (Deuteronomy 8: 3), so it is that we read, over our daily bread, the narrative of the crossing of the desert and the gift of the Promised Land. With the fruit of creation, we eat together the fruit of history and that of the covenant. We eat the Book and we read the bread. That is not all: if creation is a universal act, so must salvation be proclaimed and appear to all men in order that they make their choice between life and death. This aspect of permanence and universality is the element of creation in the act of salvation.

Having established these two sides, their relations, their "exchange" is going to help us come back to the language that we have used. When I spoke about near creation, I was talking about salvation. This was always mentioned at the "point of frailty" of the living being, in the most intimate part of his being. But it was so close and so intimate that it could only be for me. What creation gained as a concrete reality, in taking on this quality of "near," it lost in universality. Conversely, when I talk about universal salvation that transforms the entire world, this act does not differ at all from the creation that snatches everything from chaos. But I have no experience of such an act.

But to speak in this way is really too easy! My near salvation is not truly just for me. What is universal does not happen completely outside myself. Were that the case, I would live outside all reality. In fact, I live according to some reality. The abstraction that I have just formulated only helps me understand what I lack. I do not live according to ultimate reality, which would be the complete fusion of the universal and the near. But I do not live quite outside it and that is why I desire

28. B. Distant Creation: Psalm 74 and Psalm 89

it. Without coming together completely, the universal and the near are not strangers in me. I would otherwise die. They exchange their qualities, and in this way I exist.

It was to make it possible to live according to some reality, between the near and the universal and at some distance from these terms, but not without entering into their mutual relation, that God has established, between each of us and universal humanity, the different peoples to which we belong

It is in the people, in the terms of our two Psalms, that a point of frailty becomes manifest. It is the Temple and the city that are at the gates of death:

At the upper entrance they hacked the
    wooden trellis with axes.
And then, with hatchets and hammers,
    they smashed all its carved work.
They set your sanctuary on fire,
    they desecrated the dwelling place of your name,
        bringing it to the ground.
They said to themselves, "We will utterly subdue them";
    they burned all the meeting places of
        God in the land. (Ps. 74: 5-8)

Evil reaches walls, fortresses, and fences (Ps. 89). Israel sees everything that constitutes it as a people and a city disappear. The birth of the city was a solemn movement in the Bible; the moment of its undoing is also solemn. For the city is the place where distant creation and near salvation are able to cohabit, even if their union remains unfinished, unfinished in Israel, as long as Israel has not completed its mission. Its route, even today, continues, unfinished in the Church, as long as it journeys. Under one form or another, sin consists in the forgetfulness or in the refusal of this incompleteness. Faced with ordeals, creation-salvation shows its distance. Then, instead of a distance under the form of a past, an absence for which there is no remedy, creation-salvation reveals itself to be absent from us in the future, to which our existence is truly connected through promise and through hope. Creation is not quite here: it is what we await. The combination creation-salvation can, in this perspective, change its name and be called "new creation," a formulation where the word "new" takes upon itself the dimension of history and salvation.

C. Creation to Come

29

Psalms of the Kingdom of God

There is a series of Psalms in which the Lord, God of Israel, under his name of YYWH, is called "King." This title is placed in relation to the work of the Creator. Exegetes often attach these Psalms to the celebration of the principal sanctuary, or even to its construction. By proclaiming its God as King, the political and collective Israel at once celebrates the God of creation and the God of history. In these traits we recognize those of the epic poem of our "B series." A new distinctive characteristic, however, is going to open "series C" for the Psalms of YHWH King; it is their orientation towards the future. A hope that looks to the return of God is heard; his actions, when he will come, have him recognized as Creator. The reality that we now call, following the Gospels, "Kingdom of God," was formulated through similar texts. Since I am not able to give this series in its entirety, I am only going to reproduce, below, one of its most characteristic poems, Psalm 93:

1 The Lord is king, he is robed in majesty;
   the Lord is robed, he is girded with strength.
 He has established the world; it shall never be moved;
2   your throne is established from of old;
   you are from everlasting.
3 The floods have lifted up, O Lord;
   the floods have lifted up their voice;
   the floods lift up their roaring.
4 More majestic than the thunders of mighty waters,

> more majestic than the waves of the sea,
> majestic on high is the Lord!
>
> 5 Your decrees are very sure;
> holiness befits your house,
> O Lord, forevermore.

There is sound and festive light, which return to the heart through the simple act of opening the Psalter. The city is festive, as the celebration was not relegated only to the sanctuary. The people who sang the Psalms did not shut themselves inside. They sang outside. Moreover, they found very little space in the Temple and much more on its esplanades, even for the Gentiles, who had access to one of them. Since none of the great feasts of ancient Israel took place during the rainy season, one could count on good weather (with some risks, nevertheless, at Passover). That is why the Psalms that are most directly connected to the liturgy of the sanctuary evoke a coming-and-going.

> Who shall ascend the hill of the Lord?
> And who shall stand in his holy place? (Ps. 24: 3)
>
> O come, let us sing to the Lord ...
> O come, let us worship and bow down,
>   let us kneel before the Lord, our
>   Maker! (Ps. 95: 1 and 6)
>
> ... bring an offering... (Ps. 96: 8)

It is also probable that the men consecrated to the service of the Temple are those who leave it to say, "Come," "Enter" and other inviting words. We sense that rituals of dialogue unfolded between the inside and the outside, when one celebrated the reception of the Ark, in order to recall that the Lord had not always been there, and that he had also left the Temple in order to return to it. One sang amidst the trumpet blasts:

> Lift up your heads, O gates!
>   and be lifted up, O ancient doors!
>   that the King of glory may come in.

29. C. Creation to Come: Psalms of the Kingdom of God

> Who is the King of glory?
> The Lord, strong and mighty,
> the Lord, mighty in battle. (Ps. 24: 7-8)

The prayer of the Psalms states the relationship that binds men among themselves, and it seeks out men in the furthest parts:

Say among the nations, "The Lord is king! ..." (Ps. 96: 10)

Clap your hands, all you peoples ... (Ps. 47: 1)

One can well invite "all the earth" (Ps. 100: 1) to come to the house of God (verse 4) since God has made us (verse 3). And the nations can be interested in this because one goes to the Temple to celebrate creation, which necessarily concerns them.

In this place of prayer one could hear news about the world, since its creation—ancient, present and new—was proclaimed in the Temple. A divine action was celebrated and, consequently, related, in the way by which our feasts have us reread passages from the Bible that correspond to them. Since the old rituals changed several times and the texts were able to be transferred from one feast to another (because the liturgy of the Old Testament also had its reforms), scholars are not of one mind when it is a question of knowing whether this or that Psalm of collective prayer in the sanctuary was assigned to one particular feast rather than to another. In effect, the celebration of creation was appropriate for all the feasts without exception because they all celebrate salvation. Creation with salvation seeks to form a unit. One could commemorate the creative act with the feast of Tents, by mentioning the covenant and the Law, in the manner by which Psalm 19 sings about creation and the commandments. As done in Psalm 136, one could also sing about creation as about Exodus and Passover. Whatever solution was adopted, Israel always celebrated a season of nature at the same time as a great date of its history: springtime and the first vegetations with Passover and Exodus, autumn and the last harvests with its feast of Tents and the covenant. It was thus normal at each of these feasts to celebrate in song, with hymns, at once creation and salvation. But in doing this, one celebrated together the benefits common to all men ("to all flesh") and the privileges of Israel.

That is why the prayer of the Psalms is continuously expanded to the point of containing the desires of all humanity. Israel is the chosen one of God, but this choice would not have any meaning if God were only the God of Israel. God would then possess through his nature and not through his freedom. The choice only signifies freedom and it has its full meaning if God, being Lord of all peoples by his nature, becomes closer to one of them through freedom. This meaning reaches its highest point if the intimacy of only one people is the path that God takes in order, one day, to be present to all without any shade of distinction. Freedom then reconciles itself with nature according to an admirable process; intimacy, in effect, is not first experienced in a multitude but is first realized by some as a promise of the God who wants to reconcile the most universal and the nearest. Thus does God, in calling Abraham, have him sense that all the nations are interested in his benediction (Genesis 12: 3; 18: 18; 22: 18; 26: 4; 28:14), and Psalm 47 takes up this theme again:

> The princes of the peoples gather
> as the people of the God of Abraham. (Ps. 47: 9)

In order for Zion, "in the far north" (Ps. 48: 2), to serve as the meeting place for the scattered sons of Israel and, finally, for the nations, it is necessary that space and time be indicated by rather strong markers. The displacement of men who are to meet again at times set in advance is the sign and the effect of good order in the entire cosmos. Thus the series of rather homogeneous hymns that goes from Psalm 93 to Psalm 100 (Ps. 94 does not belong to this group but belongs with Psalms 24, 29 and 47) mostly considers the visible universe through its stability (or, as we shall see, through its opposite):

> The Lord is king ...
> He has established the world; it shall
>   never be moved;
>   your throne is established from of old ... (Ps. 93: 1-2)

This is the grand subject of joy, shared with every man:

29. C. Creation to Come: Psalms of the Kingdom of God

>   Say among the nations, "The Lord is king!
>   The world is firmly established; it shall never be moved.
>   He will judge the peoples with equity." (Ps. 96: 10)

The promise of the solidity of the cosmos and particularly of the seasons (submitted to the influence of the stars) was not made to Israel but, rather, to Noah, the new Adam saved from the deluge and, after Adam, father of every man. That is why Israel invites all the sons of Adam and of Noah to pray God for having been faithful to this clause of the covenant. This is the content of the terms: "The world is firmly established." It is not necessary to explain at length why the solidity of the landmarks is not only necessary for the life of every man, but constitutes the condition of possibility for every agreement, of every human convergence, of every society. This solidity is not a property of the world.

In the vision of the world that our Psalms translate, the earth does not stand firm on the waters by its nature but because it depends upon the creative word. So it is not contradictory that the same texts insist on the solidity of the cosmos and on its fragility. This contrast is even at the heart of the notion of creation. The land holds firm, but the turbulent waters "have lifted up their voice" (see Psalm 29; 93: 3). Faced with the judgment of God, the firmest elements of the world "tremble" or "melt" (Ps. 97: 4-5).

In our time, the idea that all the parts of the world are fragile cannot seem strange. We have again discovered the image of a cosmos hanging from a string. It has only become more rare to believe that God holds this string. We know how to glorify man for his power of introducing references of meaning into the chaos of the world. More recently we have learned to fear this power, since it is double, as it is also directed towards the undoing of the world. Today we would sometimes say that man holds the string from which the world hangs. And it is true that, from the lack of harmony in humanity, total destruction may arise.

This position, doubtless new, is only wrong in believing itself to be too completely new in relation to Scripture and even to the ancient beliefs of the pagans. The Bible describes the action of the creative God by borrowing rigorously the terms that serve to describe the action of man to the extent that it produces order and meaning. Man orients the world, defends it against its fragility, and constantly inscribes his word in things. The varied and rich manner by which the Bible paints the creative God is only possible if man is in a city where work is already complex and coordinated. Based on this observation many will say that man fools himself by projecting—naively or viciously—on God the power that is actually his own responsibility. But we should see things differently. If God creates or, stated in another way, if God makes meaning, only a being who himself makes meaning can understand him. What characterizes "meaning," in the sense that I understand it here, is that one cannot look at it, connect to it from the outside. To use the terms rigorously, there is no "meaning" for a spectator, but only for an actor. One cannot understand meaning without producing it, making it. That is why, as we said earlier, man, strictly speaking, does not "know" that God created the world. He says it or, more precisely, he sings it, in the poetic register, which is the way par excellence for meaning to be made, without forgetting the nonsense that churns about it like the waters that voice and breath stop. It would be foolish for a non-creative man to be able to understand a God who is.

But creation is not only an utterance. It is action with words and this "with" is not simply an addition. It is only by placing in the gestures of my hands what my lips say that the contents of my words can truly traverse me. It is only through my hands that "saying" creation will show itself more true than "knowing." But this discovery is not one that the exegete makes or the modern scholar. The song of creation, in Israel as in all religions that desire a sanctuary for a city, is accompanied by an act of the hands, by a "doing." This dubbing is not camouflaged. On the contrary, it is admitted. There is no epic of creation without the construction of a sanctuary. While man sings with his lips the words: "He has established the world; it shall never be moved ..." (Ps. 93: 1), he places with his hands the cornerstone of the sanctuary, the one that, along the Euphrates, at Mari and elsewhere, one pierced so that a large nail could go through it and push it into the earth while crushing the skull (Ps. 74: 13-14) of the turbulent monster of the waters below. At first songs of creation accompanied and then, with the passing of time, commemorated this action and many others:

> The earth is the Lord's and all that is
> in it,

29. C. Creation to Come: Psalms of the Kingdom of God

> the world, and those who live in it;
> for he has founded it on the seas,
> and established it on the rivers. (Ps. 24: 1-2)

The Psalms of the sanctuary, especially represented by the series that we are commenting on here, contain in their field of vision at once the heavenly sanctuary erected by God at the same time that he creates the cosmos, and the earthly sanctuary where men sing the song of creation in the act of creating their own image of what God creates.

Biblical man does not camouflage the place that his own creative activity holds in his faith in the creative activity of God. But the Bible not only admits the activity of man; it is submitted to a radical critique which was foundational for the faith of Israel and which remains so for our faith. Biblical judgment separates creative human activity from the idolatrous activity by which man does not know how to distinguish himself from God. We find this preoccupation in the Psalms. In effect, the sons of Abraham and the other sons of Adam place their feet on the same ground and praise the same Creator for the same blessings, but the idolatrous person is singled out, excluded:

> The Lord is king! Let the earth rejoice;
> let the many coastlands be glad! ...
> All worshipers of images are put to shame ... (Ps. 97: 1 and 7)

The horror of idols is at the center of the religion of Israel. The work of the idolatrous has no law. The work of Israel, when it does not imitate the idolatrous, is under the Law. It is a mistake to see in the Law only minute practices; the essence of the Law consists in preventing work from destroying itself and from having the land quake. Work preserves the world from chaos, but work itself can become chaos when man obeys what, in his own force, is lawless. It is then that, whatever his words, pious or atheistic, man considers himself to be a god. The Bible calls this lawless force (which often reductively degrades itself through work) by the name death and it calls the one who obeys such a force idolatrous. In contrast, the one who obeys the law of God is born to a truly human desire and becomes capable of work that does not destroy peace. The law of God introduces man to the promise.

Your decrees are very sure; holiness befits your house,
O Lord, forevermore. (Ps. 93: 5)

For the times to come ... One of the most striking characteristics of the Psalms of the sanctuary is that they show us the original covenant of creation being transformed with the expectation of a radical newness in the future. Thanks to the Law, the community was able to keep the desire that the universe end in perfection. The stability that we experience in the cosmos is only the promise of the stability to come. Creation is neither near nor distant; the cosmos itself desires and awaits its true creation:

Then shall all the trees of the forest sing for joy
   before the Lord; for he is coming,
   for he is coming to judge the earth.
He will judge the world with righteousness
   and the people with his truth. (Ps. 96: 12-13)

It was necessary that the people be constituted as a city, with work in accord with the covenant, in order that they might be able to conceive this hope:

Let the sea roar, and all that fills it;
   the world and those who live in it.
Let the floods clap their hands;
   let the hills sing together for joy
at the presence of the Lord, for he is coming to judge the earth.
He will judge the world with righteousness
   and the peoples with equity. (Ps. 98: 7-9)

Our Gospel was constituted within this hope. These Psalms contain the form and the content of our Gospel. The form is that of a universal announcement and the content is the Kingdom of God, which is stated in few words:

Say among the nations, "The Lord is king! ..." (Ps. 96: 10)

In effect, the God of Israel is often declared king during or even from the very first words of these Psalms (24: 7-10; 29: 10; 47: 2; 93:

29. C. Creation to Come: Psalms of the Kingdom of God

1; 95: 3; 96: 10; 97: 1; 98: 6; 99: 1). We find there the most distant attestation of this "Kingdom of God" under the sign of which John the Baptist and Jesus will make their first steps toward us. These Psalms teach us that their song is "new" (Pss. 96: 1; 98: 1). Jesus will not do away with the title of King. He will apply it to himself when his mission approaches its end, but he will teach us the unheard way by which God reigns.

Recapitulation
Psalm 22

When we introduced the Psalms of "distant creation," we said that distinguishing the different elements only aimed at having us appreciate the richness of their encounters. Psalm 22 may help to illustrate this principle. If we have already quoted it several times that is because the fullness of praise and of supplication in it are equal to each other. But it accomplishes yet other syntheses, especially between the individual and the collective, between the lyric dimension where the voice of only one person resonates and the epic dimension, where the voice of a city or even that of all humanity is heard. We can add a characteristic of "series C" to these aspects of "series A" and "series B"; according to Psalm 22, God will be, in the future that is proclaimed through a hymnal form, recognized as king by all peoples.

Because of its universality, which includes all the nations, this Psalm approaches the Psalms of creation and yet it is not one of them. We do not find in it the themes of the presence of the cosmos, of its origin, and of its end.

What we do find is irreplaceable. Never, probably, has a Psalmist described so closely the struggle against death and approached victory so closely. It is from this point that an immense future is promised. In order for this point to be revealed fully as a "point of creation," we shall have to consider other texts of the Old Testament to which Psalm 22 introduces us directly; therefore they will appear in our commentary. It comprises two parts: a "reading" which will show the coherence of the text and an "interpretation," which will situate it in relation to history and to ourselves.

Although Psalm 22 belongs to the Psalms of creation, it opens up for us a good path toward the place where the unity of praise and of supplication, of night and of day, is given to the "new creature."

On that day there shall not be either cold or frost. And there shall be continuous day (it is known to the Lord), not day and not night, for at evening time there shall be light.

On that day living waters shall flow out from Jerusalem, half of them to the eastern sea and half of them to the western sea; it shall continue in summer as in winter.

And the Lord will become king over all the earth; on that day the Lord will be one and his name one. (Zechariah 14: 6-9)

A. Commentary

Psalm 22

1 My God, my God, why have you forsaken me?
Why are you so far from helping me,
from the words of my groaning?

The Jewish commentary of the Psalms (*midrash Tehillim*) wonders why the supplicant calls two times upon his God. It is, the commentary states, because he called on a first day, "My God," and then, "My God" on a second day with no answer from God, in order that, on a third day, he would be able to say, "... why have you forsaken me?" When we talk about abandonment, we do so because memory has looked to the past. The past of the Psalmist is at first the long duration of his unanswered prayer. Salvation is distant, not only in the future but also in the past.

The Jewish commentary also says that the first "Eli," "My God," of verse 2) means: "My God, you are the one who saved us at the Red Sea," and the second "Eli" means: "My God, you are the one who spoke to us at Sinai," and today you are silent. The contrast between the good deeds of God, yesterday, and his silence today in our misfortune is what constitutes our abandonment.

2 O my God, I cry by day, but you do not answer;
and by night, but find no rest.

3 Yet you are holy,
enthroned on the praises of Israel.

To talk about the benefits of yesterday, at least for what concerns the words that are used, is to recite a hymn. As for the substance, this means entering into the secret union of the hymn and supplication. It is saying to God: I am grateful and my gratitude itself begs you, just as my confidence praises you. We praise God when we call him "holy" and remember his hymns, but we are also begging him:

4 In you our ancestors trusted;
    they trusted, and you delivered them.
5 To you they cried, and were saved;
    in you they trusted, and were not put to shame.

This Psalm presents a very special characteristic; the abandonment that strikes the Psalmist not only interrupts the benefits that have come to him individually. His misfortune, which he experiences as an individual, interrupts the series of benefits that the history of Israel relates, a series that is longer and more ample than the biography of the supplicant. The content of the "hymns of Israel" is the history of Israel, and the *midrash* is not wrong to evoke the Red Sea and Sinai, for the Psalmist says: "our fathers" have hoped, cried out, and you have delivered them, and their confidence has not been disappointed.

Certainly, it is not impossible to understand that the Psalmist alludes to the individual ordeals in which the forefathers, known but isolated, cried out, and that God heard them; our supplicant would take them as an example in order to argue with God and to give himself courage. Yet the words contain more than this. All the schemas which list the grand lessons of the covenant in order to teach them to the children of Israel include the moment when their prayer has been answered: "... we cried to the Lord, the God of *our ancestors*; the Lord heard our voice ..." (Deuteronomy 26: 7; emphasis of Beauchamp). God said to Moses: "I have also heard the groaning of the Israelites whom the Egyptians are holding as slaves, and I have remembered my covenant" (Exodus 6: 5). Joshua said to the people: "When I brought your ancestors out of Egypt, you came to the sea ... When *they cried out* to the Lord, he put darkness between you and the Egyptians ..." (Joshua 24: 6-7). Samuel addresses all of Israel and says, "... *your ancestors* cried to the Lord ..." (1 Samuel 12: 8); rescued, they sinned before being punished and cried out again, "... but now rescue us ..." and he "rescued you" (1 Samuel12: 10-11). Given the somewhat normative character of these formulas, it suffices to compare them to Psalm 22 to see that this text aims at designating the prayers of all the people in the framework of the covenant. And it is possible to verify that this is also the content of the hymns of Israel; thus does Psalm 99 recall: "Moses and Aaron were among his priests,/ Samuel also was among those who called on his name" (verse 6). The rhythm of the history of Israel is the rhythm of the prayers of Israel.

The supplication of Psalm 22 thus goes back to words of hymns whose content states that God has heard supplicants. This hymn celebrates the history of Israel as the history of answered supplications, and the supplication takes up the hymn again; the same substance thus turns on itself in order to have us delve into it. Life comes only from God. Here we have something like an immobile center from which every movement flows:

6   But I am a worm, and not human;
    scorned by others, and despised by the people.

You are God; I am no man. You are holy; I am a worm of the earth. You are praised in hymns; I am mocked. However, these are hymns of Israel, since Israel has in its hymns a mirror. While mocking me, Israel excludes me from the hymns where it recognizes itself: "We have heard with our ears, O God, our ancestors have told us, what deeds you performed in their days, in the days of old ..." (Psalm 44: 1). We can even say that the hymns of Israel are transmitted from fathers to sons, and are handed down like life, because the transmission of the hymns of Israel is what makes Israel: "... things that we have heard and known,/ that our ancestors have told us. /We will not hide them from their children ..." (Ps. 78: 2-4). Israel recognizes itself in its hymns and in its fathers. Israel and the supplicant have the same fathers: the supplicant calls them "our ancestors" (and not "my" or "your" ancestors). On the other hand, Israel does not recognize itself in the supplicant who is "despised by the people," an unknown man whose presence puts one off:

7   All who see me mock at me;
    they make mouths at me, they shake their heads;
8   "Commit your cause to the Lord; let him deliver—
    let him rescue the one in whom he delights!"

The supplicant is quite the opposite of the hymns of Israel. But how do we indicate this contrast if not still with the words of the hymns, taken up again, in reverse order, so as to become mocking? The hymns say; "Our fathers hoped and you delivered them." Today derision says; "He counted on the Lord, let him deliver him!" Why change words? A happy Psalmist said in Psalm 18: "... he delivered me, because he delighted in me" (verse 19). The derision of Psalm 22: 8 is almost a quotation of this thanksgiving. When addressed to God, words become fewer, and for men they become empty and fall lifeless. The death of words announces the death of man. The words that we have just talked about are threatening. The refusal to believe quickly sets off a process of acceleration, which is that of death. The one who does not believe in life asks for proof of it and, from that point, finds that he is quickly led to provide himself with proofs to the contrary. The one who does not believe in life works quickly for death. How many times do lips proclaim that a good is unverifiable, while the heart is used to destroy it. It is from this side that the Psalmist feels death approach.

9   Yet it was you who took me from the womb;
    you kept me safe on my mother's breast.

A new and a surprising aspect of this Psalm: the supplicant who grafted himself so spontaneously on all of Israel does not at all do away with the mark of his own individual life. He evokes "*our* fathers" with the great biblical texts. But he says "my mother," and this distinguishes him from the people. He thus experiences the dangers and the anxieties which are strictly his own, because the anxiety of being born is shared with no one. He remembers that God has delivered him from them, and this giving of thanks is not confused with the hymns of Israel. This Psalm thus resists the classification that separates the collective complaints from the individual ones. But this does not do away with the separation. It rather confirms it in the manner by which it posits the two opposite colors: this Psalm is individual and collective. It unifies near creation and distant salvation.

The colors are very sharp and remain so when they are contrasted. This is true in several areas. The death of the Psalmist is near, but he talks about his birth as though he were reliving it. He is able to relive it since all his being was in question in the first moment as it is in the last. If every supplication calls on the memory of something good, the cry made when one faces death has the moment of birth come back as a salvation, when the supplicant was taken "from the womb," "kept safe" (or perhaps in a more literal sense, "placed in confidence") on the breast of his mother. This is the movement from the blind attraction of life to the first request for nourishment, founded on confidence. The first of all saving moments, this salvation which consists in being born gives God the initiative; the birth of man being always anterior to his prayer, he could not receive this goodness other than through grace. It is in this radical anteriority that he recognizes God as God: "Elî attah," "You are my God." The same form for naming God ("Elî") ends in praise what had begun as a complaint, another indication of the mixing that combines both.

10 On you I was cast from my birth,
    and since my mother bore me you have been my God.

Between "our fathers" and "my mother," it is a fact that the person who would be called "my father" is missing and, without hurrying to try to conclude, we shall situate this absence on a very tight network of verbal coherence, spread throughout the entire text. This absence, moreover, is only in what is visible, for the one to whom the child "is confided" may well be, as the adoptive father, this God who was, "from the womb," his God.

11 Do not be far from me, for trouble is near
    and there is no one to help.

The God of salvation (verse 1), the God of birth (verse 9) is distant. What is near is anxiety. Nothing else, no one else, is near because "there is no one to help." In effect, abandoned by God and by man, the one who is "not human" is not surrounded by people, but, suddenly, by animals, and this circle closes in on him. The distribution of the words between verses 12 and 18 correspond to the strategy of this attack:

12 Many bulls encircle me, strong bulls of Bashan surround me;
13 they open wide their mouths at me,
    like a ravening and roaring lion.

14 I am poured out like water,

and all my bones are out of joint;
my heart is like wax,
   it is melted within my breast;
15 my mouth is dried up like a potsherd,
   and my tongue sticks to my jaws;
   you lay me in the dust of death.

16 For dogs are all around me;
   a company of evildoers encircles me.
   My hands and feet have shriveled;
17 I can count all my bones.
   They stare and gloat over me;
18 they divide my clothes among themselves,
   and for my clothing they cast lots.

This is the moment of imminence. The hostility of the animals means that the time for speaking has passed. Their mouths open to devour and make one afraid. This is the time for fear because the victim is like the prey of a hunt in reverse where the big beast would use dogs against man, whereas men use dogs against beasts. But this is not all: the "dogs" are in reality the human agents of evil. They are men, as the parallel structure of dogs/evildoers in verse 16 (and, further on, verse 20 power of the dog/sword). The dogs are men carrying a sword. The poem traces a kind of parable: the dogs are pushed along by hunters, but the evildoers are men commanded by beasts, that is to say by the bestial forces of hate and silence that destroy man. The "Beast" delegates man against man.

As in hunting, the physical harm only takes place at the end. That is why the victim, who is surrounded, encircled, and threatened by noise (verses 12-13) has all the time to be afraid, to have his mouth become dry, and to squirm and collapse with fear. The symptoms of fear are described longer than the wounds. At first the soul is ill and through it the body suffers and is undone "like" water, "like" melted wax. The interior emotions are described only by their physical effects. What once was dry liquefies; the wet tongue dries up, hence the two opposite images of water (verse 14) and dust (verse 15). This is death.

The word is not pronounced, as we would expect, at the end but in the middle of the description of the danger (verses 12-22), because it signals the moment when the chase ends (verse 16). Once the prey has been caught, everything is over. What is imminent has become certainty and the horror, for the victim who reads his fate in the will of another, is precisely that death is no longer even a danger when its steps encounter no obstacle along the way; death has become what the victim experienced. The condemned person led to the gallows dies before dying.

Man is no more than his body. He is immobilized. This is the result produced by the wounds (whatever they might be; the Hebrew verb is not clear) that affect his hands and feet. It is impossible for the body to go anywhere. The first and the only physical wound mentioned in the Psalm has to do with "the hands and the feet." This becomes very understandable if it is caused by the fangs of the dogs who have been trained to stop the prey without killing it, since it must be handed over intact to the hunter for its execution. The low reliefs found in the palace of the kings of Assyria, at Khorsabad near Nineveh, show us what ferocious dogs the successors of Nemrod (Genesis 10: 9) unleashed against the lion during their famous hunts. We can well see how the powerful Assyrian or Babylonian kings could appear to Israel as lions unleashing their dogs against men. We also know that they often judged any vassals who had betrayed them (2 Kings 25: 6-7).

The condemned is now only his body, his bones that he counts. And the body is only a thing for those who pursued it and found it, a thing for the eye. It is a body seen, looked at (verse 18), naked—a body already treated as though it were dead, since one shares his clothes under his own eyes. The moment of imminence is no more and from this past a cry bursts forth:

19 But you, O Lord, do not be far away!
      O my help, come quickly to my aid!
20 Deliver my soul from the sword,
      my life from the power of the dog!
21 Save me from the mouth of the lion!

   From the horns of the wild oxen you have rescued me.

"... quickly!"; the cry is addressed to "my God." In effect, joined by the pack, surrounded by the animals that have hunted him down, he called out, not to them, but to God that he said, "I know that you will bring me to death ..."(Job 30: 23; emphasis of Beauchamp). This is an accusation, this language of Job or of Psalm 88. But, at this same moment, there is hope. Who will snatch away, if not the one who pushes down? Who will heal, if not the one who strikes? Animal hunters and human dogs find the man for his death and God finds man at the same time: "... you will bring me ..." God dominates death because he cannot, in any manner and absolutely, be implicated in any one of its causes. God can only "bring" to death as savior. Once death is there, God shows more how death is foreign to him by only intervening after it. If God had intervened sooner in the hunt, there would be more to relate and the agitation would be more visible, the complaint less long. But then one would stay in the sphere of what we call "figures" of salvation, said differently, in the mixed shadows of light. What classifies our Psalm differently is that God lets things go so far, so far towards the moment when shade and light have to become separate. In this Psalm, the time of the answer is almost the threshold of death. That is why the answer comes without the least transition. The movement from tears to joy is abrupt and without any apparent cause. A space suddenly opens up for the divine response:

21 From the horns of the wild oxen you have rescued me.
22 I will tell of your name to my brothers and sisters;
    in the midst of the congregation I will praise you ...

"... you have rescued me" echoes "you do not answer" of verse 3. Immediately, just as death was abandonment, solitude, and separation, life shows itself to be communion, and the saved turns towards another. As quickly as the newborn child turns towards his mother, the saved one turns toward his brothers in order to "proclaim" the name of his savior. The supplicant spoke to God about his enemies. The man who sings a hymn speaks to his brothers about God. The veritable thanksgiving is this hymnal proclamation, going from the "brothers" to the distant nations (verse 28), then to the future of Israel, represented by the children (verses 31-32).

Until now, the Psalmist was alone; we did not see that he had any brothers. Hardly has he been saved that he intones his song towards them and even becomes the center of an assembly that has been convoked in order to give praise. The one who was not recognized by the group calls it together. The one who was the opposite of a hymn

Recapitulation Psalm 22: Commentary

intones the hymn. This is a situation that we frequently encounter in the Psalms:

> The stone that the builders rejected
> has become the chief cornerstone. (Ps. 118: 22)

23 You who fear the Lord, praise him!
   All you offspring of Jacob, glorify him;
   stand in awe of him, all you offspring of Israel!
24 For he did not despise or abhor
   the affliction of the afflicted; he did not hide his face from me,
   but heard when I cried to him.

25 From you comes my praise in the great congregation;
   my vows I will pay before those who fear him.
26 The poor shall eat and be satisfied;
   those who seek him shall praise the Lord.
   May your hearts live forever!

The words that assemble the groups is a hymn in good and due form. It has a form that makes one think of the Gospel. The people are invited ("praise," "glorify," "fear") in order to hear good news. But we know this good news rather well. It is that God draws near to the poor and hears his cry. Why change words? Earlier considered as a "horror" (verse 7) from whom one should hide his face, the Psalmist tells everyone that God himself was not horrified. He did not "cover his face." The Gospel of the Psalms is that God hears the poor and the needy.

The Psalmist designates himself as being "afflicted" or downtrodden. This general term announces that he is not alone. The unhappy person and those who are unhappy, the poor person and all the poor can understand each other. Those whom, in verse 23, he called upon were descendants of Jacob, of Israel, because they are able to say, as the Psalmist does, "our fathers" and are therefore "his brothers." But the fathers cried out in their poverty; the poor are thus their true descendants, the most authentic brothers. Thus is the Psalm taken up once again for them. The Psalmist had just said: "… in the midst of the congregation I will praise you" (Ps. 22: 22) (*betokh qahal ahalelékhah*, v. 22); pronounce *Kh* as in German *Ach*! Didactic and poetic assonance express the relationship of *qahal* (assembly) with *halal* (to praise). Talking more particularly about the poor, he then says : *mé'itekha tehillâti beqahal* ("From you comes my praise in the great congregation" verse 25), as though this assonance and this relationship of praise with the assembly and of the assembly with the poor made him laugh with joy.

During the time of his misfortune, he made the promise to share a hymn and a meal: "The poor shall eat and be satisfied ..." (Ps. 22: 26). They will praise with the supplicant who has been heard and will proclaim the opening words of the banquet, literally: "May your hearts live forever!" (Ps. 22: 26). Similarly, on hearing that Joseph was not dead, the spirit of his father Jacob "revived" (Genesis 45: 27). "... be cheerful ..."' is said elsewhere when there is an invitation to eat (1 Kings 21: 7; see Psalm 69: 32).

> 27 All the ends of the earth shall remember and turn to the Lord; and all the families of the nations shall worship before him.

The Psalmist is with his own when he is among the poor. It is more surprising and even stupefying to see the entire earth and every nation suddenly come together in order to intone a hymnal formula that, in Hebrew, begins with "yes," just like the formula of verse 29, which is translated as "indeed." Insignificant explanations may be given for this: literary habit, or a very general hope, for an undetermined time, without any direct relation to the event of salvation that is mentioned and celebrated here. This is almost a refusal to understand, what is only allowed in case of necessity. Here, on the contrary, the coherence is quite solid, since we know that the Psalmist speaks from two different points of view. His individual point of view has put him in conflict with his community and his people; so it is normal that his salvation is celebrated first with his brothers, in his people. But he also begs to the extent that his fate puts into play the continuity of the "descendants of Israel" with the Israel of "our fathers." His fate is also a moment of history because the poem is individual and also collective. Just as the collectivity celebrates what concerns the individual, so does the collectivity of the nations celebrate what concerns the nation Israel. And we have found, in the Psalms of the Lord King, the convocation of the nations called to say that the Lord is King of all the earth, since he created it. Here they attribute to him the same title:

> 28 For dominion belongs to the Lord,
>   and he rules over the nations.

In effect, the nations frequently recognize the Lord in what happens to the people of God and praise him for this motive: Israel says, "Praise the Lord, all you nations! ... For great is his steadfast love toward us" (Ps. 117: verses 1-2). According to God's plan, what happens to Israel happens for the world.

> 29 To him, indeed, shall all who sleep in the earth bow down;
>   before him shall bow all who go down to the dust,
>   and I shall live for him.

After Israel, people of the poor, and the nations (two categories which have each intoned their hymn, verses 24 and 28), what remains? An answer cannot be given without any nuance since, unfortunately, some obscurity makes it difficult to understand lines 29 and 30, up to "Posterity." However, it is certain that it is a question of man to the extent that death snatches him up. The poor will eat and will live. Those who not only eat but have a good time (the Hebrew used here is a pejorative word) will die. The contrast, though it is not developed, still speaks loudly. These rich people will bow before God but not give any praise. Their silence is not surprising if they are in Sheol, the underground sojourn for mute shades.

> 30 Posterity will serve him;
>   future generations will be told about the Lord,
> 31 and proclaim his deliverance to a
>   people yet unborn, saying that he has done it.

"... and I shall live for him ..." Here we come up against the only truly serious difficulty in the Hebrew text. So this translation is conjectural. Another translation is possible: "He has not made them live," or the equivalent: "He has not given it, the people, (collective singular) life." It would follow that death is understood as the irremediable punishment of men stuffed with the good things of life and fighting against the poor. The meaning is not evident and the tradition, Greek as well as Latin, has understood it differently. In any case, let us keep this: those who are the farthest from God die, whereas the promise made to those whom God saves is a promise of being born.

To whom is this promise made? To a descendance (literally a "seed" or a "race") which, in the Latin and Greek tradition, is that of the Psalmist. (The Hebrew is not precise and has one understand that Israel will continue in its descendance.) In any case, the poem looks to the future without coming to a conclusion.

While the proclamation to the people touched what is near (verses 23-26), the hymn of the nations comes from what is distant in space (verses 27-28). What concerns the dead takes place in the depths (verse 29), whereas the end of the Psalm concerns prolongation in time, the salvation to come. The complete inventory of the dimensions related to the individual and the people, quite differentiated from each other, make one think about what certain Pauline epistles call the "pleroma" (height, depth, length, width of the entire cosmos). This poem inscribes an act of salvation in the framework of near creation, distant creation, and creation to come.

The extension in time is perhaps even more striking. What is this about if not the transmission, from father to son, of a praise whose content is found summarized in two words which ring out, at the end of the Psalm, as the proclamation par excellence: "kî asâh!" "He has acted!" ("That is his work!" ... "...he has done it"). The maximal extension in space and time gives this impression of satisfaction that the Bible so often celebrates. The more true it is that God is the conqueror of death, the more true are time and space concerned. This must, therefore, be announced to them: "God has acted, he has conquered death." Who would keep this news to himself?

It must be announced to the brothers, throughout space, and to the sons, throughout time. We are familiar with this double problematic, and the Psalm does not let us forget it. It is written into the framework of other Psalms: "... our ancestors have told us ..." says Psalm 44: 1. What "our ancestors have told us" will be told "to the coming generation" (Ps. 78: 3 and 4). We shall see that Psalm 22 radically modifies these first data. But it turns them into the most rigid schema of its text:

our fathers

my mother
my brothers
descendance of Israel
families of the nations
descendance (?)
generations to come
people to be born

This chain is first of all one regarding time. Its beginning and end indicate it as a chain of successions, of tradition that goes from fathers to sons; the word and life are at once transmitted along this line. But they are also transmitted along another line that crosses the first one and cuts it. The word is transmitted in space as it is in time. It comes from the past but is exchanged with our contemporaries. Life is transmitted in time through the seed of the father, but it is transmitted in space and is shared with our brothers and, finally, with all the nations, under the form of bread, or of all nourishment. These two modes of transmission can come into conflict.

The same men call themselves Israel because they descend from the same fathers and recognize themselves in the same hymns handed down from father to son. However, they separate from one another when the praise of hymns is used in derision against anyone who is needy and when life is refused, because no one helps him. As Psalm 69 says, nourishment turns into poison and drink into vinegar. There is a separation in the people between those who are enemies of the just man and the poor with whom he shares his food (verse 26), his bread. Life shared through the bread of thanksgiving is, here, more true than the life that is communicated from father to son. Those who use bread while feasting only for themselves may well be from the nations or from Israel (it is a fact that the poem is not specific as to whom), but they will not live. The posterity that, according to the terms of the promise, transmits praise is only the posterity of the poor. The Psalms do not use the term in a manner that is rigidly applied to an economic category; it is completed by mentioning those who "seek him" (verse 26). What happens to the Psalmist is the veritable judgment that is going to define and determine who is the poor person. So we are far from the perspective of Psalm 44 or Psalm 78 that we quoted earlier. All the newness comes from the fact that a gallows for the just man has been set up, as an isolated judgment seat, in the middle of the people. The individual character of the Psalm does not only rest on a distinction with the collective element but on a conflict. The break in the chain of praises is also a rift in the people. Can the action of God be reduced to sewing up again what was unsewn? Would the "doing" of God be a "doing as though nothing had happened?" Does the Psalm end with the assurance, which would be quite banal, of a "rerun of the activities" of praise? In this case, salvation would be practically the equivalent of an obliteration of past ordeals. We would not be able to recognize the mark of God in that.

If the past is sewed up again to the detriment of the newness of salvation, God is not in it. But if salvation has us forget the opening, the evil, the hope and the life of the past, there is no salvation and God is also not there. So the divine truths are not complicated, but they are usually "composed." How could the visit of God leave us anything other than the mix of suffering and joy, of newness and memory? However new this salvation may be, it has to be transmitted to those who will not have seen it and exposed to the alternative of forgetfulness and memory. We hand on to our brothers a begetting, and, to our sons, a brotherhood. Such is the mark of God. Did we not find, while reading Psalm 136, that if the book must be eaten, the bread must be read? It must be read, since it becomes a memorial of salvation.

There is another way of saying this. What the seed of the father hands on is individual, unique, and marked with a name. It is the body, which is truly no longer a body if it is shared. What the sharing of bread transmits is the same for all. Our word carries in it a division between the mark of the individual body from which it comes and the indefinite multiplication, often called "universal" when it is only indifferent. In that the word remains in bread that is body, in a body that is bread, we recognize the mark of God.

Before we know whether we can inscribe precisely this mark on this Psalm, we will have to change levels and go from commentary to interpretation.

30

B. Interpretation

WHO IS SPEAKING IN THE PSALM?

The text of Psalm 22 provides us with little information as to its origin. It is quite different from autobiographies that begin with something like: "I, Mr. So and So, born to ... in the town, of ... etc." An epigraph begins the text: "To the leader; according to The Deer of the Dawn. A Psalm of David." In the opinion of most, this inscription is much more modern than the text and it is not reproduced in liturgical editions; but no one identifies the origin of the Psalm according to this addition of one or several later editors.

We can only say that any man who considers himself the success or the failure of his own life as a date and a turning point in the history of his people is no ordinary man. When he expects to see "all the families of the nations" confess the one God, if God has indeed liberated him, then only one person can answer to these possibilities and fill the slot that the anonymity of the Psalmist has left empty, and that is the person of the king. In effect, not only can the life or death of a king be a turning point in the history of his people, but it can also affect the nations of the world, because every king turns one way towards his subjects and, in another way, towards all the kings as towards his partners, enemies or allies. In fact it is almost only as having been conquered that the kings of Israel or Judah had the honor of passing into the annals of their great contemporary kings, but this at least confirms that the fate of a king can interest other kings. Let us add a note that is not at all necessary, but which is not insignificant: in Israel no one but the king has God as an adoptive father (see Psalm 2: 7; 89: 27). We could explain verse 11 this way.

However, the one detail of the solution that we are advancing increases our difficulty. Which king of Israel was ever dragged to an infamous death by his enemies and then saved by a resounding rescue? Hezekiah, threatened by Sennacherib when his capital was under siege, did not experience this. Josiah died in war and his death was celebrated for a long time, at a fixed time, with lamentations (2 Chronicles 35: 25) whereas not even the tragic part of our Psalm is a lamentation over the dead. So it is normal to look for an answer in the narrative of the worst moments of the ancient history of Israel, at the end of the second Book of Kings. Let us look carefully at the name of Zedekiah. At the very beginning of the sixth century before our era, Zedekiah was put on the throne in place of his nephew by the order of the king of Babylonia. This reign that began so poorly did not leave any good memories, but the one merit the king did have was to have shown some regard for the prophet Jeremiah while he himself hid from his ministers who had thrown Jeremiah into prison. At the end of the siege of Jerusalem, Zedekiah fled but was pursued by the troops of Nebuchadnezzar, captured, judged by the king, and condemned to watching his own sons slaughtered before being blinded and placed in irons. He experienced the worst fate. But he was never heard to proclaim his deliverance to his brothers nor seen to share with the poor his bread or any thanksgiving of a man who has been spared. His nephew Jehoiachin was treated a bit better, because he was let out of prison and granted "a seat above the other seats of the kings who were with him in Babylon" (2 Kings 25: 28). But these kings were all vanquished and enjoyed no freedom, spared only to recall everyday the victory of their enemy. The final situation of Jehoiachin, though it may have given some hope to the editor of the Book of Kings, offered Israel no sufficient motive for singing a hymn. Then there is Zorobabel, too good of a candidate to fill the different spaces found empty by history, because we know very little of him beyond his name (retained in the genealogies of Christ in Luke and Matthew) and the mysterious fact that he returned from exile at the end of the sixth century with the title of a royal personage. What ordeals preceded this and what others was he to experience? No one can say.

The question that has concerned us looks towards the past. The slab that has closed the past and its darkness is at times too heavy and almost impossible to lift up. That is the general opinion in this case as soon as it is a question of assigning names and describing circumstances.

Nevertheless, it was not useless to ask questions. In effect, we are less ready than our ancestors to conclude that God granted the Psalmist a direct anticipated vision of the passion and resurrection of Christ. The idea of an indirect prophecy seems to us to carry more weight. By "indirect" I mean the prophecy that has, as its object, near realities, the experiences by which these participate in advance in the ordeals of Christ and his salvation. Through the examples we mentioned earlier, we can at least sense at what period the image of a humiliated king of Israel, and then glorified before the nations of the world, was able to concern certain people and give them hope. But if the different areas of knowledge that history has in hand are too weak to give us some verification, we suppose that this extraordinary song of complaint and triumph has effectively led the real Israel to a turning point of its history and into one of the crises of its survival, somewhat like the column of clouds which went ahead of the people of the Exodus and helped them leave the waters. Not all the conditions that produced this poem are impossible to imagine. We know that it is not necessary that a king compose a royal Psalm. The misfortunes of the monarchy were able to produce a prayer that an inspired person of the temple, a prophet or a Psalmist consecrated among the Levites, was to proclaim in the name of the king before receiving an oracle for him. Psalm 22 would then be the prayer of an intercessor, not the prayer of the victim himself. This intercessor would have been able to pray, like many others, far from the temple or, because of exile, placed at a great distance, temporal and spatial, from his king. But are we not already saying too much?

We also know, and this time with more precision, that an ensemble of Psalms exists which, by their formulas and structure, are related to Psalm 22, such as Psalms 69, 71, 102 and perhaps 42 and 43. Since Psalm 102 certainly dates from the time of the Exile, we can infer a date for it that is very close to Psalm 22.

Other possibilities remain open to us. Some think that the extreme dimensions of the final expansion, beginning with the invitation to the nations, can be explained by the intervention of a writer who is more modern than the Psalmist. We cannot discuss here the technical difficulties that this hypothesis raises. But, if the hypothesis were a good one, we would have to admit that the author of the addition himself gave an openly messianic meaning to a more particular experience and one that is less universal. This author of a second edition would thus be the witness of a very important moment in the on-going journey of his people.

The essential point to keep is this: even if it were a question of a text composed entirely and directly as a prophecy, it would be indispensable to understand it in the light of the historical experiences that, before its being said, the people and the prophet traversed.

MASK AND FIGURE: ESTHER

The mysterious character of the reality designated by the Psalm is not only due to the centuries that separate us from it. The very way in which it is written keeps it at a distance from an event that is too special. The Psalm would not exist without a certain distance from the awaited salvation or commemorated misfortune, thus in both cases, without an interval which keeps it separated from the event (as we said in chapters 17 and 18). This position and the general character make the Psalm apt to be taken up in varied circumstances and by different people, and this happened from the beginning of the biblical period, as soon as the Psalms were placed in one or several collections. In the beginning of this book, chapter 4, I compared the Psalms to a piece of clothing. But similar texts even cover what expresses what is most intimate in our soul, that is our face. And I shall now risk comparing the Psalms to masks, and all the more so since the same mask can be worn successively by several actors.

The most representative mask of the Psalter would be the one on which a double face is painted. It would then be necessary to trace in the middle a bar, a vertical line, and keep one side in tears, the other laughing. This would correspond to another aspect of the nature of every mask. Without being a lie, a mask hides the truth. Likewise, the alternation of our laughter and our tears keeps hidden the true face of the inexpressible unity towards which God leads us. The mask is temporary. Truth will come. We await it.

Psalm 22 was attributed, in the tradition and by the most ancient uses that Israel made of it, to successive "actors." Among the interpretative repetitions of our poem, the one that has the favor of the *midrash Tehillim* may seem to be unexpected. According to this Jewish commentary, the words of this Psalm are best applied to the character and story of Esther. The commentary develops this application, verse by verse, longer than any other. Naturally, this choice has to be situated within the convention of a commentary that distances itself from any preoccupation of a historical inquiry. But it does merit our attention. In effect, it gives a place to the double characteristic of our text, collective and individual. Esther is very much a royal personage since she is the wife of the great Artaxerxes whose empire stretches "from India to Ethiopia." The fate of the entire people depends on the queen, because the book does not indicate that there are any Jews living beyond the borders of this immense territory. A death sentence has just been pronounced against this entire people and the date for the collective execution has been set. The people already live their own death in advance. Esther places her own life in danger in order to save her people, and then she herself is saved and saves all Israel, as exultation follows tears and fasting; then comes a "time for feasting and gladness and for sending presents of food to their friends and to the poor" (Esther 9: 22). After this, the Jews put to death those who had plotted against them. Haman, in particular, who had foreseen and organized the extermination of the Jews, will be hanged on the gallows that he had himself set up for Mordecai, the adoptive father of Esther. This will not be without having first had Mordecai led about on a royal horse and dressed in royal garments, an honorable gesture that he had planned in advance for himself. This contrasted and violent narrative seeks to report the origin of the Jewish feast of "Lots" or Purim. Given its popular celebration, this feast resembles our carnival. Certainly going from fasting to a banquet, in our case, is done in the opposite order. But in both cases we are dealing with disguises.

This commentary encourages us to return to the comparison that we made earlier when we compared the Psalms to a mask, and more particularly Psalm 22. This special characteristic should not be exaggerated, but Christians will not deny that Psalm 22 played a rather marked role (not unique) in the meditation of the final fate of Christ, and this from the beginnings of their faith. If they wonder why this Psalm was chosen, they discover that it exists for itself with its own density, independently of its use by the Gospel. They then realize that no other Psalm has presented so clearly, not so much the details as the constitutive traits of a situation, which is the gradual progression of death towards its prey. Perhaps no other text has known how to render the end so present in describing so clearly the progression.

But the dramatic acuity of the text, by making the limit so noticeable, also draws attention to what is beyond the limit. If God is capable of saving man who has come so close to death, what does he do for the man whom death has already found? It is clear that Psalm 22, which approaches this limit the closest, does not touch it. But we can say that, the closer it gets, the more it increases our impatience. By a rather natural paradox, the more the end is near, the more we feel that it is not yet here. This is what makes our Psalm typical of the Psalmist's situation: it shows where the other Psalms are going.

Verses 8 and 9 converge to impress in us this agonizing sensation of marked time, time that is counted out. Mocking men state their challenge: the encounter is set! "If God loves him," he should act now. The victim "counted" on the Lord but it was while "counting" time; each second is a victory for his enemies, and time accelerates, since the body is the measure of time that flees and that finally stops. The challenge gives God time to act. Biblical history gives numerous examples of this. But the situation of the Psalm is here one of radical simplicity. What measures time is not a sand clock that becomes empty. Time is measured by a human body where life ends. The "mockers" pretend that they will believe if God acts before the body comes to an end! It is true that the Psalmist, several times, declares that God will follow him beyond death: "Do you work wonders for the dead?" (Ps. 88:10). But this question is asked in faith. On the contrary, those who "make mouths" at him while saying, "let him deliver—/let him rescue the one in whom he delights!" "Let him save him!" exhibit their lie: they will believe, they say, if God intervenes now. But it is a manner of affirming brutally that God can do nothing when death is there. We could say that this challenge is going to oblige God to act in such a way that his action be invisible. This Psalm is presented as a kind of ultimate thrust towards the threshold of truth, towards the location of the word that is not sonorous ("... their voice is not heard ..." Ps. 19: 3) but whose sound, nevertheless, will traverse the entire earth. But in relation to the threshold, the situation of the Psalm is kept within a certain distance, and it is maintained with a double point of view.

The texts are not at the point that they designate. This point is the extreme limit, death, from which comes no sound or text because death makes one speak but does not speak. This point is also the salvation that snatches from death, but no text comes from this point, because those who are saved from death do not speak. But, if they are truly saved from it, it will only happen that the texts that spoke about their salvation, although they had spoken at some distance from death, will be made completely authentic. They will speak about death that was traversed.

Recapitulation Psalm 22: Interpretation 245

The distance can be grasped in the fact that the subject who has experienced the ordeal to the very end does not speak to us. He only reaches us through his writing, which is not he. This written intermediary receives its existence from all the conditions that society places in an exchange. This is especially made clear when the Psalmist writer is an individual who is distinct from the victim and "ordered" to communicate his word to us. He is an intercessor. Society is then authorized to exercise its rights on the word of the victim, and the same Psalm that has served for one can serve for others.

Distance is thus maintained, notably in Psalm 22, with respect to two limits: one that makes death a unique moment, the other which has the individual live a unique existence. These two limits meet with an impassable precision from the fact that the individual dies alone. It is also in relation to these two limits that the comparison of the Psalm to a mask can be justified. By describing a salvation that is not yet victory over death, when faced with some misfortune that is not yet death, the text masks the ultimate moment, the last moment. But, by being interchangeable between several individuals, the text is also a mask and not a face.

This comparison can surprise us and even be disconcerting. Let us reveal its meaning more fully by exchanging the term mask for that of figure which, this time, is traditional. When the represented loss is not truly the lost, because death is at a distance, then the represented salvation is not yet salvation, and one calls it a "figure" of salvation, the figure being (in the use of the word that Christian tradition has given the term) a reality which has not yet reached its final truth. The figure is more of a role than a face: one "is seen as" a hero or a traitor; one "figures" on a list of invited guests or of suspects.

By saying that our Psalm bears a figure of salvation, we thus affirm what at once separates it and what places it in solidarity with the radical victory of Christ as with the irreplaceable unicity of his person. But we still have to gather, by way of words that have come to us from other places, other promises that are even more complete. To do this, we shall have to make a detour through the prophets as we did, earlier, in the Book of Esther.

THE SUFFERING SERVANT

To say that the Psalms keep a distance from the limit where the individual reveals himself to be absolutely unique and at a distance from the limit where the veil of death is raised would not have much meaning if this limit were not reached one day and formulated in the message of Israel. We would not even speak of distance if the term were not known, and we would be able to believe that the Psalms are the last word of the Bible. But the path to the last word is long. As it somewhat happens when we are in the mountains, when we think that we have come closer to the summit and continue our hiking, new valleys and new heights separate us from the pinnacle. This grand summit is the victory of Christ, but several stages separate it from the Psalms.

One of these stages cannot be passed without saying something. This is the prophecy of the Suffering Servant (Isaiah 52: 13-53, 12), a text that was later placed in the book of "Deutero-Isaiah" (Isaiah 40-55), and which dates from the time of the exile. So the reader is invited to return to the well-known text in order to appreciate its words and, then, to compare its message with that of Psalm 22. As readers, we shall be able to verify what change is produced when the "limit" is, in effect, reached. We do not know very well what difference of historic reality separates Psalm 22 and this text, but we do see what newness is carried by the words of the most recent text, the prophetic text. From a point of view that is at once exterior and essential, the principal newness is that, in this prophecy, we no longer hear a man speak about himself. The imprisoned person, the condemned, has died, having passed the "limit:"

> By a perversion of justice he was taken away ...
> For he was cut off from the land of the living ... (Isaiah 53: 8)

The "Servant" spoke in the first person in the preceding poems. Once he is dead, we only hear him speak about himself through others. It is around this newness that all other newness of the prophetic text is organized. It has five principal characteristics.

1. One of the voices that talks about the Servant is that of God, who declares that the victim put to death is just and proclaims for this just person light, power, riches and posterity. The other voice belongs to men, but it is polyphonic and it is not very easy to distinguish with precision the different parts of the chorus. But there is no doubt regarding what is essential: God proclaims the victim to be innocent, and men declare themselves to be guilty.

Recapitulation Psalm 22: Interpretation

Already a "silent sheep" before his death, the Just Man is, after his death, the silent one (Isaiah 53: 7). He recites no Psalm. But God and men speak to themselves about him. The marvel of this prophecy is that God does not accuse men. "He is just," God says while showing the victim. Men say, "We are guilty," and they talk without God accusing them. And how do they know that they are guilty? It is because God pronounced a judgment that contradicts those who accused the just man and declared him to be a sinner. If they had not been led to that point, they would never have discovered their fault. The evil that they attributed to the just man is suddenly revealed to them in its truth, by a moment of clarity that could only have come from God alone and which enlightens them; it was their own evil. Thus, although the Servant no longer recites any Psalm, we hear those speak who, in the Psalter, are the regular partners of the Psalmist. We do not leave the universe of the Psalms. First of all because the divine sentence that glorifies the supplicant and proclaims him innocent is able to occupy the place the Psalms generally left empty for the response (see chapter 17). And then because the men who accused, in the name of lying, the sick and dying man recognize that they are saved by the appearance of evil, because they were lost by the appearance of the good. No one speaks about them any more; they are the ones who talk, for they know their evil.

But the one who knows his evil, on the condition, however, that it be in the light of God (who alone can truly enlighten him), that one is healed and made just because, as Saint Paul says it so admirably; "... for everything that becomes visible is light" (Ephesians 5: 14). Therefore, it is by the death of the Just One that God justifies men: "Yet it was the will of the Lord to crush him with pain" (Isaiah 53: 10). The prophet even says that, by choice, the Lord has led him to this suffering; this suffering body of the Servant is the book, written by man and not by God, where God, like a master who knew how to wait, shows man his fault in order that, seeing it, he might correct himself more radically than he would have been able to do it when suddenly blamed.

2. That is why God does more than just declare to men the justice of the accused. He also tells them that this justice has become their own:

> The righteous one, my servant, shall make many righteous,
> and he shall bear their iniquities. (Isaiah 53:11)

God has given to the innocent one the sin of men while having him carry "the resemblance of sin" (see chapter 9) and he gives men the justice of the innocent one.

This exchange is even much more extraordinary than the one that Israel celebrates while commemorating Queen Esther under the disguises of the feast of Purim. There were the gallows, a place of dishonor, and there was a place of honor for the one favored by the king. But the person whom the pagans expected to be hanged is found in the place of honor and inversely: Mordecai and Haman change places, because there are two places, and that is what the noisy joy of the feast celebrates. The prophecy of the Servant has advanced by one degree further than the limit. Only one place is left, the gallows, which becomes a throne and inversely. It is only when the Just One has died on the gallows that God, who sees it as a throne, gives men his own gaze.

3. How does God give men his own gaze if it is not by talking to them? What moment in the history of men if not the one when, from all the nations, this voice is heard:

Who has believed what we have heard?
And to whom has the arm of the Lord been revealed? (Isaiah 53: 1)

The ear which hears the sentence of God is that of faith and, on the day when the announcement of an exchange between the Just One and the sinner will be heard, on that day, "Who will believe?", who will have this faith? The limit is, in effect, crossed. This is why the proclamation is that of the Unique, the unique moment of death, the unique mark of the individual:

… kings shall shut their mouths because of him;
for that which had not been told them they shall see,
   and that which they had not heard
      they shall contemplate. (Isaiah 52: 15)

Only the voice that is voice most of all and not simply sound, only the voice "not heard" is able to transform one's gaze. Are the kings to whom the word of God has been addressed and whose presence indicates that that word has traversed several nations the same ones who have talked about their conversion? Or is it rather about one people

Recapitulation Psalm 22: Interpretation

whose transformation is related to the kings as an incredible fact, which will then transform them? In any case, some men ("we") talk about what they have heard. The gaze that the word transforms is a gaze that no longer has anything in front of it, a gaze directed towards what is no longer there. The disappearance has truth appear. What is marvelous is that men who relate multiply the terms which belong to "seeing," but they do not have to tell about any vision which would directly justify their conversion; they have not seen the Servant raised up to God in his justice. To have heard a voice of God which is not a sound (just as the creative voice is silent) is enough for them to see something else in what, yesterday, struck their eyes; they "contemplate" (Isaiah 52: 15), they learn. The sign that the suspect, yesterday, was just was that they, today, leave their sin as they see with other eyes. His justice is in them. He has not left and they are able to hear God say to his Servant that he was "numbered with the transgressors" (Isaiah 53: 12). To no longer be a sinner and to be "numbered" with the Just Man is what happens at the same time.

4. To see with other eyes is already to change bodies. The place that "seeing" holds in the narrative of the Servant is, we have just said, all the more extraordinary in that, with the Servant gone, there is no longer anything or anyone to see. But we have to say also that, when the Servant was there, his appearance denied to the eye everything that made it want to see. His appearance "astonished," his face was "marred," he was "beyond human semblance" (Isaiah 52: 14-15):

> ... he had no form or majesty that we should look at him,
>   nothing in his appearance that we should desire him ...
> and as one from whom others hide their faces. (Isaiah 53: 2-3)

The spectators of yesterday do not see the Servant under different traits; they only see him with other eyes. Used to looking at the face, they see the "disfigured" one. They see the same body, but such as it is. They see it as the body of justice; it seemed to them to be a body of dishonor and of shame. But why do they see in this way? May the Lord help us to understand this! Because whoever does not want to know himself as sinner is in the absolute necessity of attributing his sin to another, and of transforming himself, like Satan, into an accuser (see chapter 9). And why does one not want to know oneself to be a sinner? Because every sin is a lie and man is ashamed to lie. And what does this lie consist of? In believing death. Our eye is made to look at the good. Since we cannot look at death in which we place our faith, we are obliged to lie. To sin is to believe in the power of death. The Bible has never ceased teaching that. Because we believe that death steals us from ourselves, we steal others from themselves and that is how our sin always does wrong to others. Death does have a power and it is to accuse us. We believe death; it takes what we give it, and it then accuses us. That is why it is impossible for us not to accuse those whom we want to steal from themselves.

> Surely he has borne our infirmities and carried our diseases;
> yet we accounted him stricken, struck down by God, and afflicted.
> But he was wounded for our transgressions,
>   crushed for our iniquities;
> upon him was the punishment that made us whole,
> and by his bruises we are healed. (Isaiah 53: 4-5)

Complicity with our death takes us from ourselves and, lost to ourselves, we lose others. It is striking that the men who speak in the prophecy of the Servant do not accuse themselves to have killed him but only to have accused him (as so many "adversaries" do in the Psalms) because his body was struck. To be complicit in their own death alienates them in such a way that they believe the sinful just man because he is dying. That is the very same alienation that leads one to kill, but few men have been able in fact to kill the just man, whereas everyone carries in himself or herself what does kill him. The infernal drama of history has even been organized in this way, that those who did not kill the Just One with their hands wanted to construct their justice by accusing those that they judged closest to this act. These accusers thus revealed that death was in their heart.

5. Death takes us from ourselves and we believe it. The Just One gives us to ourselves for the life that is his own, if we believe him. The prophecy of the Servant carries the proclamation of a victory of the Servant over death, but it tells it in a rather implicit way, rather indirect, whereas his death is told without any ambiguity. Certainly we cannot see how he could then benefit from diverse promises, unless having been dead, he not now be living. However, the emphasis

is placed on the new relation that is established after his death between him and the multitudes. They would not be healed of their sin if the justice of the Servant did not extend to them. But the prophecy does not say that the Servant belongs to the multitudes. We know that this is a discourse often held today by those who think that, since Christ left us his inheritance and all the best that he had, we would have nothing more to find in the word "resurrection" other than this meaning: "Christ belongs to us." But, on the contrary, the prophecy says that the multitudes are "for the Servant" and belong to him. It is probably true that everything is for us, including Christ, but "we belong to Christ," because Christ is living and lives for God. There is an important consequence in this: our faith in the resurrection of the Just One is mutilated and precarious if we do not believe at the same time that we belong to him, if we do not recognize sin as our property which he takes from us by freeing us from our attachment to death. To believe Jesus saved from death and to convert oneself from one's sin are one and the same act.

"… the firstborn within a large family" (Romans 8: 29)

A big step was taken from Psalm 22 to the prophecy of the Suffering Servant. But we well knew that, in order to understand the Psalms in the Christian faith, it was necessary to go farther than the Psalms. Jesus goes through the entire Bible with his disciples of Emmaus and not just one book isolated from the others. So it was necessary "to open the Book" of the Psalms, as we did to begin this present work, but it was also necessary to leave the Psalms, as we have just done. The path is only completely known by the term, the end, and the space is only measured by its limits. We can say that the prophecy of the Servant and some other texts delimit the Psalms or stop them. Once God has seized the Just One at the limit of death, then all the other limits of the Psalms are crossed. Avowal and pardon are particularly given free reign. In Psalm 22, the disdain of the people for the condemned and the derision which empties praise of its meaning were certainly to be read as sins. It was not forbidden, and it was certainly not required to understand that the "brothers" of the Psalmist had been his enemies before being reconciled with him. But their transformation remains in the shadows. The sorrow of the broken heart, such as Psalm 51 expresses it, is not introduced into the drama. In the prophecy, on the contrary, the people admit and the Servant forgives.

And yet this difference of density between the two texts does not keep Psalm 22, far from the limit, from being forever associated with the moment of the limit. And here we come, perhaps, to the most beautiful of our surprises: the most marvelous paradox is that the Unique, attaining the unique moment of the limit, says nothing unique. He says what is for everyone. Matthew and Mark place the first words of Psalm 22 on the lips of Jesus, and they are his last: "Elî Elî lemâh sabachtanî." The Unique enters the model (see chapter 5); he puts on his face the mask that was worn by so many supplicants. He has come, he who had the "form of God," to bear our figure. But in him, our figure, our face, becomes the unique face; after that it remains marked by his imprint. By giving life to men, the Servant, the Unique, the Christ gives truth to their words. There is no need to change words, for in the "terms" of the Psalms all that was missing was for them to reach their "term," their limit where words are true. The text is forever transformed by this new mark because the community is also transformed. We would not see that it is transformed if it were not its words that had been kept. The mask of the community becomes its truth, and this truth is no longer a general truth, because it has crossed the double distance which separated it from the Unique, that of the moment and that of the face. But the unique is not reduced to Jesus Christ, since Jesus Christ died in order to give himself to all. A grain could have remained alone, but it died in order to become a numerous grain. However, when he extends himself, he does not lose this quality of being unique and it is even this very quality that he communicates. The question arises, "How can one communicate what is unique?" But what does one want to communicate, if not what is unique? It is for the incomparable price of this communication that men esteem love more than anything else. It is, in God, the function of the Spirit to communicate what, from God, is incommunicable and what we call holiness: what belongs only to God. But it is also because of this that the Holy Spirit is called Spirit of love. Once the unique moment of Christ, his term, his "time," has come, then is this Spirit communicated. To share what is unique ... that is divine, and faith teaches us that such is the mission of the Holy Spirit: to inscribe in the people of Christ the face of Christ that is not exchangeable. Neither Matthew nor the Letter to the Hebrews are mistaken about the true meaning of Psalm 22 when they use it to say that Christ found brothers for himself.

Jesus purifies the Psalms by reciting them; their letter does not have to be changed in order for the Spirit to pass through them. But the letter has always been able to be used as a mask, and the mask is other than truth. The mask is not without some lie. The words that everyone uses hide the slowness that people have in understanding them. Since man is a sinner, how is it that lying and violence would not be able to abuse the letter, the written word, and not even find shelter in Sacred Scripture? Jesus comes to chase sin away from this shelter. He does it by putting on Scripture. As long as truth is not revealed, suffering and joy take a little of their truth from each other. Truth and justice, on the contrary, by invading suffering and joy, unite them and that is where there is no longer any mask, because there is no longer any duality in man. The line, the dash that separated, unites from here on. The writing on the cross is no longer distant from what it says: Scripture is accomplished. Death becomes only the suppression of all that hides, the end of the mask and of the figure. The moment of Christ's Passion removes from the eye all that it thought it could grasp: "... beyond human semblance ..." (Isaiah 52: 14). Christ has taken, even to the point of death, the words of the Psalms that had been pronounced on this side of death, and, conqueror, first-born among the dead, he returns to us the very words that he had borrowed from us. The new birth of Christ makes him the author of the Psalms and verifies that the Spirit had inspired their words. Henceforth, the corporal goods that the Psalms describe are those of our body of justice, the corporal ills are those of our body of injustice, and we do not desire any victory over other enemies except evil. We first recognize it in ourselves and it is against it that we ask for justice in the name of the just Christ. The opaque letter, instead of having us wander about in the duality of the mask, in the ambiguity of the figure, has us enter into the night that is light:

> "... the night is as bright as the day, for darkness is as light to you." (Ps. 139: 12)

Here the Christian puts on at once the Psalm of a people, the Psalm of one person, the Psalm of Christ. He can recite this Psalm like an "Our Father," not only because of the divine goodness, but also because having a share at the moment of the limit, in the salvation without figure, in the resurrection, is to be born anew by God and to have him for a "Father." The Christian then follows the lesson of the Son, who has taught us magisterially how to unite praise and supplication, by begging in order that the name of God be praised through our lives, our deaths: "… hallowed be thy name …." He cries out with the Spirit towards the creation to come: "… thy kingdom come …" but for all that his feet do not leave the path on earth, since it is "on earth" that he wants to see the will of God accomplished "as it is in heaven." Distant creation does not make him forget his body nor does near creation, in the instant, where he will be maintained if God gives him every time "daily bread." He is not ashamed to declare his justice before God because he dares to tell him that he "forgives." But he declares his sin at the same time, since he asks "to be forgiven." Here the confidence to receive justice from God and the act that makes this justice my gesture and my decision become indissolubly connected. The struggle is not over. We are still in danger of "tempting" God, instead of praying to him, and the enemy who "tempts" us, each time that human history approaches its end, is in any case stronger than we. And then, how can we not pray? Because what we would be able to forget to see behind our ills as also behind every kind of good, "evil," is what only God can free us from when he will have conquered "the last enemy … death" (1 Corinthians 15: 26).

The Psalms, like the "Our Father," are at once the prayer of the living person and of the dying. They can be taken as a prayer for the dead and as a prayer for the living. It is quite beautiful that these two prayers be one.

The resurrection of Christ would have no meaning if it did not open the door that has the divine life communicate with our own in both directions. Death is a threshold that one can cross towards God, but this is only one feature of Christian teaching. The life towards which we are going is also, and the one that is coming towards us, to reach us "on this side," right here. Life is a path. This is true of the life of the Psalmist, of the life of Christ, and of our own. To believe that God manifests himself at the end, on the limit, and that he is absent along the way is to leave the Christian faith. If someone said, "Christ has risen, but the Psalmists deluded themselves in believing that God could intervene in the affairs of their life," it would not only be insulting the faith of the Psalmist but also the faith which believes in the resurrection.

Christ, whom God made the "first-born within a large family" (Romans 8: 9), joins us when we become mortal through the power of his resurrected body.

So, finally, God waits for the end in order to give a definitive answer. But by responding at the very end, he responds to all that has preceded. It is by responding to his Christ that God has answered forever the Psalmists.

The Psalmist who, with the transitory responses of God, desired God and his definitive answer lived in faith since his desire was directed at what went beyond all provisional signs. We are also quite near the Psalmist since, if our ear has heard the ultimate message, our own faith is again lived through the daily signs in order to attain what is invisible and definitive.

"... the firstborn of all creation ..." (Colossians 1: 15)

The definitive response is given once and only once through all history to the One on whom "God the Father has set his seal" (John 6: 27). These words of Psalm 22, "Elî, Elî, lemâh sabachtanî," already expressed the contrast between the history of wondrous deeds and a unique moment. Psalm 77: 11 had already proclaimed, "... the right hand of the Most High has changed" (see chapter 1). In his cry Jesus takes up once again the memory of all the great deeds of God at the time when this same God lets perish from an unjust death the very one whom he has chosen and loved among all. The entire history of the Old Testament accompanies the Messiah of God all the way to Calvary, before this history encounters a radical newness, a unique moment.

All men have cried before God, in his presence. In the Garden of Eden, Adam and Eve, before any fault, gave a meaning to the verb "to die" (Genesis 2: 17; 3: 3) and the sons of Adam and Eve placed this word in many of their prayers. But the man on whom God had "set his seal," as the Evangelist John says, is the only one to whom God has given an answer in such a way that it would be able to be proclaimed to all men as an event of victory over death.

A change, a newness that is quickly replaced by another change and another newness is a rhythm that we know. But this is not the way by which we can decide whether a newness is radical. Whereas, on the contrary, a newness that triumphs over death will never be replaced by another. This newness will never seem old. A newness that no other newness will replace introduces a permanent "now" into the world. All that precedes the news of this now is ancient. This now is forever new.

The elements of this proclamation are found in all the Psalms. We know how much the themes of creation are always oriented towards the most precise benefits and the most personal ones, particularly those regarding birth. Psalm 22, faced with death, resurrects all the cries of a coming into the world, and the happy outcome, even if it is lived by only one man, is transformed into a message for all the nations. Other Psalms establish a link between the creation of the world and the salvation of the Nation threatened with death. They sing of creation under the form of a battle against chaos and obscurity, against "tohu wabohu" and "tehôm," against Leviathan and other monsters (see chapter 28): creation is a figure of salvation. Yet other Psalms (chapter 29) cry out towards salvation as towards a new creation, the creation named "Reign of God."

We could expect, and we almost do expect to find a Psalm that summarizes all these types of Psalms. An individual placed by history as a kind of marker for the masses would satisfy this kind of expectation, at the threshold of the doors of death, by recalling the victory of the God who created the universe by his power. This victory would see itself changed into a disaster because the supplicant whom God has marked "with his seal" would perish. But God would then answer him, and the supplicant would announce to the world that his own salvation initiates a new creation for everyone.

No Psalm makes such a synthesis. The grand harmonies of the Psalms of creation are missing in Psalm 22. At most, we could propose Psalm 89 as a possibility, because it does bring together the theme of cosmic creation and that of the individual misfortune of a king. However, the verses that describe this misfortune (verses 39-46) have much less relief when we compare them to Psalm 22! Nor do we find in Psalm 89 the exultation of the saved Just One. And so the composition of words that we imagined does not exist.

If this is a frustrating experience for us, it is certainly not the first time in the analysis of the biblical tradition. The incredible rigor of the language of the Scriptures traces, with the greatest precision, the placement of a possible text that would be obtained by prolonging logically the lines of real texts, but this placement remains empty, at least in the series from which it can be constructed. Nothing is more rich as a teaching, nothing more biblical, than this brake that is imposed on the autonomous functioning of logical necessity, not to distort it but, rather, to control it in its own movement.

It is imposed by experience and is its sign. The time had not come, in the Psalms, to say this in truth, even in the form of an announcement. When the time comes, we shall not find the Psalm that we made up. We could say that, for the supplicant to have the right to proclaim, correlatively to his own salvation, the marvel of a new creation, he would have to have seen the doors of death close in on him. No one speaks like that in the Psalms.

We recognize the "Psalm" that is awaited in the prophecy of the Suffering Servant. But, as a sign that one can be mistaken as to what is logical, this prophecy respects the reserve of the Psalter, since once "cut off from the land of the living," the Servant does not speak again (Isaiah 53: 8). Different from Jonah who preaches after he has been rescued from the depths, the Servant no longer speaks, but one speaks about him in a word of faith. This characteristic of real prophecy emphasizes what remained imaginary in our projection of a "logical" text.

At the same time, the prophecy of Deutero-Isaiah fulfills our expectation. The person it speaks about has crossed death and his salvation is announced to all the nations in a proclamation that relies on faith: "Who has believed ...?" (Isaiah 53: 1). By its position in the prophetic collection, this Gospel before the letter is of the same nature as the message of all creation, at once original and new. The grand prophetic voice of exile constantly speaks the language of the Psalms of creation: their summation is thus made, not at the level of the Psalter itself, but in another textual group, and it is there that a perfect connection is made between the message of the origin of the world, which concerns all the nations, and the proclamation of a victory over death, which has taken place in Israel in order to be proclaimed to kings and peoples.

It is at this level of the prophecy of exile that a harmony is constructed, harmony between the silence of the Servant, silent before death, silent in death, and the faith that alone hears. There is harmony again between silence and the word of creation, because it is not a closed and positive language that would designate God as some particular being.

Deutero-Isaiah rightly lets unfold the grand waves of cosmic silence in order to make silent every god who is not God. The language of creation is a language without words (Ps. 19), a luminous night (Ps. 139), a path in the sea that has no trace of footprints (Ps. 77). This is what comes forth from the origin. But the language of creation is also not closed and negative: the utterance without words bounds from the Levant to where the sky ends in order that the origin appear at the end, which washes it of its appearances:

> Its rising is from the end of the heavens,
>   and its circuit to the end of them;
>   and nothing is hid from its heat. (Ps. 19: 6)

Between East and West, the rising and setting of duration, history extends everything that is unique and places it in order that the absolutely Unique appear. Thus, from horizon to horizon, from letter to letter, the Scriptures are accomplished.

Index

A

Aaron 20, 227
Abel 71, 73, 160
Abraham 16–17, 216, 219
Absalom 48
Abyss 206
accuser 28, 30, 65–67, 249
Acts of the Apostles 134
Ahab 134
Amos 77
Ancients 100
appearance 47, 62, 69, 184, 209, 247, 249
Ark of the Covenant 19, 87
Assyria 231
Auschwitz 158
Azariah 88, 128, 136

B

Babylon 87, 240
Beast of the Abyss 208
Ben Sira 48, 73, 86
Bethel 121, 128
birth 36, 68, 74, 85, 88–90, 104, 131–132, 138, 141, 186–187, 206–207, 211, 228–229, 253, 256
body 16, 25, 51, 53–59, 62, 67, 69, 80, 110, 133, 135, 145–147, 150, 158, 182–183, 205–206, 208–210, 230–231, 238, 244, 247, 249–250, 253–255
bread 22, 41–42, 60, 89, 129, 131, 134–136, 145–147, 153, 172, 199–201, 210, 237–238, 240, 254
breath 16, 25, 93, 108, 131, 172–173, 175–178, 204, 218
Brothers Karamazov 126

C

Cain 71, 73, 160
Christ 8, 16, 25, 30–31, 33–40, 43, 45–47, 50–51, 69, 75, 82, 88–91, 107, 111, 113, 117, 131, 133, 135–136, 141, 146–147, 152–153, 166, 168–169, 177, 185, 201, 240–241, 243, 245–246, 251–255
Christians 7, 25, 29, 33, 78–79, 133, 141, 186, 243
Church 16, 20, 27, 29, 38, 81, 85, 90, 93, 129, 211
Colossians 91, 255
community 88–89, 127, 178, 209, 220, 234, 252
compassion 30, 141
complicity 31
covenant 94, 116, 195, 199, 208, 210, 215, 217, 220, 226
Creator 96, 101, 156, 158–159, 168–169, 175, 200, 203, 207, 213, 219
curse 30, 60, 66–67, 69, 133

D

David 16, 19, 48, 71, 73, 86–87, 101, 207–208, 239

detour 156, 161, 165, 167–168, 190, 245
Deutero-Isaiah 204, 246, 257–258
Deuteronomy 73, 80–81, 151, 167, 185, 210, 226
devil 73–74
dialogue 28, 40, 140, 214
Doctors of the Church 79
Dragon 74, 81, 206

E

Ecclesiasticus 73
Eden 255
Egypt 17, 79, 128, 143, 151, 193, 195, 204, 226
Elijah 93, 134
Enuma Elish 205
Ephesians 88, 99, 185, 247
Esau 71
Esther 242, 245, 248
Eucharist 129, 134–136, 143, 146–147
Euphrates 218
Eve 74, 190, 255
Exile 241
Exodus 17–18, 20, 72, 74, 79–82, 151, 209, 215, 226, 241
eye 54, 56, 59, 99, 169, 181–183, 231, 249–250, 253

F

flesh 18, 22, 38, 48, 53, 68–69, 110, 124, 133, 194, 199–200, 205, 209, 215
forgiveness 31–32

G

gaze 47, 57, 81, 86, 151, 158–159, 183, 186, 248

Genesis 16, 48, 73, 121, 128, 159–161, 166, 168, 173–175, 178, 196, 198–199, 205, 208–209, 216, 231, 234, 255
genre 28
Gentiles 93, 214
Gibeon 121
grace 46, 81, 88, 120, 124, 146, 150, 229
Great Babylon 31

H

Haman 243, 248
Hannah 121–122, 134
Hebrews 7, 124, 137, 253
Hezekiah 125, 240
Hokhmâ 167
hope 9, 24–26, 31, 78–79, 96, 103–104, 117, 128–129, 131–135, 140–141, 177, 211, 213, 220, 232, 234, 238, 240–241

I

idol 116
image 43, 46, 56–57, 65, 74, 80, 88, 102, 105, 116, 126, 145, 159, 161, 164, 168, 176–178, 181–183, 197, 204, 208–209, 217, 219, 241
individual 17, 24, 95, 145, 155, 189, 207, 223, 226, 228, 234, 236, 238, 243, 245, 248, 256
Isaiah 62–63, 122, 125, 141, 160–161, 204, 246–250, 253, 257
Israel 7, 16, 19–20, 25, 61, 72, 74, 79, 82, 87–88, 90, 93, 95, 103–104, 110, 120, 128, 151, 155, 167, 169, 184,

Index

193–196, 198–200, 211, 213–220, 225–228, 231–237, 239, 241–242, 246, 248, 257

J

Jacob 7, 121, 128, 233–234
Jehoiachin 240
Jeremiah 30, 72, 240
Jerusalem 13, 40, 87, 89, 155, 224, 240
Jesus 16, 25, 30–32, 34–43, 45–47, 50–51, 65, 69, 71, 73, 81–82, 89–91, 95, 107, 111, 117, 123–124, 128–129, 133, 135–136, 141, 147, 161, 165, 168–170, 184, 201, 220, 251–253, 255
Job 28, 61–63, 66–67, 133, 185, 204, 232
Jonah, 80
Joseph 40, 71–73, 234
Judaism 93
Judas 31, 41–42
justice 29–30, 32, 51, 62–63, 69, 102, 169, 200, 246–251, 253–254
Just One 42, 51, 120, 247–248, 250–251, 256

K

Khorsabad 231
kingdom 65, 135, 153, 254
Kingdom of God 153, 213, 220
Kings 2 73, 125, 134, 231, 234, 240

L

Last Judgment 182
Lazarus 117, 128
Leviathan 172, 174, 203–204, 206, 208, 256
Levites 122, 128, 241
liberation 71, 77–78, 93, 116, 200
limit 187, 190, 243–246, 248, 251–252, 254
Liturgy of the Hours 15

M

Maccabees 88
Malchiah 72
Malta 61
Marduk 205
Mari 218
Marys 35
mask 29, 242–243, 245, 252–253
materiality 133
memory 95, 102, 121, 139, 151, 198, 200, 207, 225, 228, 238, 255
Messiah 36, 40, 66, 87, 255
Micah 77
Michal 87
Michelangelo 182
Middle Ages 66
model 40, 42–44, 46, 92, 94, 103, 166–167, 198, 205, 209, 252
Mordecai 243, 248
Moses 17, 20, 34, 36, 40, 43, 69, 167, 169, 205, 226

N

Naboth 73, 134
Nathanael 40–42
Nazareth 40, 165
Nebuchadnezzar 87, 240
Nemrod 231
New Testament 16, 31, 34–35, 46, 68, 74, 123, 185
Nineveh 185, 231

Noah 217
nourishment 143, 145, 174, 176, 199, 229, 237

O

Old Testament 8-9, 29, 31, 34-36, 39, 41, 43, 46, 68, 82, 128-129, 133, 138-139, 141, 215, 223, 255
Orient 54

P

parable 18, 28, 230
Paradise 103, 190
passion 37, 46, 100, 129, 141, 241
Passion 30, 34, 39-41, 46-47, 50, 82, 201, 253
path 19-20, 35-36, 43-45, 47, 80, 82, 105, 113, 127, 129, 144, 149-153, 155-156, 177, 179, 183-185, 200, 205-206, 216, 223, 246, 251, 254, 258
Pharisees 75
Philistines 19, 48
Phillip 40, 42
presence 33, 51, 55, 58, 101, 111, 117, 121, 125, 134, 158, 169, 179-181, 183-185, 197, 220, 223, 227, 248, 255
Promised Land 196, 199, 210
prophecy 43, 46, 62, 103, 241-242, 246-248, 250-251, 257

Ps. 1
22   34

Ps. 2
1   48
7   239

Ps. 3
     87
1-2   121
4-5   121
5   26, 124

Ps. 4
1   92

Ps. 5
1   92
3   121
8   150
9   73

Ps. 6
3   59, 107
5   138
6   100
7   54
8   123
10   59

Ps. 7
     48, 93
1   92, 94
2   23
3   77
8   27
15   67
16   82

Ps. 8
1-9   157
2   161
3   158, 189
4   158
5-9   159

Ps. 9
13-14   101
15   67, 82, 150

Ps. 10

Index

51		3-4	117, 166
7	50	4	113, 114, 168
8-9	72	4-6	168
		5	115, 187
Ps. 12		6	114, 169, 258
6	115	10-14	164
		12	169
Ps. 13		12-14	189
4	99	13	170
Ps. 14		Ps. 20	
4	73	6	123
Ps. 16		Ps. 22	
7	121		60, 123, 223, 239, 241-
10	137		243, 251-253, 255
		1	34, 96, 252, 255
Ps. 17		1-3	225
3	121	2	136
5	27	3	95, 232
15	121	4-5	103, 226
		5	114
Ps. 18		6	227
	48, 87	7	233
1-2	93	7-8	227
3	78	8	228
4-5	74	8-9	244
9	228	9-11	131
16-17	77	9-14	229
17	49	12	229
18	48	12-13	230
19	228	12-22	230
24	27	15	53
29	80	15-18	230
33	80	17	49
36	80, 150	18	22, 41, 42, 229
48-50	101	18-21	231
		20	230
Ps. 19		21-22	232
	215, 258	22	35, 233
1-2	165-170	23-26	233
1-10	163	24	235
2	109-113	25	104
3	114, 117, 244	25-26	136

26-27	234	Ps. 30		
28	232	3	137	
28-31	235	8	126	
29	234	9	137	
30-31	104	12	89, 108	
31-32	232			
		Ps. 31		
Ps. 23		9	54	
3-4	150	10	54	
4	132	12	57	
5	101	13	59, 71, 75	
Ps. 24		Ps. 32		
	216	3	55	
1-2	219	5	126	
3	214			
7-8	215	Ps. 33		
7-10	220	1	109	
		3	103	
Ps. 25		10	49	
4	152			
9	152	Ps. 34		
15	150		48, 87	
19	48, 71	1	90	
		3	90	
Ps. 26		19	41, 132	
6	28	20	41	
12	150	21	82	
Ps. 27		Ps. 35		
2	73		59	
11	152	3	122	
		4	49, 71	
Ps. 28		13-14	122	
1	140	15	49	
6	123	19	51, 99	
14	216	25	73	
		27	100	
Ps. 29		28	108	
	216, 217			
6	73	Ps. 36		
10	220	4	49	

Index 265

Ps. 37		2	138-139
	161	4	96
3	153	5	138
5	153		
9	153	Ps. 43	241
11	153		
14	67, 71	Ps. 44	
14-15	67	1	95, 102, 116, 227, 236, 237
15	82	3	93
23	153	8	102
34	153	9	116
		18	116
Ps. 38		25-26	116
7	22, 53		
10	54	Ps. 46	
11	57, 59	4	152
12	59-60, 71	6	48
19-20	48		
20	59	Ps. 47	
		1	215
Ps. 40		2	220
2-3	103, 140	9	216
3-16	100		
6-10	37	Ps 48	
4-17	100	2	216
6-10	37		
10	102	Ps. 51	
14	71		87, 251
Ps. 41		Ps. 52	
	42, 87		48, 87
1	236	3	49
4	126		
4-5	60	Ps. 53	
6-7	48	4	49, 73
8	22		
9	41, 60	Ps. 54	
10	32		48, 87
11	100	1	48, 123
13	102	3	71
		4	123
Ps. 42			
	241		
1	236		

Ps. 55		Ps. 65	
4	22	5	41
6-7	47		
9-11	48	Ps. 66	
23	50	6	151
		9	150, 151
Ps. 56			
	22, 48	Ps. 68	
5-6	50	22-23	30
6	71		
9	123	Ps. 69	
13	150		22, 241
14	77	1	125
		1-2	72
Ps. 57		3	55
	48, 59, 87	4-5	41, 51
6	22, 82	12	49
8	108	13	120
		13-15	74
Ps. 59		15	77, 140
	48, 87	17	140
14-15	48	21	30, 41
16	121	22	60
		25	31
Ps. 60		26	237
7	123	28	30
		29	24
Ps. 61		32	234
2	151	36	104
5	123		
		Ps. 70	
Ps. 62			22
3	48	3	48
11	123		
		Ps. 71	
Ps. 63		5-6	132, 241
	48, 87	7	49
2	122	8	102
6-7	122	10-11	50
		24	108
Ps. 64			
8	67, 82	Ps. 73	
		8-9	49

Index

Ps. 74		7	123
	207	13	77, 140
2	208		
5-8	211	Ps. 88	
12-15	203		136
13-14	218	3-5	56
19	207	9	54
		10	244
Ps. 76		18	57
10	15		
		Ps. 89	
Ps. 77			203, 207, 208, 211
	258	1	95, 204, 209
1	16	10-12	204
4-5	18	12	209
5-9	17	27	239
6	19	39-46	256
8	19	47	23, 207
11	255		
18-19	19	Ps. 91	
19	105	3	77
19-20	20		
		Ps. 93	
Ps. 78		1	216, 218, 220
	237	2	216
2-4	18, 227	1-4	213
3-4	108, 236	3	217
		4-5	214
Ps. 81		5	220
5	123		
10	143	Ps. 94	
11	144-146		216
13	143	18	150
16	143, 147	23	82
Ps. 84		Ps. 95	
5	151	1	214
7	151	3	221
		6	214
Ps. 85			
8	123	Ps. 96	
		1	103, 221
Ps. 86		8	214
	87	10	215, 217, 221

12-13	220		11	174
			12-18	173
Ps. 97			14-30	172
1	219, 221		19	174
4-5	217		22-23	174
7	219		24	208
10	220		27-28	174
			28-29	176
Ps. 98			30	175, 177
1	103, 221		30-35	173
6	221		33	108, 177, 189
7-9	220			
			Ps. 106	
Ps. 99			47	102
1	221		48	102
6	227			
			Ps. 107	
Ps. 100			7	152
	216		9	144
1	215			
3-4	215		Ps. 109	
			2-3	66
Ps. 102			6-7	67
	241		6-15	30
3	53		8	31
5	23, 55		17	30, 67, 82
7	57		17-19	67
8	60			
13	120		Ps. 113	
18-10	104		3	108
27	105			
			Ps. 115	
Ps. 103			17-18	138
14-16	139			
14	140		Ps. 116	
17	102		8	141
			9	146
Ps. 104			10	111
	183, 207		12-14	111
1-4	173			
1-13	171		Ps. 117	
1-6	173			110
8	173		1-2	90, 235
9	74, 204-205			

Index

Ps. 118		7	185
	210	9-10	181
17	141	11	183-184
22	233	11-12	183
22-23	40	12	253
		13-15	182
Ps. 119		15-24	180
143	132	115	184
		16	186
Ps. 121		18	186
1	78	24	152, 185
3	78, 150		
8	150	Ps. 140	
		9	67
Ps. 124		10	82
2	81		
5-7	81	Ps. 141	
		10	32, 82
Ps. 129			
2-3	22	Ps. 142	
			48
Ps. 136		5	146
	215, 238	6	49
1-3	195		
1-14	193	Ps. 143	
4-9	198	7	140
5-9	197	8	152
5-24	195		
10-22	198	Ps. 144	
15-26	194	7	77, 104
25-26	199	9	103, 104
17-18	200	13	144
23-24	201		
26	200	Ps. 145	
		16	145
Ps. 138			
7	132	Ps. 146	
		1	108
Ps. 139			
1	182, 189, 258	Ps. 149	
1-14	179	1	103
4	185		
5-8	181		
6	156		

Matthew
4:2   93
5:39   82
5:44   31
6:7   93
8:16-17   133
10:28   56
18:10   184
21:26   161
22:15   51
23:13-29   31
25:41   31
26:30   34, 201
27:34, 48   30
28:10   35

John
1:18   37
1:45   3
1:46   40
3:14   69
4:2   43
5:46   43
7:19-20   72
8:16   38
8:44   50
11:41   128
11:56-57   51
13:18   39, 41
13:27   42
15:25   39, 41, 51
17:5   117
19:23   42
19:24   39
19:28   39, 41
19:36   39

Purim   243, 248

Q

Qumran   166

R

Racine   206
Rahab   203-204, 206, 209
Red Sea   74, 79, 193-194, 225-226
religion   32, 55, 68, 126, 139, 181, 219
Resurrection   32, 46, 82, 187
Revelation   28, 31, 65-66, 68, 74, 81, 146
ritual   122, 134
Romans   31, 38, 68-69, 75, 166-167, 185, 251, 255
royal   159, 240-241, 243

S

Saint Paul   31, 33, 38, 48, 61, 68-69, 75, 91, 99, 134-135, 166-167, 185, 247
Saint Peter   31
Samuel 1   86-87, 121, 134, 226
Satan   28-29, 42, 50, 65-66, 68-69, 74, 133, 206, 249
Saul   48, 71, 73, 86-87
schema   50, 67-68, 82, 89, 185, 205, 209, 236
secret   35, 57, 62, 71-72, 93-94, 96, 119, 158, 167, 170, 180, 182-184, 187, 197, 226
Sennacherib   240
Servant   245-252, 257
Sheol   56, 74, 80, 119, 137-138, 140, 179, 181, 235
Shiloh   121
silence   54, 81, 114-115, 137-139, 157, 161, 164-165, 167-169, 181, 184, 225, 230, 235, 257
Sirach   48, 73, 86
Solomon   73, 93, 121, 128

Index

Song of Solomon 93–94
Sophia 167
soul 54, 56, 62, 86, 101, 122–123, 131, 133, 137–140, 150, 158, 163, 171, 173, 207, 230–231, 242
Spirit 25–26, 32, 37, 44, 46, 89, 152, 177, 252–254

T

Tehillîm 107, 184, 225, 242
Tehôm 205–206, 208
Teresa of Avila 32
thanksgiving 85–87, 91, 96, 123, 126–128, 135–136, 200, 228, 232, 237, 240
Tiamat 205
tradition 7, 18, 25–26, 33, 47, 56, 102–103, 109, 111, 114, 167, 169, 175, 198, 235–237, 242, 245, 256
tribunal 28–29, 68, 75

U

Unique 39, 43–44, 46, 248, 252, 258

V

victory 75, 87–90, 101, 110, 116, 141, 158, 161, 208–209, 223, 240, 244–246, 250, 253, 255–257
violence 31, 47, 50, 71, 73–74, 160–161, 206, 253

W

war 30, 79, 160–161, 203–204, 207, 209, 240
Wisdom of Solomon 73, 128

witness 7, 39–40, 43, 73, 88, 90, 102, 108–109, 120, 132, 189, 201, 241

Y

YHWH 93–94, 213

Z

Zechariah 66, 224
Zion 101, 151, 208, 216
Zorobabel 240

ACKNOWLEDGMENTS

Matthieu Saulière and Peter Du Brul encouraged me to undertake this translation. I am beholden to them for having answered many questions about my choice of words and for offering their own. Mr. and Mrs. Paul Haddon were also keen on having Paul Beauchamp's reading of the Psalms available in English.

I am grateful to Colette Friend, Cassandra Mabe, Kay Labauve Rees, and Richard Snow for their many remarks, corrections and musings. The Jesuit community of St. François Xavier in Paris and the Benedictines of Abbaye Notre-Dame, in Tournay were always most hospitable. Bernard Gillibert and Allain Pierre were as resourceful as ever in helping me tackle the nuances of French.

Avia Alonzo, Maria Calzada, Bob Dewell, Eileen Doll, Isabel Durocher, Alice Kornovich, Claire Lebas, Clifton Meynard, Josefa Salmón and Leopoldo Tablante were always generous when I needed their assistance. Besides these Ignatian companions, the Loyola Jesuit Community in New Orleans and my family in the Teche country of Louisiana always provided me with a good blend of humor and gravity.

The patience and goodness of Dr. Andy Tallon and Ms. Maureen Kondrick were often called upon. Their interest and support have given this project the shape of a book. Any mistakes in the text are definitely my own.

My hope is that *Psalms Night and Day* will invite readers to open the Psalter and find in it words to express their own grief, joy, or complaint, and to know that, in doing so, they are, like Jesus, not alone.